# 144 Talks for totally awesome kids

# 144 Talks

## for totally awesome kids

### Messages with a meaning for 8-12s

Chris Chesterton
& David T. Ward

MONARCH
BOOKS

Oxford, UK & Grand Rapids, Michigan, USA

Originally published in the UK as *77 Talks for 21st Century Kids*
and *77 Talks for Cyberspace Kids*.

Illustrations by James Walton and Greg Clifton

First published in the UK in 2006 by Monarch Books
(a publishing imprint of Lion Hudson plc),
Mayfield House, 256 Banbury Road, Oxford OX2 7DH.
Tel: +44 (0)1865 302750    Fax: +44 (0)1865 302757
Email: monarch@lionhudson.com
www.lionhudson.com

ISBN-13: 978-1-85424-789-6 (UK)
ISBN-10: 1-85424-789-1 (UK)
ISBN-13: 978-0-8254-6147-7 (USA)
ISBN-10: 0-8254-6147-2 (USA)

Distributed by:
UK: Marston Book Services Ltd, PO Box 269,
Abingdon, Oxon OX14 4YN;
USA: Kregel Publications, PO Box 2607,
Grand Rapids, Michigan 49501

**British Library Cataloguing Data**
A catalogue record for this book is available from the British Library.

Printed and bound in Malta by Gutenberg Press

# Contents

---

### THIS BOOK IS AN INTERNATIONAL EDITION

Since currencies vary so much, we have retained the British currency and £. Please "translate" into your local currency as necessary.

# Acknowledgements

The authors would like to thank Sheila Chesterton, Peter Goodyear and Anna Gibbs for ideas which have been used in this volume. They would also like to express their gratitude to Sue Aldridge, Franck and Rebecca Fama, Tony and Georgina Clay, and David Lant for permission to use their true-life incidents and stories. Nigel Lee, David Smith, Malcolm Rogers, Pat Gutteridge, Catherine Aldridge, Allan Tibble, Ian Blake and Alex Marsden.


Note to 2006 edition:

Sadly Chris Chesterton died, quite unexpectedly, in 2005. He was a wonderful man and an excellent communicator, and is profoundly missed.

# Introduction

"Look at this belt," says Jeremiah, holding the rotting strip under the noses of his hearers. "The man who wore this would end up with his trousers round his ankles!"

"Look at these beautiful wild flowers under your feet," says Jesus. "Look at that flock of birds feeding over there…"

CRASH! goes the mud brick wall of Ezekiel's house as he kicks his way through it. It is a wordless parable that brings a crowd running to peer through the dust.

That's how God's word goes out. That's how the great communicators of the Bible unblocked ears to hear the message.

But surely the eyes of today's kids are too dazzled by flickering screens to see? Surely their ears are too blasted by techno-beat to hear? Surely we can't compete with marketing men, budgets of billions, cutting-edge electronics?

WRONG!

This generation of kids is force-fed on entertainment and information coming through a glass brightly. It is a diet high in sugar and spice but low in real nutrition. These children are starving for meaningful human contact. Just being there in the flesh carries a premium, being there with a message to share and a love that burns to break the communication barrier.

What was the greatest act of communication of all time? – the Word made flesh. "We saw it," says John, getting excited. "We heard it. We touched it." Interactive? Absolutely!

These 144 messages for kids are modelled on the examples of Jesus and the prophets. They take the stuff of the world and use it as a lens to focus truth from beyond time. They are interactive in a way the touch-pad and keyboard can never be.

Adapt them to your own circumstances, expand them, or use them as a spur to developing your own ideas. Tell them with humour and humility. Communicate with confidence in the Creator, and with an awed respect for the sacred right of each precious child both to hear and to choose freely.

"We write this to you so that you can be full of joy with us," John continues in his First Letter. That is my motivation for writing these "messages with a meaning." I hope you will share it as motivation for taking them out to a spiritually hungry generation.

Chris Chesterton
Nottingham

# Five keys to understanding cyberspace kids

## KEY 1: I WANNABE A CELEBRITY

Back in the 1960s, Andy Warhol said, "In the future everyone will be famous for fifteen minutes." Warhol's future is now.

Today's "royals" are the personalities created by the media and sports industries. Many children aspire to join them. And fifteen minutes – or, at least, fifteen seconds – of TV fame has never been easier to achieve. You can apply to get on a quiz game or a reality show; you can raise money for one of the big TV charity nights; you can join a protest or a blockade. Beyond the limit, you can even go out and shoot fellow schoolkids.

If you have the right sort of face or personality or skills, you can make it. But that brings with it the fear of being excluded, of being a nobody. It narrows the horizons and devalues the gifts and qualities of the majority of "ordinary" people.

How do we respond to the instant fame culture? How do we interact with our young celebrity wannabes, their hopes and their fears?

In considering our response to each of these keys to understanding cyberspace kids, we take our cue from the counsel of Jesus to be **"in the world, but not of the world"**. There are ways in which, with scriptural integrity, we can "go with the flow" and recognize God-given impulses and needs. But equally, to be true to the revelation we have been given, we have to take a stand and declare truths which are counter-culture. As we do the former, we gain a hearing for the latter.

### Going with the flow
Jesus took children on his knee and blessed them when the disciples were trying to shoo them away. At Passover, Jewish children have a central place, finding the hidden bread and asking, "Why is this night special above all nights?"

Knowing the unique value that God places on every individual, we can seek ways to make children feel special. We can examine our church services and find ways to include children in active roles. We can bring them out to take part in the message – as in many of the talks in this book – and applaud them for doing so. We can ask them to prepare sketches or prayers or artwork. We can celebrate their achievements, including secular things like being part of sports teams or passing exams. This also underlines that Christianity is part of everyday life and not just for Sundays.

## Taking a stand

The virtue of humility, of deliberately choosing **"to take the lowest place"**, is totally alien to our celebrity culture. We can only start by directing children's eyes to the greatness of God the Creator. This is where talks like "Cataclysmic love" and "10,000 trillion stars" are important. As children begin to appreciate the awesome power of the Creator, they can start to see themselves as they really are.

Then we shall want to help our children to see Jesus as the greatest man who ever lived, besides whom all our celebrities fade into shadows. And this extraordinary man and incomparable teacher is our best friend! But here we have a problem. The 20th century church largely lost contact with the Jesus of the gospels and could only see the Christ of the epistles.

So we pay lip-service to the Sermon on the Mount, but rarely preach on it. And the houses built on rock and sand, or Jesus' encounter with Zacchaeus, are good for bouncy kiddies' songs but seem to have no relevance for grown-ups. It is no wonder that young people turn their backs on the church when the adults in the pews and pulpits pay so little regard to the acts and words of the Master they claim to follow! Before we speak to children, we need prayerfully to ask Jesus to open our own eyes to see him as he is. If we are to take a stand against the culture of the world, we need first to take a stand against the culture of the church.


## KEY 2: LIVING IN CYBERSPACE

To an ever-increasing extent, a child can live in the web of relationships he or she chooses. You no longer either walk home alone or in the company of a classmate (if you walk at all) – you switch on your mobile and walk home in the company of the friend of your choice.

At home, you log into a chat room on the computer. You are now part of a group whose members may be in the USA or Korea or Argentina. Geography and physical distance have no meaning. You no longer inhabit body-space, but cyberspace. Very shortly, even language barriers will have disappeared as translation software allows instant communication.

This accelerates the trend for social groupings to be less and less constrained by the place in which people live. The child whose passion is a particular form of computer gaming or music finds like-minded people on the web. The outsider in the classroom becomes an insider in an online community of soul mates. The disabled child finds others with a similar condition whom she can share her feelings with, or else enters a world of freedom where physical attributes have no meaning at all.

## Going with the flow

Look at the images cyberspace gives us: the worldwide web of prayer, instant communication with God, sharing intimately with the friend you cannot see. These are the kind of parables that are developed throughout this book.

When we think about the possibilities that are opened up to the lonely or to those with unusual medical conditions, for example, we realize the value of cyber community to minorities and the marginalized. One columnist said this about Silicon Valley: "It's about kids who couldn't walk down the hall in high school without being beaten up or insulted. Nerdy and reclusive kids who are nevertheless yanking the rug out from under 21st century civilization."[1] Does that have echoes of the Old Testament prophets or the early church? Maybe Elijah would not have thought he was the only one not to have bowed the knee to Baal if he had had access to the Internet! Cyberspace technology is just as powerful a tool for good or for evil as the printing press. It is up to us to push the good for all we are worth.

## Taking a stand

**"The Word became flesh and made his dwelling among us. We have seen his glory."** The immaterial became material. The beyond-space became space-bound, wrapped in three dimensions tighter than any swaddling bands.

The incarnation teaches us the immense premium God places on meeting us "in the flesh". He knows our needs. When we relate to children through midweek groups or uniformed organizations or more informal contacts, we continue and extend what God did in Jesus. Stories of how children respond to things like table games and dressing-up show that we do not need to be ashamed of offering "old-fashioned" activities. Indeed, the more children become immersed in cyberspace, the more they will need and welcome direct human contact. A pendulum swing back to valuing such opportunities may not be far off.

## KEY 3: LIMITLESS CHOICE

Hundreds of TV channels, music of any kind to download onto your personal player, vast online libraries of films…choice is exploding. In education, it is no longer necessary to follow the teacher or textbook from A to Z. You pick your package, decide how you want to use it, begin at P, jump to F, check out how that relates to X, and finish your session with an Internet link that was updated just hours ago.

Because there are endless different groups of like-minded people online, you do not have to wear the same clothes or listen to the same music as the other kids in the neighbourhood to feel part of an "in" crowd. You can choose which particular crowd you want to be part of. It is not surprising that a "pick-and-mix" spirituality has become enormously popular, too.

---

1. Chris Gulker, article in *The Independent*, 14 February 2002.

Now think what it feels like to come from a world that offers choice on that scale to the kind of set programmes we lay on in church. For some, it feels like an intolerable restraint. For others, it is a relief to have someone else take the responsibility of choice off their shoulders. But that has its own dangers.

## Going with the flow

Choice is one of God's fundamental gifts to humanity. In Genesis 2, Adam is given the choice of eating the fruits of any of the trees in the garden – except one. He is also given the task of choosing names for all the animals and birds. Within the limitations of our resources, we need to look for ways to offer choices to the children in our care. Following teaching with the options of creating a drama, artwork, or a word-based activity (poem or story) not only gives children that choice but it allows them to use their own preferred learning style. We can restructure our children's programmes to give them that sort of choice.

One of the most important things we shall want to do with our children today is to help them learn how to choose wisely, as in "Dangerous attachments" or "Are we blind?" That means teaching them to think for themselves and allowing them to make some of their own moral choices. That may seem risky, but it was the risk God took with Adam and Eve in the garden.

## Taking a stand

God gives us choice, lots of choice. But some of those choices are wrong. There is absolute truth and absolute morality. That runs entirely counter to today's hedonistic and libertarian society. Telling children that something is wrong cuts very little ice unless they have learned to trust and respect us. We need to give reasons, tell true-life stories that show the results of certain actions, accentuate the wonderful benefits of listening to conscience or to the wisdom of God in the Bible. Pieces like "Robots don't win prizes" and "Some adults never live" highlight some of those benefits.

## KEY 4: COMMUNICATION IS VISUAL

Our window on the world is now the screen, from the giant cinema screen to the 6cm$^2$ of the mobile phone. Communication is primarily visual. It is colourful, it moves fast, it has an excitement factor that the everyday world rarely has, and it is increasingly interactive.

A futher key factor about this visual world is that it communicates through stories. In Britain, the majority of TV ads don't say much at all about the product. Instead they place the product in the context of a 30-second story told in a sequence of very rapid images. Children are highly adept at decoding these stories and get the point – often humourous – much more quickly than adults. It is hardly surprising that sitting through a fifteen-minute sermon does not rate too highly on children's wish lists!

## Going with the flow

God puts a rainbow in the sky, attracts Moses's attention through a burning bush, and prepares his people to understand salvation through the story of Passover with all its visual and sensory aids. The psalm-writers and prophets can barely open their mouths without images spilling out, and Jesus never spoke to the crowds without using parables. Have you noticed those two-sentence story-line ads for the kingdom that Jesus keeps slipping in? "The kingdom of heaven is like treasure hidden in a field..."

With a Bible full of such examples in our hands, we should be rejoicing that cyberspace kids are forcing us to go back to our roots. If your message isn't visual or interactive, or if it doesn't feature a story – bin it and start again.

## Taking a stand

How much of the latest blockbuster movie you saw was real and how much of it was created inside a computer? The art of illusion is constantly reaching dazzling new levels of mastery – and we love it!

There is nothing wrong in this. Our imagination and technical skills are God-given abilities. The dangers lie in losing sight of the real world and in images that are deliberately manipulated in order to deceive. Once again, teaching children to think for themselves and to evaluate what they see is so important.

Illustrations from the cinema and TV are generally too ephemeral to be included in a book of this kind, but that is the only reason for their absence. We should seek to include them in our messages, but always draw our audience back to the world of real people, real pain, real joy, and the real wonders of a life infused by a supernatural God.

## KEY 5: WE'RE SEVEN YEARS OLD – WE DON'T PLAY WITH TOYS

That is a quote from a documentary entitled Getting Older Younger. It looked at childhood through the eyes and with the tools of modern marketing. There were some sobering images, such as a group of toddlers, some barely out of nappies, who could not only instantly shout the names of products whose logos were shown to them, but could recognize them backwards through the thickness of the paper before it was turned round!

One of the findings was that Britain has an unenviable lead in the world: nowhere do children stop playing with toys younger than here. The seven-year-olds quoted above were into fashion clothes and make-up. Yet if they are just given the excuse that adults are into something, then kids will enthusiastically take up a toy and express their unfulfilled need to play. That explains why 2001 saw hulking teenage lads pushing themselves along the pavements on ridiculously undersized scooters!

Another of its findings was that children's favourite TV programmes are not those specially made for them, but soap operas. Previous generations learned about the adult world through hearing the gossip of their parents around the table and over the garden fence. Our children learn what it means to be grown up through their daily diet of soaps.

## Going with the flow

Knowing how children view themselves helps us avoid the trap of talking down to them. None of the illustrations used in the talks in this book is particularly childish. That is why they can be used effectively in all-age worship. When we look at the ministry of Jesus, we see that he rarely, if ever, addressed himself directly to children. Yet references to them make it clear that they were part of the crowds who followed him. That simply underlines the fact that parables – stories and images – speak to people of whatever age.

As for soaps, some of us love them, some of us hate them. Either way, what we need to see is that they provide the meeting ground where we can engage with children and talk about their perceptions of the world. TV soap may be super-concentrated, but lurching from crisis to crisis, relationship to relationship, is exactly the way many people live. Let's come at this from a biblical perspective.

## Taking a stand

Did Jesus have anything to say about soaps? Yes, a lot. The Sermon on the Mount is all about the kind of day-to-day community relationships that are portrayed in soap operas. (The exception is the discussion of the public aspects of religious practice which are part of most societies but not of most Western countries today.)

Look at how angrily people speak to each other in some soaps and with what contempt. That is where Jesus starts in his discourse. Adultery, divorce, disputes, money, stress and anxiety, blame and condemnation, dangerous friends – it is all there in Jesus' teaching. And his answer is not (as sometimes portrayed) to give us a new and impossibly difficult "law" to keep, but to tell us that an inner life of relationship to the Father and obedience to the Son is the only thing that can keep us whole in the struggles of day-to-day living. That must be the good news for today's cyberspace kids!

Aspects of this good news are brought out in many of the pieces in this book, but to really rediscover the relevance of the beatitudes and Sermon on the Mount we urge you to read *The Divine Conspiracy* by Dallas Willard.[2]

To quote from Willard's own introduction: "[Jesus] comes where we are, and he brings us the life we hunger for. As an early report reads, 'Life was in him, life that made sense of human existence' (John 1:4). To be the light of life, and to deliver God's life to women and men where they are and as they are, is the secret of the enduring

---

2. Dallas Willard, *The Divine Conspiracy* (Fount Paperbacks, 1998).

relevance of Jesus. Suddenly they are flying right-side up, in a world that makes sense."[3]

To which we would simply add: Jesus comes to deliver God's life to the women and men *whom our precious cyberspace kids are rapidly becoming.*

---

3. Dallas Willard, *The Divine Conspiracy* (Fount Paperbacks, 1998), p. 20.

# God, You, and Me

# God is eternal

## Theme
Thinking about the nature of God has always been part of human life.

## You will need
- a board or OHP to write on
- examples of some hieroglyphics or Chinese characters

throw-stick     ox     water     eye     Palm of hand     house

## Presentation
Write silently as children watch:

**"You shall give Abubu eight portions of..."**

Those words were written on the wall of an Egyptian turquoise mine in the Sinai Desert 4,500 years ago. We do not know who Abubu was, or what he was to be given eight portions of. The end of the sentence has been lost with time. Presumably it wasn't a take-out pizza! **(Children might like to make some guesses.)**

But the words are very important, not for *what* they say but for *how they were written*. The words carved on the walls of this Egyptian mine are the earliest in the world to be written in an alphabet of just a few letters. Before that, all writing was in hieroglyphics – a different picture or symbol for each word (show examples). Just imagine what it would be like in school if instead of making words out of just twenty-six letters you had to know a different picture-character for every word! It would be like writing in Chinese. The alphabet is one of the great human inventions of all time.

## A timeless message
There is another sentence carved on the wall of this mine. This is what it says (write silently):

**"God is eternal."**

God is eternal. He never changes. He is beyond time. He existed before the Universe was created and will continue after it has ended.

Written words can be used for simple practical messages like, "Please remember to lock the door when you go out" or, "Give Abubu eight portions of sweet and sour camel." They can also be used for messages that are for all time and for all people. Not far away from this mine is Mount Sinai, where God gave Moses the Ten Commandments. But a thousand years before that a humble miner knew and wrote a great truth: "God is eternal."

## A prayer
Here is a prayer from a letter in the Bible written 2,500 years after that miner lived:

**Now to the King, eternal, immortal, invisible, the only God, be honour and glory for ever and ever. Amen.** *1 Timothy 1:17,* New International Version

Adapted from an article by Jamie Buckingham in GOOD NEWS Newsletter.

# 2 Thunder from heaven

## Theme

For the morning after the thunderstorm the night before, we link some factual information with one of David's biblical songs of praise.

## You will need

- the means of creating "virtual" thunder and lightning. For lightning, flash some lights or use a camera flash. For thunder, hold a large sheet of cardboard by the edge and shake it, or drum on the side of a box.
- a Bible: 2 Samuel 22:5–20. Have a group or individual prepare to read this dramatically. Treat it as a piece of theatre, to be read with as much power and drama as possible.

## Presentation

Refer to any recent thunderstorm, or to an experience you had in the past. Thunder and lightning frighten some people and excite others. Whichever kind of way you react, you can hardly ignore lightning if it strikes close to you. Lightning is a giant spark leaping between a cloud and the earth. The temperature generated by that spark reaches around 30,000°C (55,000°F). This causes the air to expand at supersonic speed. It is this explosion of hot air along the lightning's path that we hear as thunder.

Most people know that you can tell roughly how far away the lightning is by counting the seconds between seeing the flash and hearing the thunder. Does anyone know why?... It is because light travels so fast we see the lightning virtually at once, but sound travels much slower, around one-third of a kilometer (one-fifth of a mile) per second. That gives us the answer to how far away the storm is: one-third of a kilometer (one-fifth of a mile) for each second we count, or three seconds for each kilometer (five seconds for each mile).

Try that out. Teach the children to count roughly seconds using the word "seconds" in between each number: "**one second, two seconds, three seconds**", etc. The stopwatch function on a wristwatch is useful. Now present your "virtual thunderstorm." Get the children to count between the "lightning" and the "thunder" and then tell you how far away the "storm" is.

In the past, people sometimes thought of thunderstorms as the work of the gods. The Norse god Thor was the god of thunder. But even when we know the scientific explanations, the awesome power of a thunderstorm can still make us realize how small we are. The power of natural phenomena like this has often reminded people of the power of God. If you know that God is loving, then that power can be reassuring rather than frightening.

This was true for David, the same David who killed Goliath and later had to run and hide from the anger of King Saul. He once wrote a song about a time when everything seemed so bad that he felt like giving up. Then a great thunderstorm reminded him of the power of God, the God he knew cared for him and protected him. Now listen to part of that song.

**Present the reading of** 2 Samuel 22:5–20.

# 3 Kangaroos and manna

## Theme
Examples of God providing in desperate situations.

## Presentation
Tell children you have a game for them to play on teachers, parents, or other unsuspecting adults: when asked a question to which they don't know the answer, they reply, "Kangaroo."

Practice with a few suitable questions, e.g. Who was number one in the charts on January 1st 1983?...

How many languages are there in the world?

How high is the tallest mountain in Africa?...

When the teacher or parent becomes exasperated with this silly behavior, they can explain that they are simply practicing the Australian Aborigine language. Captain James Cook and his expedition were the first Europeans to set foot in Australia. They made contact with the Aborigines and began to learn a few words of the Aboriginal language. When Cook asked what the funny jumping animals were, the Aborigines replied, "I don't know." In their language that is pronounced "kangaroo". So to this day there are millions of "I don't knows" hopping about Australia!

## Breakfasting on Wotsit
Another strange word like that comes from the story of the Israelite people when they were in the desert after escaping from slavery in Egypt. Food was short and the Israelites began to complain that they would die of hunger. Their leader, Moses, prayed to God, and in the morning the ground was covered all over with white flakes, like frost. The people were all saying, "What is it? What is it?"

Finally someone dared taste it – it was like honey-flavoured wafers. If you had been an Israelite child your parents would probably have given you a jar and told you to go and collect some of that...er...some of that "wotsit." The Israelite word for "wotsit" was *manna*. So the Israelites were saved from starvation by eating honey-flavoured manna or "wotsit."

You might still hear that word today. On a highway outside Nottingham, England, for example, is a farm called Manna Farm – that is m-a-n-n-a not m-a-n-o-r. It is a place where drug-addicts can go and learn how to live without drugs. Manna Farm was set up by Christians, some of whom had problems with drugs themselves in the past. They called it Manna Farm because, just as the Israelites believed God sent the manna to rescue them when they were in a desperate situation, the farm helps rescue people today who are desperate.

**A possible final word:** By the way, don't overdo it with the kangaroo game – you might just find an exasperated parent sends you to bed early with a kick on the…er…*manna*!

## Something to think about
David's experience when he was in a desperate situation:

> **I asked the Lord for help and he answered me. He saved me from all that I feared. Those who go to him for help are happy. They are never disgraced.**   *Psalm 34:4–5*

# 4 With our own eyes

This little demonstration of balance is hard to believe, but very easy to do. Try it and amaze yourself – and the children!

## Theme
Some things are hard to believe until you see them with your own eyes.

## You will need
- an ordinary 30cm (12 inch) ruler, a hammer, and a length of string about 24cm (9 inches) long tied in a loop of about 16cm (6$^1$/2 inch) circumference. Experiment with balancing the ruler and hammer as in the illustration, adjusting the size of the loop if necessary. A good position for the loop is around 9cm (3$^1$/2 inches) from the end of the ruler. The fulcrum is likely to be near the 20cm (8 inch) mark. This sounds more complicated than it is.
- A Bible: 1 John 1:1–2.

## Presentation
Balance the ruler on an outstretched finger – or get a volunteer to do so. Show a coin and ask what will happen if you place it on the end of the balanced ruler?... Demonstrate... As expected, the ruler overbalances and falls on the floor.

What happens if you move the ruler so that more sticks out one side than the other?... Demonstrate again.

"Now what would happen if I moved the ruler along and hung something really heavy like this hammer from the end on the longer side? Would it balance? Of course it...*would*! You don't believe me? Okay, see for yourselves."

Slip on the loop of string and the hammer as in the illustration. Do it yourself first, then balance it on a child's finger to show you are not cheating. Ask the children if they would have believed it if they had not seen it for themselves.

## Almost unbelievable
John, one of the closest friends of Jesus, once got very excited about something he had seen that was almost unbelievable. He had realized that Jesus really was the Son of God. Jesus was the meaning of life itself. And he, John, had seen him, walked with him, listened to him, and known him as a friend. He tried to get across something of the wonder of that in a letter he wrote.

**Read** 1 John 1:1–2. (Please, not in a dreary "Bible voice." In verse 4 John says, "We write this to you so that you can be full of joy with us.")

> **We write to you now about something that has always existed. We have heard. We have seen with our own eyes. We have watched, and we have touched with our hands. We write to you about the Word that gives life. He who gives life was shown to us. We saw him, and we can give proof about it. And now we tell you that he has life that continues for ever. The One who gives this life was with God the Father. God showed him to us.**

## Conclusion

Seeing this ruler balancing with a hammer hanging on the end is amazing. You probably need to try it yourself to convince yourself that it really works.

Seeing the things Jesus did and hearing the things he said was amazing to the people around him. His closest friends became convinced he was the Son of God. **"We saw him,"** says John, **"and we can give proof about it."**

## Something to do

Children could try this at home and show family or friends. They could tell how Jesus' friends came to believe he was the Son of God because they saw the amazing things he did with their own eyes.

# 5 All the colours of white

## Theme
Holiness is neither dull nor boring.

## You will need
- an OHP; a prism and a multi-coloured disc which appears white when spun (see if you can borrow these from a school science department); a card mask with a prism-sized cut-out
- as much colour as you can muster: children's art, posters, flowers, objects, clothes, etc.

## Presentation
Show white light from the OHP and then make a rainbow using the prism. Introduce children to, or remind them of, some facts about light and colour. Show the reverse of the prism process by spinning a rainbow-coloured disc.

Talk about colour: brightly coloured clothes for parties or beachwear; Christmas decorations; flowers; art; etc. Talk about the effects colours have on the way we feel.

When artists paint pictures of Jesus, what colour robe is he most likely to be wearing?... White. Why?...

We associate white with purity, goodness, holiness. Very often we go on to think of goodness and holiness as being dull, unexciting, boring – very different from the things we associate bright colours with.

But Jesus said,

> **I am the light of the world.**

John described Jesus in his vision like this:

> **His head and hair were white like wool, as white as snow, and his eyes were like blazing fire... His face was like the sun shining in all its brilliance.**
>
> *Revelation 1:14, 16*

Is white light colourless? No! It is all the colours of the rainbow. The Bible says that Jesus was involved in the creation of the world, so everything colourful, everything exciting, every true pleasure, was made by him and for him. Purity and holiness are not boring, they are all the riotous kaleidoscope of colour in the world spun into one dazzling white light – the light John saw in the face of Jesus.

## A dance
A group of children might prepare and perform a dance to some lively music using brightly coloured streamers.

# 6 Everywhere he went he left a song

## Theme
The compassion of Jesus.

## You will need
• a couple of roughly torn strips of old cloth
• A Bible: Mark 1:40–45.

## Presentation
You want a volunteer, a good actor. Ask the children to put on a really sad face and choose one who does it well. Sit him/her on a chair. Wrap the cloth strips as rough bandages around his hands.

Tell how this man was ill and everyone was frightened to go near him. Talk about the effects of leprosy – feelings deadened so that when he suffered cuts or burns or accidents he did not feel any pain, and so could lose the ends of his fingers or toes or nose.

Stress that no one would go near him, certainly not touch him, for fear of catching the disease. He had to live in a cave because people would not let him come into a town or a village. Nobody had given him a hug or a cuddle for years. Dramatize with body language.

Tell the story in Mark 1:40–42. When you get to, "Filled with compassion, Jesus reached out his hand and touched the man," act this out. Jesus did not have to touch him to heal him, he did it to show the man how much he cared for him.

Take off the bandages, and demonstrate how the man had to go to the priest (like going to the doctor) to show that his hands were healed of the disease (v. 44).

Jesus strongly warned the man not to tell anyone what had happened (v. 43). Why? Because if people knew Jesus had touched a leper, they would be afraid he might have caught leprosy and not go near him. But the man was too excited to keep it a secret. He told everyone. "As a result, Jesus could no longer enter a town openly, but stayed outside in lonely places" (v. 45).

Jesus' mission was to go from town to town telling people about God's kingdom. But he was prepared to put that at risk because one poor man hadn't had a hug in years

31

and needed to feel a human touch. Fortunately, people still came to see Jesus, even outside the towns in those lonely places.

This was just one of many times Jesus healed people – and often he reached out his hand and touched them as he did so.

# 7 Holy joker

## Theme
Laughter and worshipping God can go together.

## Presentation
Children love jokes, so why not have a "World's Worst Joke" competition, with the winner being the one who elicits the loudest groan? Jokes should be submitted in advance, of course, or whispered first to an adult to weed out unsuitable ones!

Follow this with the story of St. Philip Neri, the saint who loved a good joke. Philip started out in business, but then he had a real experience of God. He decided to live a very simple life, keeping only the barest essentials for himself. First he studied theology in Rome, and then he turned to telling other young businessmen like he had been about God.

His greatest joy was to be alone worshipping God. However, he never neglected helping people in need. But instead of doing it with a serious face, he went with a smile and a joke on his lips. Sometimes he would go around with half his beard shaved off, or dance in public. Many people came to ask his advice, from the very poorest to cardinals and kings. When an important person came, he would get someone to read a funny book to him. Perhaps that was his way of telling important people not to take themselves too seriously.

Someone wrote this verse about him:

> **Two books he read with great affection,**
> **The Gospels and a joke collection,**
> **And sang hosannas set to fiddles**
> **And fed the sick on soup and riddles.**
> *Ronald Knox*

Being a Christian does not mean walking around with a long face and being a killjoy. Philip Neri showed that you can laugh and worship God and help other people all at the same time.

By the way, who was the quickest runner ever? – Adam. He came first in the human race!

# To think about

Happiness makes a person smile.
But sadness breaks a person's spirit.
*Proverbs 15:13*

 **Courage to go blind**

## Theme
It takes courage to live by what we believe.

## You will need
- a blindfold; a jug filled with milk; a glass; a plate and a knife; a slice of bread and a tub of margarine; a cloth to clean up with!

## Presentation
**Blindfold a volunteer.** He has to imagine he is blind and is getting his snack ready. His tasks are to pour a glass of milk and to butter a slice of bread. Of course, he has to do all this by feel.

Having seen the difficulties our volunteer has got into, ask children to think what it would be like to climb a high mountain blind, a mountain with snow and ice. Ask them to suggest some of the problems and joys of such a challenge.

The highest mountain in Europe, Mont Blanc in the Alps, stands at 4,807 meters (16,000 feet). In 1988 Dave Hurst and Alan Matthews became the first blind climbers to reach the summit of Mont Blanc, a major achievement that must have given them great satisfaction.

## It takes courage
The early Christian leader Paul seemed to view life as the same sort of exciting challenge Dave Hurst and Alan Matthews faced when they climbed Mont Blanc. He said that the mountain-top we are aiming for is heaven and what he calls "an eternal glory." He puts it like this:

> **So we set our eyes not on what we can see, but on what we cannot see... We live by what we believe, not by what we can see. So I say that we have courage.**
> *2 Corinthians 4:18; 5:7–8*

It must have taken a lot of courage to climb Mont Blanc blind. It takes courage to set out on a journey when you can't see the destination. Christians believe that life is a journey and that heaven is the unseen destination. They accept the challenges and difficulties on the way, as well as the joy and excitement when they look back and see how far they have come. They believe there is going to be even greater joy when they finally make it to "the top."

# A prayer

Father God, help us to keep our eyes fixed on what we can't see: heaven, where you are. Give us the courage to keep going when the going gets tough. We really want to make it to the top with you! Amen.

 # A tale of two fish

## Theme
Explaining some of the basics of Christian belief.

## You will need
- an OHP
- a drawing of a fish symbol and the Greek letters to spell ICHTHUS (see illustration)
- 8 matches, toothpicks, or similar.

## Presentation
Show the fish symbol. Have children seen it on lapel-badges, the back of cars, etc.?…

It is thought that the sign was by Christians to identify themselves to each other when they were being persecuted in Rome. The common language of the time was Greek, and the Greek word for fish was "ichthus." The five letters that spell ichthus are also the first letters of Greek words meaning: "Jesus Christ, God's Son, Savior." So Christians in Rome could use the two curved lines that make a simple fish drawing as a secret sign to show they were believers in Jesus Christ.

Now for a fishy puzzle. Display the matches on the OHP arranged to make a fish as in the illustration overleaf. Ask for a volunteer to solve a puzzle. They have to move just three matches to make the fish swim in the opposite direction. The answer is shown in the illustration.

## God gives the power to change
These two fish sum up the whole core of the Christian message.

First, Christians believe that God sent his Son into the world as Jesus, the Christ, the promised Messiah. He is called "Saviour" because he came to save us from the mess we get our lives into.

What do people do when they believe that about Jesus? They turn their lives around and "swim" in the opposite direction – God's way instead of their own way. This is an impossibly big change, but Christian experience is that God gives the power to do it.

St Paul put it like this in a letter which we have in the Bible: **"You were raised from death with Christ"** – that is to say, Jesus has become your Saviour – **"...now put these things out of your life: bad temper, doing or saying things to hurt others, and using evil words when you talk. Do not lie to each other. You have left your old sinful life and the things you did before. You have begun to live the new life"** (Colossians 3:1 & 8–10). In other words, start swimming in a new direction!

## Something to do

Try the matchstick puzzle out on some friends and tell them what it means.

# Escape

## Theme
The Christian concept of salvation.

## You will need
• a ruler or tape measure

## Presentation
Ask children to think of a situation where they have wanted to escape. An example might be being cornered by bullies. Nature gives us many different examples of ways of escaping from danger.

Explain the meanings of the words "predator" and "prey"... Animals that are preyed on by others have developed many ingenious ways of escaping. We are going to meet an animal that escapes by jumping – even though it does not have any legs!

Ask for one or two volunteers to do standing jumps and measure the distance they jump. This will provide a comparison with the exploits of the legless jumper, the fruit-fly maggot.

Fruit-fly maggots escape from possible predators such as ants by jumping enormous distances. Even though it has no legs, the maggot can jump up to thirty times its own length. If we could do that, we could do a standing jump of fifty meters (fifty yards)!

The maggot does it by curling into a ball and gripping its rear end with a pair of mouth hooks. It then tenses its whole body with powerful muscles, lets go its rear end, and flips through the air as if fired from a catapult. It is a good thing that the maggots fishermen use cannot do that!

## Escaping from the mess
All down through history, people have felt that they needed a different kind of escape, not from some enemy but from the results of the mess they have got themselves into. Christians believe that we shall one day stand before God and be judged for what we have done in this life on earth. The early Christian leader Paul put it like this in one of his letters:

> **For we must all stand before Christ to be judged. Each one will receive what he should get – good or bad – for the things he did when he lived in the earthly body.**
> *2 Corinthians 5:10*

People look at themselves and ask what will happen when they face God on judgment day. They wonder how they can escape. The Bible offers a means of escape; it calls it "salvation". Salvation means being saved from evil or the results of sin – the wrong things we ourselves do. Christians believe this salvation comes through believing in Jesus and what he has done for us.

One early Christian wrote: "How…shall we escape if we pay no attention to such a great salvation? The Lord (Jesus) himself first announced this salvation, and those who heard him proved to us that it is true" (Hebrews 2:3, *Good News Bible*).

The events of Jesus' life convinced his followers that salvation comes through him. They believed that the way to escape from sin and its consequences was being offered by God through Jesus. This is what Christians all over the world still believe today.

## A Bible passage to think about

This is what John the Baptist's father said about his new baby son, looking forward to the time when John would prepare the way for Jesus and his salvation:

> **You, my child, will be called a prophet of the Most High God. You will go ahead of the Lord to prepare a road for him, to tell his people that they will be saved by having their sins forgiven. Our God is merciful and tender. He will cause the bright dawn of salvation to rise on us and to shine from heaven on all those who live in the dark shadow of death, to guide our footsteps into the path of peace.**
>
> *Luke 1:76–79,* Good News Bible

# 11 Under the knife

## Theme
Trusting God to perform "heart" surgery.

## You will need
- If anyone can perform a circus act of some kind, juggling or plate-spinning for example, that could be used as an introduction.

## Presentation
Talk about circuses and the children's favourite acts. Include a demonstration if such is available.

Although juggling is the kind of thing anyone can try, some acts are very dangerous and should never be tried in play. One of those is knife-throwing. One lady assistant to a knife-thrower said that she had "only" been hit three times!

Did you hear about the doctor who agreed to be a knife-thrower's target to prove how steady his nerves were: Here's the story:

Dave Flame, a professional knife thrower, had a heart problem and needed an operation. He wanted to know if the surgeon's hand was as steady with the scalpel as his was with his knives. You know what he did? He challenged the doctor to stand and have knives hurled at him. Dave reckoned he wasn't prepared to put his life in the surgeon's hands unless the surgeon was prepared to trust his life to him. And, believe it or not, Dr Peter Reid agreed.

Isn't the doctor in the story a bit like God? Christians believe we all have a kind of "heart problem." We all have an inner drive to do things that are stupid and hurtful. God wants to put that right. The Bible puts it like this: God says,

**I will give you a new heart and put a new spirit in you.** *Ezekiel 36:26*

In order for God to perform that "heart surgery," we have to put our lives in God's hands, to trust him. For many people that is not an easy thing to do. We would rather live with the problem than risk the operation.

Would God be prepared to do what Dr Reid did, put himself at the mercy of the "patient"? Christians believe that is what he did when Jesus came.

41

First, Jesus showed us what God is like.

**Anyone who has seen me, has seen the Father.**   *John 14:9*

If Jesus is the kind of person you can trust, then so is God.

Second, he put his life in people's hands. But unlike Dave Flame, they couldn't be trusted. Instead of throwing knives to just miss him, they hammered nails into his wrists and into his feet and they crucified him.

This is where God did something no doctor could do. Read Isaiah 53:4–6.

**He was crushed for the evil things we did.**

It is almost as if the surgeon donated his own healthy heart as a transplant for the sick patient!

Christians are people who realize that they have a heart problem and trust God as the heavenly surgeon to give them a new one. How wonderful that Jesus was prepared to put his life in our hands to prove that we can trust him completely.

## A prayer

**Lord Jesus, you are better than the best doctor in the whole world. Help us to trust you completely and put our lives in your hands. Amen.**

# 12 Beauty and the beast

## Theme
Transformation; a fresh start.

## You will need
• any visual focus you can find referred to below, e.g. video, book, picture of a dragonfly.

## Presentation
Most children will have seen the Disney version of *Beauty and the Beast*. Talk about the story.[1]

*Beauty and the Beast* is what we sometimes call a "fairy tale." But like many other fairy tales it has some real truth within it. There are some amazing "beasts" which turn into "beauties" in the natural world. One of the most dramatic transformations is that of the dragonfly. This is a real-life Beauty and the Beast story.

Like several other insects, the dragonfly spends up to the first three years of its life underwater. This part of its life-cycle is called the larval stage. At this point it is a real "beast." Dragonfly larvae are among the most fearsome of predators. (Explain what "predator" means.)

The dragonfly larva preys on other insects, tadpoles, and even small fish much larger than itself. Its method of catching them is unique. The dragonfly larva has an extraordinarily long, folding lower jaw which ends in two large hooks. When a suitable prey is located by its rangefinder eyes, this lower jaw shoots forward in a lightning movement that takes only 1/400th of a second. Few horror films have come up with anything worse!

In midsummer the larva crawls up a reed out of the water. Its skin splits and the adult dragonfly emerges. Its crumpled wings unfold, dry and stiffen in the sun, then yesterday's monster turns into a brilliant neon tube hovering and darting over the surface of the pond.

Perhaps it is natural transformations like this that encourage us and storytellers to believe that humans can have a real change of heart. Jesus talked about the need to be "born again," to have a completely fresh start.

---

1. *The Water Babies*, written by the English clergyman Charles Kingsley in 1863, is another fictional variation on the same theme.

The dragonfly changes from living underwater to flying in the air. It is transformed from a beast into a beauty.

**Christians believe that something similar can happen to people on the inside – they can be "born again."**

Here is how one of Jesus' followers described that transformation in a letter he wrote:

**If anyone is in Christ, he is a new creation; the old has gone, the new has come!**
*2 Corinthians 5:17,* New International Version

## Follow-up

Suitable follow-ups to this talk could be: Dickens' *A Christmas Carol*; Saul's conversion and adopting the new name, Paul (Acts 22:1–21); various drug-addicts and gangsters in *Crack in the Wall* by Jackie Pullinger (Hodder & Stoughton, 1989); other true stories of changed lives (Christian bookshops will recommend stories). Telling such a story as a serial can be very effective.

# Valuing Ourselves

# 13 Made of stardust

## Theme
Our origin and destiny.

## You will need
• a candle, matches and a saucer. Try out the demonstration below in advance.

## Presentation
Who is a science-fiction or Star Trek addict?… Who has travelled to the stars in their imagination?… Did you know that we all came from the stars, that everyone of us is made of stardust?… **Would you like to see some stardust?**

Light a candle and hold a saucer over the flame. Show the black deposit on the saucer.

**What is this?**… Carbon. Holding the saucer over the flame prevented all the carbon from burning and formed a thin layer on the saucer. This is stardust!

When a star comes near the end of its lifecycle, it throws out carbon, one of the essential building blocks of the universe. When God made man out of the "dust of the earth", he used the same material that made the stars, and planets, and everything that we see in the starry night sky!

That is amazing to think about. Even more amazing is to think that the Bible says we shall still be alive long after our own sun has grown into a red giant, consumed the earth, and died itself. This is the promise that Jesus made in one of the best-loved verses in the Bible:

> **For God loved the world so much that he gave his only Son. God gave his Son so that whoever believes in him may not be lost, but have eternal life.** *John 3:16*

"Eternal life." That does not mean just existing forever like a speck of stardust. It means the real you outlasting the stars in a life beyond our imagination. That is better than any sci-fi story ever written!

## Time for reflection
Play some quiet music with a science-fiction feel about it if possible. Children might like to think about what they have heard, where they have come from and where they are going to.

# 14 A loveable Teddy

## Theme
We often talk about God loving us, but tend to overlook the corollary, that we are essentially loveable (despite the loss of some of our moral stuffing!).

## You will need
- Either collect a bunch of cuddly toys or ask the children to bring in their favourites. You need one very old Teddy, obviously the worse for wear.
- A Bible: Psalm 139.

## Presentation
Show your soft toys one at a time, talking about them. For fun, you could liken each one – tongue in cheek – to one of the children or adults.

Finally, bring out the old Teddy. Explain his history. He is like... (if he's past his prime and his stuffing's coming out, he may well be like you!)

**Why are these soft toys like us?** Because they are loveable. And we are loveable. God loves us. He doesn't just love us, he actually likes us. Not just when we are new, either. Some of us may be old and battered and have been in all sorts of scrapes, but that doesn't make us any the less loveable.

Psalm 139 in the Bible tells us that God planned us and knew us before we were born:

> **You saw my bones being formed as I took shape in my mother's body. When I was put together there, you saw my body as it was formed. All the days planned for me were written in your book before I was one day old.** *Psalm 139:15–16*

Like this old Teddy, God has had us around for a long time. Each one of us is an old favourite in God's collection.

## A prayer

> **Thank you, Lord God, for making me – not as a toy but as a real person. Help me to really know just how loveable I am to you. Amen.**

# 15 Are you disposable?

## Theme
People may reject us, but God will not.

## You will need
- a waste-bin, preferably metal, and a selection of disposable items such as tissues, pen, razor, drink can, yogurt container, plastic cutlery, etc.
- a few figures of people cut out of paper
- a Bible: 2 Peter 3:9 and Psalm 70.

## Presentation
Silently use various articles – or find them unusable – and throw them away. You could start by blowing your nose and throwing the tissue in the bin, then lifting the bin on the table. Try writing with a pen which (apparently) doesn't work and throwing that away, and so on. The items should make a loud noise hitting the side of the bin if possible.

Hold up one of the paper figures and say to it (in an appropriately childish manner), **"I don't want to be friends with you any more."** Crumple the figure up and throw it in the bin.

Treat another figure similarly, this time saying, **"We don't want you on the team any more. You're not good enough."**

And a third: **"We can't afford to keep you working here. I am afraid we are going to have to fire you."**

Talk about how hurtful it is being rejected.

We are all used to things being disposable – we throw them away when we are finished with them. Sadly, some people treat others as if they were disposable, too.

But for God, no one is disposable. One of Jesus' disciples, Peter, explained in a letter what will happen at the end of the world. Everything that is wrong and evil in the world will be like rubbish. It will be thrown away and destroyed. People were asking then, as they do now, why God didn't do it right then.

Peter explained it like this:

**God is patient with you. He does not want anyone to be lost. He wants everyone to change his heart and life.**

*2 Peter 3:9*

God does not want a single person to be lost when the evil rubbish of the world is burned. He is patiently waiting for us to allow him to clean us up and put us right. No one is rubbish in God's sight.

Take one of the crumpled figures out of the bin and smooth it out. This is what God wants to do for us: smooth out the hurts where other people have rejected us and sort out the wrong things we have done. Then he wants to take us into his eternal life in heaven. For God, no one is disposable.

## A prayer

Psalm 70 makes an appropriate prayer to accompany this message. It is one of David's songs when he was feeling rejected and attacked by others. It could be read by a child. Recommended version: International Children's Bible.

# 16 Name above all names

## Theme
Our importance alongside Jesus in God's eyes.

## You will need
- a dozen or so strips of paper or card. On some write the titles of "important people" – e.g. Queen, President, Pop Star, Millionaire, Sportsman. On another card write JESUS. Leave the rest blank and have a marker pen on hand.
- a Bible: Philippians 2:9–11 and Ephesians 2:6.

## Presentation
Ask the children what sort of people are important. If they come up with actual names, fit these into categories as above. Write new categories as they are suggested. Have a child hold up each category as they arise. You should end up with a line of eight or nine children holding up "important people."

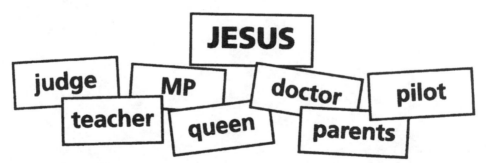

Is there anyone more important than all of these?... Read Philippians 2:9–11 – the name of Jesus "is above every name."

Ask another child to hold the card with the name JESUS on it – and stand him/her on a chair so that "JESUS" is above every other name.

Ask for two more volunteers to come and write their own names on cards. Ask the children where they think these two – and themselves – come in this group of important people. Sitting down on the floor, perhaps?

Where does God want us to be? In another letter St. Paul wrote to Christians. He said that God

**raised us up with Christ and gave us a seat with him in the heavens.** *Ephesians 2:6*

Stand the two children on chairs on either side of "JESUS." This is what God wants for us and why he sent his Son, Jesus.

**Who do you think is important now?**

## A reflection

You might try this if it feels right for your group. Play some quiet music. Ask the children to close their eyes and imagine Jesus on a throne in heaven, with themselves sitting beside him. Then imagine looking down and seeing all the "important" people way below like little ants on the earth. This is a picture of what the Bible says God wants for us.

 **Chicken run**

## Theme
Valuing things we do and make ourselves.

## You will need
- things made by yourself or a child, e.g., a cake, a picture, etc., and similar bought items.
- if you can find one, a video of *Chicken Run* or a picture of Wallace and Gromit or one of their videos.

## Presentation
Talk about the relative merits of bought and homemade items and show your examples. Stress the pleasure that comes from personal achievement.

There can't be many people who have not seen *Chicken Run* or *A Close Shave* by Nick Park, or his previous successes, *The Wrong Trousers* and *A Grand Day Out*. Three years running Nick won Oscars for his films – an amazing achievement.

Nick began making animated films when he was thirteen. He discovered that his dad's cine camera would take single frames – one picture at a time. The art of animation is to take one frame, move the model slightly, take another, and so on. Nick's first character was Walter the Rat, made from his mum's cotton-reels (thread spools), and his first film was *Walter Goes Fishing*. It featured Walter's friend, a Plasticine worm who ended up as the bait.

Nick turned his attic at home into a studio and by the time he was fifteen had made half a dozen films. When his school found out about his talent they asked him to show the films in assembly.

**"People loved it,"** says Nick, **"which was great because I loved making people laugh but I wasn't much by way of a performer."**

As so often, some of Nick's talent clearly comes from his parents. Nick's dad was always out in the garden shed making things. He once made a wooden caravan and took the whole family, including five children, on vacation in Wales in it. There is clearly something of Nick's dad in Wallace, creator of the infamous techno-trousers.

**"Everything was homemade,"** says Nick, **"my mum even made my school blazer."** At the time he wished he could have had a bought one like everyone else. Looking back he feels glad. His parents' do-it-yourself approach to life has blossomed in Nick into a talent which has made millions of people laugh.

Ask children to think about things they enjoy doing or making themselves. Or what about other members of their family? Do we sometimes think these things are not worth much because they don't seem as good as the ones we can buy in the shops?

## A prayer

God the Creator of all things, help us to feel really good about the things we do and make ourselves. Stop us when we are tempted to make fun of someone else's efforts, but help us learn how to appreciate them. Amen.

# 18 Red faces

## Theme
Failure is not the end of the world.

## You will need
• a Bible. Refresh your memory of the story of Peter's denials of Jesus in Mark 14:66–72.

## Presentation
"Was my face red!" "I wished I could have sunk through the floor." "I felt like an idiot." These are the kind of things we say when we have made a mess of something. It is a pretty awful feeling. Here are a few red-face stories reported in the newspapers.

• A life-sized cardboard policeman was set up in a supermarket in Ripon, North Yorkshire, to try to make people think twice about shoplifting. Clearly it did not work, though – thieves stole the cut-out constable himself!

• The army was testing a heat-seeking anti-tank missile. An old tank was used as a target on an army firing range. Unfortunately, the test was an expensive failure. The missile missed the turret of the tank it was supposed to home in on and blew up a beer can instead!

• A man by the name of Jeffrey McLeod robbed a gas station in Florida, America. The garage alerted the police who sent out a patrol car to chase him. We've all seen high-speed cops-and-robbers chases in films, but this one wasn't quite like that. It ended tamely when the robber's car ran out of fuel twenty miles down the road. "When you rob a gas station, you're supposed to fill the tank before you hold up the clerk," was the comment from the sheriff's office.

## One of the worst feelings
We can all enjoy laughing at stories like that, but it doesn't seem so funny when we do something silly. Feeling a failure can be one of the worst feelings you can have. The question is:

**Is making a mess of something the end of the world, or can we pick ourselves up and learn something from it?**

Tell the story of Peter's denials of Jesus in Mark 14:66–72. Mark brings out Peter's feeling of shame at his failure: "He broke down and wept."

Peter could have given up then, but he didn't. After his resurrection, Jesus met Peter on the beach by the Sea of Galilee. He asked Peter three times if he loved him. Then Jesus gave Peter the job of being the leader of the first Christians, the one who was to oversee the birth of the Christian church. Jesus helped Peter put his failure behind him and go on to do great things.

## A prayer
First, a moment of quiet to think about anything we have made a mess of and feel bad about.

**Father in heaven, help us not to feel so bad about our mistakes that we give up. Show us how to learn from our mistakes and go on to greater things. Amen.**

# Timeless Virtues

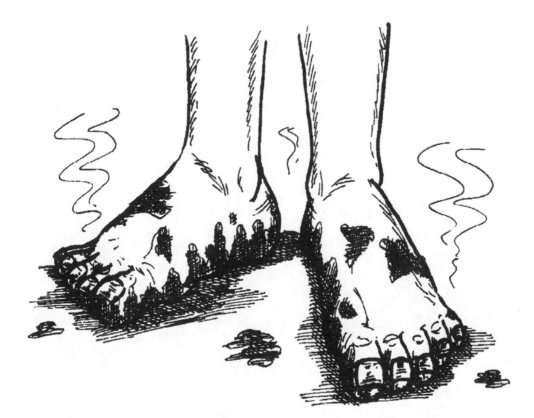

# 19 Be an encourager!

## Theme
Encouraging one another.

## You will need
- a radio
- a globe, if possible.

## Presentation
Switch on the radio and move the tuning along the medium or short wave band to pick up other radio stations from many miles away.

Do children know who made many of the discoveries that enable us to send and receive radio signals?…

**His name was Marconi.** It sounds like "macaroni" – so can anyone guess which country he came from?… Italy. However, although he was Italian, many of his famous and successful experiments were carried out in England. We are going to find out why.

**Who likes doing experiments with batteries and wires and light bulbs?…** So did Marconi, except that he did not have light bulbs to experiment with because they hadn't been invented then! He was born in 1874. One thing fascinated him. If you made a spark in one electrical circuit it caused a small amount of electricity to flow in another wire nearby, one that was not connected to the first circuit at all. It was as though the first circuit was sending a signal to the second circuit. How did that happen? It was *wire-less* communication.

Young Marconi started to do some experiments to see if he could find out what was happening. The trouble was, he got little encouragement to continue with them in Italy. He moved to England, and there he did find the encouragement he needed.

In 1896 he demonstrated the possibilities by sending signals four miles across Salisbury Plain in southern England. Later that year, he sent signals nine miles across the Bristol Channel.

That was certainly interesting, but people thought that the distance signals could be sent and received would be limited by the earth's curve – the radio waves travelled in a straight line and would go off into space. Then, in December 1901, Marconi sent a signal from Cornwall which was received right across the Atlantic Ocean in St. John's, Newfoundland. (Show on the globe.) That caused a worldwide sensation.

**Imagine, when the fastest means of communication was the time it took a steamboat to carry a letter, suddenly discovering that a message could be sent thousands of miles instantaneously!**

In 1909 Marconi was awarded the Nobel Prize for Physics.

All our modern TV and radio flows from that. What might have happened if nobody had encouraged Marconi in England either? He might have given up. It might have been years before someone else got as curious. We might still be watching TV in black and white!

Geniuses and inventors and top sports men and women take the headlines, but behind them are the encouragers, the ones who have faith in them and help them carry on when things go wrong. Not everyone can be a genius, but anyone can be an encourager.

## A famous encourager

One of the most famous men in the Bible is Paul, who took the Christian message to large parts of the Roman Empire. He had a friend who first introduced him to the leaders of the early church, and then went with him on some of his journeys. We only hear this man's real name – Joseph – once (Acts 4:36). The rest of the time he is called by his nickname, Barnabas. Guess what that means? – **The Encourager**.

**How do you become a Barnabas The Encourager?**

By saying things like: "That looks really great." Or: "You've done a good job there." Or: "I think you can do it. Go for it!" Or: "Try it, I'll give you a hand."

One of the rewards of being an encourager is the smiles of thanks you get. And then, you never know, you might just be helping a Marconi or a Paul or a future international player along the road to some really great achievement! Go for it!

## Something to do

Make a "Barnabas" badge. Award it in a week's time to someone who is nominated as the week's best encourager. That way we can encourage each other to be encouragers!

#  **20 Formation flying**

## Theme
Lessons from nature about supporting one another in a team.

## You will need
- a picture of some geese, if possible.

## Presentation
Who has seen film of geese flying in a V-formation?... Who has seen them in real life?... Does anyone know why they fly like that?... It gives them several advantages. We can learn some valuable lessons from them.

First, as each bird flaps its wings, the air currents it creates help the bird immediately behind it. So each goose except the lead bird uses less effort and can fly further. Cyclists racing together as a team get a similar effect. If one goose on its own could fly 100 miles, geese together in V-formation could fly 171 miles!

**LESSON NUMBER 1: WORK TOGETHER AS A TEAM, YOU GO A LOT FURTHER.**

Second, as the lead goose gets tired, another takes its place. By taking it in turns to lead they share the load. No one drops out from exhaustion.

**LESSON NUMBER 2: SHARE THE LOAD SO THAT WE ALL MAKE IT TO OUR GOAL TOGETHER.**

Third, if one goose has to drop out because it gets sick or is wounded by someone shooting at it, two other geese leave the formation and follow it down to help and protect it. They stay with the hurt goose until it can fly again.

**LESSON NUMBER 3: WE ARE ALWAYS GLAD OF SOMEBODY STICKING BY US IF WE GET HURT. ARE WE READY TO DO THE SAME FOR OTHERS?**

Fourth, if you have seen geese flying like this, you will know that they honk as they fly. It is the geese at the back who honk. They do it to let the leaders know they are following and keeping up. Anyone who has played hockey or football knows how much it helps when the team shout encouragement to one another. That is true whatever sort of group we are in.

## LESSON NUMBER 4: SAYING THINGS LIKE, "THAT'S REALLY GOOD," MAKES PEOPLE FEEL HAPPIER AND WORK BETTER. THE WHOLE GROUP OR TEAM BENEFITS.

Did you ever hear anyone called a "silly goose"? It seems geese aren't that silly at all. In fact, there are a lot of very sensible lessons we can learn from them.

## A prayer

Lord God, Jesus told people to "look at the birds in the air." Help us to take that advice and learn some lessons that will help us to go a lot further in life. Amen.

Adapted from an article by Nigel Lee in the UCCF newsletter, Fellowship Link. Used by permission.

# Mother's Day pet

## Theme
Appreciating what our Mothers do for us.

## You will need
- a large cardboard box with a hole cut in the back for your forearm to go into the box. Punch a couple of holes in the lid and tie with string so that it does not come open until you are ready.
- a hand-mirror inside the box.

## Presentation
Talk about pets and say you have a very unusual and special pet who needs a new owner. Show the box. Your arm is inside, but this is hidden from the children. Make scratching and movement noises inside the box.

Explain that looking after this pet is very demanding. Ask for a volunteer. Go through the details below slowly. Keep asking your volunteer if she is prepared to go to this much trouble. If she backs out at any point, ask for another volunteer to take her place.

When this pet is young it needs feeding six to eight times a day, including in the middle of the night. (**"Could you do that?"**...) It also makes a nasty smelly mess that has to be cleaned up...and it needs bathing every day.

As it gets a bit bigger, you have to spend a lot of time talking to it, playing with it and taking it for walks. It is also quite mischievous and can make quite a mess of your things if it is left to itself.

## Worry and sleepless nights
This stage lasts several years, and all the time it is growing. As it gets older, it will quite likely get into trouble sometimes and cause you lots of worry and sleepless nights. Eventually it will grow as big as you are.

Then there is the cost. Feeding this pet and giving it all the other things it needs costs as much as £3,000 per year. **Can you afford it?**...

Children being as optimistic as they are, you should end up with a volunteer who is prepared to say "yes" to all this. Tell her you are going to let her see this special pet now. Ask her just to look at it, but not say anything. Open the lid and hold the mirror at an angle inside the box so she can see her own face, but the other children cannot see the mirror. (Practice this at home with a member of the family.) Enjoy the expression on her face!

Now show the rest of the children the mirror. For those who are slow to catch on, explain how all you have said applies to them. Very few of them would really want to take on the responsibility of looking after a "pet" like that, but that is what their mums have done.

Commandment number five of the Ten Commandments says:

**Honour your father and mother, so that you may live long in the land the Lord your God is giving you.**

Realizing that a big job it is looking after a child helps us understand why it is good to honour our mums on Mother's Day.

# A prayer

A group of children might be asked in advance to prepare some prayers for their mums. Or perhaps we should pray to be the least difficult pets possible!

# 22 Gorillas and aliens

## Theme
The Bible shows us how to treat people who are different from us.

## You will need
- A picture of a gorilla if you can find one.
- Some children could be given the Bible verses to read.

## Presentation
Find out which children have seen gorillas at a zoo or on TV. Show a picture if you have one.

One toddler had his first experience of a gorilla at a zoo. The toddler was looking through the massive glass window which forms one wall of the gorillas' pen when a large male raced up and flung himself against the glass. The child concentrated for a moment to find words to describe the frightening incident. "Big monkey," he said solemnly. "Dang'rous!"

In the spring of 1996, another small boy suffered a much more serious experience. The three-year-old (his parents asked for his name not to be released) was on an outing to Brookfield Zoo in Illinois. He climbed over some railings and fell six meters (4 yards) onto a concrete floor of an enclosure which was home to seven gorillas. You can imagine his parents' horror seeing their son lying unconscious on the ground below them. **What would the gorillas do?**

The first one to approach the limp body was eight-year-old Binti Jua, a mother with her own infant. Her name is Swahili for "Daughter of Sunshine." With her baby on her back, Binti Jua picked up the unconscious boy and carried him to the door of the pen. She handed him over to waiting first-aiders who were able to look after him and call an ambulance. While she was doing this, keepers sprayed the other gorillas with water to keep them back.

For a gorilla, a human is another species, a sort of alien. What prompted Binti Jua to rescue a human child? Was it maternal instinct? Was it because she herself had been raised by humans? (She had to be taught how to look after her own baby.) Unfortunately, she cannot talk to tell us.

When we look at how human beings treat other humans who are different from them, it seems that we need to be taught the right way to do it. Perhaps that is why there are lots of rules in the early chapters of the Bible on how to treat "aliens". "Aliens" are strangers, people who look different or talk differently to us.

Some of God's rules say that aliens should be treated fairly:

> **Do not ill-treat an alien or oppress him, for you were aliens in Egypt.** *Exodus 22:21*

> **The community is to have the same rules for you and for the alien living among you... You and the alien shall be the same before the Lord.** *Numbers 15:15*

Other rules were meant to make sure strangers or foreigners without jobs had enough to eat in the days when there were no shops:

> **Do not go over your vineyard a second time or pick up the grapes that have fallen. Leave them for the poor and the alien. I am the Lord your God.**
> *Leviticus 19:10*

> **When you reap the harvest of your land, do not reap to the very edges of your field or gather the gleanings of your harvest. Leave them for the poor and the alien. I am the Lord your God.** *Leviticus 23:22*

Strangers are not to be left out when there are meetings – or even parties!

> **Assemble the people – men, women and children, and the aliens living in your towns – so that they can listen [to the law].** *Deuteronomy 31:12*

> **Be joyful at your Feast – you, your sons and daughters, ...the aliens, the fatherless and the widows who live in your towns.** *Deuteronomy 16:14*

These rules were written for people who lived very different kinds of lives to ours. But it is very clear how God wants us to treat aliens or strangers: we should treat them the same as us, look after their needs, and make sure they don't get left out. Do we need a gorilla to teach us a lesson to do that?

## Something to do
Draw up a list of "rules" on how to make someone welcome who has just moved into your street or your class.

# 23 Swimming against the current

## Theme
Drifting with the crowd is not really living.

## You will need
- a whole dead fish (from a fish shop)
- a Bible: Matthew 7:13–14.

If possible, suspend the fish on a length of string so that it hangs in the air at the front of the room, preferably a foot or two above your head. This will intrigue the children and ensure their close attention.

## Presentation
Begin by standing under the fish, but do not acknowledge it or make any reference to it. This adds to the intrigue.

Talk about the kind of temptations that can arise when people just drift with the crowd. Relate to any specific local or topical issues, e.g. bullying, shoplifting, vandalism.

Ask the children if they have seen film of salmon swimming up-river to breed. Pictures of the great fish leaping into the air as they try to climb waterfalls are very impressive. Sometimes they have to try again and again to fight their way through rocks and against powerful currents. This is life at full stretch.

**Now compare that picture with the dead fish.** Dead fish don't do much – just hang around! They float downstream and decay, instead of leaping up waterfalls.

Real life is often a question of swimming upstream, against the current and the opposite way to dead fish floating past.

Jesus once painted a similar kind of picture. In his picture it wasn't fish in a river, but people on two different kinds of roads. He said:

> **Enter through the narrow gate. The road that leads to hell is a very easy road. And the gate to hell is very wide. Many people enter through that gate. But the gate that opens the way to true life is very small. And the road to true life is very hard. Only a few people find that road.** *Matthew 7:13–14*

67

It seems like we have a choice in life. One way is tough and sometimes lonely, but exciting. It leads to finding out what life is all about. The other way is easy, just drifting with the crowd, but it ends in shame and disappointment and misery.

**Which sort of fish do you want to be?**

## A prayer

This prayer is by David, the shepherd boy who became a king:

> **Lord, tell me your ways. Show me how to live. Guide me in your truth. Teach me, my God, my Saviour. I trust you all day long.**            *Psalm 25:4–5*

Original idea by David Smith.

# 24 Unselfish clockwork

## Theme
The contrast between selfishness and being ready to help others.

## You will need
• a wind-up toy or alarm clock.

## Presentation
Show your clockwork toy or set the alarm clock ringing. Discuss with the children the relative merits of powering toys and clocks by clockwork or by batteries.

Now think if you lived in a village in Africa with no electricity, a long walk to the nearest shop, and very little money. Would clockwork or batteries be best?

People who live in African villages might not put toys or clocks very high on the list of things they would like to own.

**One thing many people do want is a radio.**

And some of the information they could listen to on a radio might save their lives. There are lots of things they could learn which would help them to avoid catching diseases. One of Africa's greatest disasters is the spread of AIDS. If more people had radios, governments and health workers could get vital information to them and save people from getting infected.

**But radios need batteries. Or do they?**

Inventor Trevor Baylis saw TV reports on AIDS in Africa and started thinking about how to make a radio that doesn't need electricity or batteries. Winding up a spring to power a clock or a watch or a toy has long been used as a way of storing energy and releasing it slowly.

**Could a clockwork spring run a mini-generator and make enough electricity to power a radio?**

Trevor Baylis started experimenting and managed to make it work.

His original model was shown on *Tomorrow's World*. There were still lots of problems, but a businessman liked the idea, and money was found to explore it further. In the end they succeeded in making a radio which gives forty minutes listening from twenty seconds winding.

A company called BayGen built a factory in South Africa to produce the new Freeplay radios. They employ handicapped people on the production line making thousands of radios every month. Aid agencies are buying the radios to give away to people who could not get information any other way.

**Trevor Baylis could have been selfish with his talent for inventing things. Instead, he used it to help others.** James (who was probably one of Jesus' brothers) wrote about this in a letter in the Bible.

> **Where there is jealousy and selfishness, there will be confusion and every kind of evil.**
> *James 3:16*

How different this is from people who have real wisdom that is

> **...always ready to help those who are troubled and to do good for others. This wisdom is always fair and honest.**
> *James 3:16–17*

Some people in the Third World now have the voices on Trevor's clockwork radios to warn them of the dangers of AIDS and other diseases.

**We all have a little voice built into our heads to warn us of the dangers of selfishness. It doesn't need either batteries or a spring. It is called our "conscience."**

## A prayer

> **Spirit of God, speak to us and warn us when we are tempted to be selfish. Give us that true wisdom so that we may always be ready to "help those who are troubled and to do good for others." Amen.**

 # The "UGH" jobs

## Theme
Serving others.

## You will need
- a bowl, water, soap and towel.
- prepare the story of Jesus washing the disciples' feet in John 13:1–20.

## Presentation
Ask for two volunteers and ask one to wash the other one's feet. Hopefully the other children will go, "ugh."

Tell the story of John 13:1–20, including the following explanations. Ask the children to go "ugh" when you raise your hand.

Explain how the disciples' feet were dirty and smelly ("ugh") from all the walking where the pollution was not car exhausts but donkey and camel droppings ("ugh"). When you ate your dinner you lay out on a couch and someone else's feet were in your face ("ugh") – that was not very nice when they were dirty and smelly ("ugh"). Slaves washed people's feet which was an ("ugh") job.

**But in this story there are no slaves, so who is going to wash the disciples' feet? Jesus did, and Jesus said we should do the same.**

Not literally – these days we usually wear shoes and socks instead of sandals, and we do not have camels. Rather it means that we should think of others as better than ourselves, not be afraid to do the dirty jobs and the boring jobs.

Children might be asked to suggest what some of these jobs might be, both at school and at home... **Who usually does those jobs?**

The foot-washer knelt at the feet of the person he washed. Jesus set his disciples an example by doing it for them.

**Are we willing to serve others and do some of the "ugh" jobs?**

## A reflection and response
Take a moment for each one to think of a particular job he or she could offer to do today, perhaps something at home.

Original idea by Malcolm Rogers of Ipswich.

# 26 People or objects?

## Theme
Treating others as people, not as objects.

## You will need
- a stone or a piece of wood
- a potted plant
- a doll
- a piece of carpet to protect the floor.

## Presentation
**Hold up the stone or piece of wood and drop it on the mat.** (Make sure it is far enough away from children not to bounce and hit anyone.)

Ask if anyone thinks that is wrong, or if the stone will object to being dropped?... No, of course not.

**Now hold up the potted plant. If you drop that, would that be wrong?...**

It would certainly cause a mess; the plant might die, but could probably be repotted and survive. Would anyone call the police?... Could you be imprisoned for plant abuse?

**Hold up the doll. Ask the children to imagine it is a real baby. Would it be wrong to drop a baby?...**

Would anyone think they ought to call the police or social services?...

## Name calling
Pick up the stone and start calling it names, e.g.:

"What a miserable, ugly little pebble you are! I'd rather spend my holidays on the local dump than sit on a beach with you....

If you were inside a volcano it would erupt just to spew you out."

That may be rather stupid, but is it doing any harm?...

**Now insult one of the children** (one with a good self-image) or an imaginary person, e.g.:

"Have you looked in a mirror lately – or are you too much of a coward?...

Quick, put a helmet on your head! Here comes a woodpecker!"...

If those comments were serious, would that do any harm?

**Is there a difference between insulting a stone and a person?**

Talk about how we can treat people as less than human – as objects – whenever we fail to consider their feelings. There is all the difference in the world between kicking a ball and kicking a person.

In a letter in the Bible, Paul gives some guidelines on how to treat each other. Here is what he says:

> **Show mercy to others; be kind, humble, gentle, and patient. Do not be angry with each other but forgive each other.** *Colossians 3:12–13*

God always treats us as people, people he loves, not as objects. He calls on us to treat each other in the same way. You can't be kind, gentle or patient with a stone! But you can be kind to someone else.

## A prayer

> **Lord God, you know how much we hate it when people are unkind to us and treat us as objects. Help us never to do that to other people. Amen.**

# 27 Giving and receiving

## Theme
God rewards generosity.

## You will need
- a packet of Smarties or thirty other small sweets; two bowls to put them in.
- a Bible: Mark 4:24.

## Presentation

Ask for one volunteer (A), then choose one other (B) who would not be among A's circle of friends.

**Give both volunteers an empty bowl and count ten Smarties into A's bowl.**

Tell A he can keep them all for himself **or**

give just one to B **or**

give as many to B as he wants.

He must decide and do it right away.

**When he has done so, say you have twenty Smarties left and you are going to give A the same proportion of your twenty as he gave of his ten to B.**

Explain this carefully to the whole group and illustrate what would happen in different cases, e.g., if A gave B one, you give A two of yours; if A gave B all of his, you give all yours to A. How ever many are left of your twenty, you are going to give those to B.

**Give A the correct proportion, then give the rest of the twenty to B.** Comment on how A has done well or badly out of this depending on his generosity to B in the first place.

**Read** Mark 4:24. Jesus said,

> **Think carefully about the things you hear. The way you give to others is the way God will give to you. But God will give you more than you give.**

In other words, if we are generous to others, God will be generous to us. If we are mean to others God will be mean to us. And as God has far more to give than we ever have, it is a very good thing to be on the receiving end of God's generosity!

**That does not mean that if we give half our bar of chocolate away today we can automatically expect a whole chocolate bar to drop out of the sky tomorrow!**

God rewards the truly generous spirit, and he may give back to us in quite different ways to the way we have given.

Jesus repeated this kind of thing several times. Clearly, he saw this as one of the basic rules of living:

**The way we treat others is how God will treat us!**

## A prayer

Give me a truly generous spirit, Lord God. When I am tempted to be selfish, remind me that you will treat me in the same way as I treat others. Amen.

# Good and Bad Choices

 **Making choices**

## Theme
We can ask God to help us when we have difficult choices to make.

## You will need
- a large bar of chocolate or other prize
- three envelopes with red, blue and yellow stickers or felt-tip marks on them; three pieces of paper with these words written on them and sealed in the envelopes:
- a large sheet of paper or card with some black ticks and red crosses drawn on (more ticks than crosses) as in the illustration
- the names of a few children on slips of paper in a hat or box.

> 1
> You have won the prize.

> 2
> Draw another name and give the prize to that person.

> 3
> Do the lunch-time washing-up every day for a week. (Or similar appropriate chore, e.g.: Clear up your class room every day for a week.)

## Presentation
**Show the prize and explain that you are going to draw a name from the hat.** This person is going to get a chance to win the prize. Draw the name and bring the child to the front. Show the three envelopes and explain what is written on slips inside (as above). Let him choose one. He either gets the prize, draws another name to give it to, or promises to do whatever the chore is. There should be people eager to ensure he keeps his promise!

**Continue like this:** We all make scores of choices every day. Some are very ordinary, such as whether to have lasagne or a hamburger for lunch, or which TV program to watch. Some are more important: who to be friends with, for example.

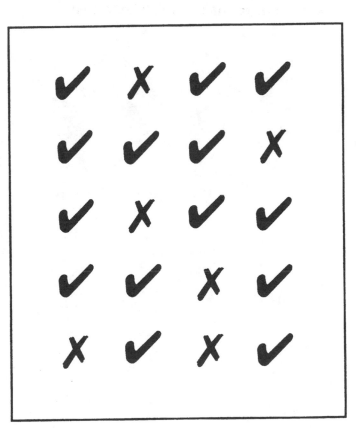

As we get older the choices we make for ourselves become more and more important. We shall have to choose what sort of job to train for, where to live, who to go out with or marry. Unlike the three envelopes, most choices are not blind. There will usually be people or information to help us to choose. Even so, big choices can feel quite risky.

## The first wrong choice

Being able to choose is at the heart of what it means to be a human being. In the Bible story of Adam and Eve, the first humans are given choices. They get to choose the names of all the animals. They can choose from lots of different fruits that are good to eat. There is just one fruit that is harmful to them. We know the story: eventually they choose the one thing they were told not to do. The consequences are very serious.

**Show the sheet with the ticks and crosses on it.** The ticks stand for good choices, the crosses for bad choices. Some of the crosses stand for things that parents, teachers and others have told us can harm us. Every one of us makes mistakes and gets a cross sometimes. But we can pray and ask God to help us make good choices. After all, he is the only one who knows what the results of our choice will be.

## A prayer

Father in Heaven, you know everything. I don't want to make the same kind of mistake Adam and Eve made. Help me to select from all the good choices in life you have given me. Help me to hear that small voice inside that warns me when I am about to make a mistake. Amen.

# 29 The right choice

## Theme
An example of making a good choice.

## You will need
• a Bible. Prepare to retell the story in 1 Samuel 24 in your own words.
• the sheet with black ticks and red crosses on it from MAKING CHOICES.

## Presentation
Show the ticks and crosses and remind children of the importance of making good choices. Adam and Eve made a bad choice when they chose the one fruit God had told them not to eat. Here is a story about a famous man and how he made a good choice one day.

After David defeated Goliath he became a national hero and King Saul became so jealous that he tried to kill David. David drew a bunch of outlaws around him, but was pursued by Saul and his army. Sometimes the outlaws had to hide in caves to escape.

**Relate the story of David choosing to spare Saul's life as recounted in 1 Samuel 24.**

Finish with Saul's words in verses 19–20:

> **If a man finds his enemy, he won't send him away with goodness, will he? May the Lord reward you because you were good to me today. I know you will surely be king. You will rule the kingdom of Israel.**

This came true some time later. Saul was killed in a battle against the Philistines. The people all chose David as the new king of Israel. David had chosen to do the right thing, and God rewarded him.

## Something to think about
How many of us have said to somebody recently, "I'll get my own back on you!"? We may even have imagined the nasty things we would like to do to that person. How about deciding to choose not to get our own back. Remember how God rewarded David when he chose to do the right thing.

# 30 The secret of being happy

## Theme
To illustrate the meaning of the Tenth Commandment: Do not covet.

## You will need
- four sheets of paper with pictures like those below on one side and readings on the other. Rehearse four readers.

## Presentation
The four children stand in a row, hold up their papers, and read in succession.

CHILD 1   I'm off to take my dog for a walk in the park. I can see some lovely gardens with their own tennis-courts in them. I'd love to live in one of those houses.

(Picture 1)

**CHILD 2**  I live in a big house near the park. I sit by the window most of the day watching the people go by. Look! There's a man jogging. I'd love to do that.

(Picture 2)

**CHILD 3**  I've nearly finished my three-mile jog. I'm so hungry. I'd love some burgers and fries, but I haven't any money to buy some.

(Picture 3)

**CHILD 4**  I'll buy some burgers and fries then go home to my apartment. There will be no one there. I'm so lonely. I'd love to have a friend, or even a cat or a dog like that girl in the park.

(Picture 4)

**LEADER**  Thank you for reading so well. Don't go away yet because we shall need you again.

So often we look at other people and want what they have: sweets at playtime, a new football, some new trainers. But other people look at us and want what we have. Let's experiment. Would our readers now reverse the order – number 4 read first. Turn and look at the next person when you finish.

**CHILD 4**  I'll just eat my burgers and fries. I'm getting a bit fat. I wish I were fit like that man jogging.

**CHILD 3**  I'll jog past this big house where that pretty girl sits in the window. She looks terrific. I wish she were my girlfriend.

**CHILD 2**  There's that girl again, walking her dog in the park. I wish I could get up and go for a walk, not have to sit in this wheelchair all day.

**CHILD 1**  Come on, dog. Why does my mum make me take you for a walk every day? It's not fair. I wish I could live on my own in my own apartment like that lady over there.

**LEADER**  We are never satisfied, are we? We always want what somebody else has. It's like a chain going round and round.

In the Bible St. Paul says,

**I have learned the secret of being happy at any time in everything that happens.**

*Philippians 4:12*

You might be thinking, "That's okay for Paul, he was a saint. You don't know how tough my life is."

Actually, Paul's life was pretty tough. Several times he got badly beaten up or thrown into prison. His secret was that he knew God was with him all the time and nothing else was as important as that. He chose to think about that, rather than thinking how badly done to he was.

## Something to think about

As we finish, let's have a moment of quiet. Think of something you have that someone else might like – even if it is just being able to walk and run – and say thank you for that. Ask God to help you choose to be thankful for what you have, rather than wanting what someone else has.

By Pat Gutteridge, co-author of *52 Ideas for Junior Classroom Assemblies* (Monarch Books).

# 31 Actions speak louder than words

## Theme
What we do is more important than what we say.

## Presentation
Ask children what they would think if someone came to their school to present a special lesson on how to survive in the wild but had to be rescued himself before the lesson could begin?

This happened in October 1992 at Allhallows School in Devon, England. The school is in a beautiful part of the country, right on the clifftops overlooking the sea. The visiting speaker, Mr. Alistair Emms, arrived early and decided to go for a walk before his talk on survival techniques. When he hadn't returned an hour later, staff at the school began to fear for his safety.

Allhallows is a very unusual school. All round the shores of Britain there are coastguards who keep a watch out for people in difficulty. Allhallows is the only school in the country to have its own Auxiliary Coastguard Unit. This group of staff and pupils was mobilized to go off in search of Mr. Emms, but they could not find any trace of him. Other coastguard units were then called, plus the police. The search party now numbered forty local people, five police officers, one tracker dog, and two helicopters!

Five hours later, a team scaling an inaccessible cliff face and cutting their way through bushes finally heard cries for help. They found Mr. Emms on a ledge. Although he had only a groundsheet with him, and no food, he then told his rescuers he wanted to stay there!

A policeman said, "It's all a bit weird, but basically he just wanted to stay there and come down when he was ready. Eventually he was talked into getting into the helicopter."

The school decided not to invite Mr. Emms back to give the lesson on survival which he had failed to deliver.

## Saying and doing
**Which is more important: what we say or what we do?** For example, who does more for the environment: the person who designs an eye-catching poster or the one who actually picks up the litter and turns off the lights?

85

Jesus put it like this in a simple story ending with a question:

**Now what do you think? There was once a man who had two sons. He went to the elder one and said, "Son, go and work in the vineyard today." "I don't want to," he answered, but later he changed his mind and went. Then the father went to the other son and said the same thing. "Yes, sir," he answered, but he did not go. Which of the two did what his father wanted?**

*Matthew 21:28–31a,* Good News Bible

An old saying goes, "Actions speak louder than words." The search party and people who read the story in the newspaper judged Mr. Emms by what he did, not by whatever he might have said in his talk. Jesus' story shows us that God judges us in the same way. Perhaps we might pray for our actions to match the best of our words.

---

This story appeared in *The Independent*, 14 October 1992.

# 32 Up in smoke

## Theme
The need to cooperate with the Creator in order to clean up the world.

## You will need
- a bag of barbecue charcoal
- a roll of paper with one of these numbers printed in large letters:
  - for a 5kg (10 lb.) bag of charcoal, **1,140,000,000,000**;
  - for a 3kg (5 lb.) bag, **1,710,000,000,000**.

## Presentation
Show a lump of charcoal. Talk about what it is made of – largely carbon. Explain about the gas that is produced when it is burned – carbon dioxide.

When we burn charcoal or fossil fuels such as coal or oil, much of the carbon goes into our atmosphere as carbon dioxide, a greenhouse gas. Some of the carbon may not burn but literally "go up in smoke" as tiny specks of black soot.

How much carbon do we put into the atmosphere each year, either as carbon dioxide or as soot? Is it equal to millions of bags of charcoal? Tens of millions?

Get two children to unroll the number. The amount of carbon that goes into the atmosphere each year is the same as this number of bags of charcoal. Imagine the size of a mountain of that number of bags of charcoal! It is 5.7 billion tons.

## No respect for God's creation
Burning all this carbon causes pollution. The worst area of the world for pollution is the former Soviet Union and its satellite countries. In Poland, one third less sunlight reaches the ground because it is cut out by pollution. One Pole said,

**"They didn't pay God's creation enough respect."**

Is it a coincidence that in the Soviet Union for three quarters of a century the government claimed that God did not exist and tried to put an end to all religion?

Of course, it is not only "they" who do not pay God's creation enough respect. We are all guilty – including those of us who go to school in a car when we could walk!

But if it was people who said that God did not exist who made the biggest mistakes, perhaps it is those who listen to God who will best be able to help put things right.

## A prayer

Creator God, forgive us for not paying your creation enough respect. Show us how, together with you, we can help clean up the world you made for us. Amen.

# 33 Population explosion

## Theme
A Christian approach to the problems caused by an exploding world population.

## You will need
• large sheets of paper with these figures written on them: 6,000,000,000 and 1,000,000,000+

## Presentation
Tell children near the front that you are going to count and to point at them. As you point at each individual, he or she is to stand up.

Start counting and pointing at one-second intervals: "One baby, two babies, three babies, four babies..." – up to thirty.

Each person standing represents a new baby who has actually just been born somewhere in the world.

**One baby is born every second.**

Bring the thirty children out to the front and say that they represent the 6 billion in the world now. Give one the paper to hold with 6,000,000,000 written on it.

Separate ten of the thirty: these represent the children.

**One third of the present world population is children.**

They need food, housing, healthcare and schools.

Now separate six of the twenty "adults." These are the ones who can't find work in the developing countries, the poorer countries of the world. Of the remaining fourteen, some are too old to work and need care. The ones who have work must support all the others.

Bring out six more children to join the thirty at the front. This is the extra number of people there are going to be in the world in the next ten years, more than one billion of them. Give one of them the 1,000,000,000+ sheet.

Where are we going to find the food, the hospitals, the work, the schools for all these as well? It sounds like an impossible task, doesn't it.

Do you think anyone knows the answer?

Do you know what is probably the most famous verse in the Bible, John 3:16? It begins,

> **God loved the world so much that he gave his only Son.**

## God knows the answers

Christians believe that God is the Creator of the world and that God loves the world and all the people in it. If he is clever enough to create the world, he is clever enough to know the answers. Because he loves us, but hasn't made us like robots, he wants us to listen to him for those answers.

Christians believe that whenever someone listens to God, the answers start to get worked out. It might be the voice of conscience inside us telling us not to be greedy or selfish.

It might be an interest or a skill that we have that, as we grow up, leads to a job God wants us to do.

It might be the feeling of excitement that some of us get when we discover new things. Maybe some of us here will discover new answers to some of the problems.

**Conscience, interests, excitement – these are all ways God can speak to us and show us what to do.**

The problems of feeding and caring for all these people in the world are vast. But God is even bigger. Christians believe that when we work with him, we can work it out. Every single one of us can be a part of God's answer.

## Something to think about

Here are some thoughts from Psalm 33. They might be read out or written on OHP to think about while some music is played.

> **The Lord watches over those who obey him, those who trust in his constant love. He saves them from death, he keeps them alive in times of famine.**
>
> *Psalm 33:18–19,* Good News Bible

## Follow-up

Work with a small group of children on presenting the whole of Psalm 33 as a dramatic or choral reading. (Recommended version: International Children's Bible.)

This can be introduced by a recap of the figures above. The people of Israel faced problems of war and hunger that were as great to them as the present world problems are to us. This is a poem or song that shows how they faced those problems.

The last three verses and the first three encourage us not to get overwhelmed by thinking about problems, but to trust God and have a good sing!

# Don't Get Caught!

# 34 Hooked!

## Theme
The dangers of being "hooked" by addictions, and how some people find freedom.

## You will need
- some real fishing tackle OR two canes and string with some suitable sweets tied on (e.g., red liquorice "bootlaces")
- two blindfolds.

## Presentation
You could talk seriously about fishing, or have a fun fishing contest between two pairs of children. One of each pair holds the cane (keeping the end well up in the air away from eyes) and the other is blindfolded and keeps his hands behind his back. He has to catch and eat the "bait" off the end of the line. Quickest pair wins.

**What do people get "hooked" on?**

Start with one or two examples; the children may be able to suggest others, e.g., video games, scratch cards, food, drugs, alcohol, stealing. It can even be things like gossiping or telling tall stories.

**What happens to people who get hooked on such things?**

Talk about how hard it is to escape. The funny thing is, those who get hooked often start by thinking they are being really free! We probably all know someone who started smoking because they thought it looked "big" and now would like to stop but can't.

## The bait the disciples used
Jesus told some of his first disciples that they were going to be "fishers of men." What sort of bait did they use to catch people? It was things like: the promise of eternal life; freedom from guilt; understanding what life is all about; being filled with the Spirit of God.

People who get "caught" by this bait find something strange: they claim they are set free! Jesus actually said about himself, **"If the Son sets you free, you will be free indeed"** (John 8:36).

A man called Rick Toseland had been on drugs for five years. One night he got "caught" at a Salvation Army meeting when he asked Jesus to take his addiction from him. The next morning he woke up free from the usual overpowering need for drugs. Rick said, "As far as I know, it is medically impossible to come off drugs overnight with no withdrawal symptoms, no medication. But with God, anything is possible."[1]

The best thing is to avoid the temptation of the bait in the first place. But if we do get hooked, let's remember that there are many people like Rick Toseland who tell us that there is a way to be set free – through Jesus.

## A prayer

Lord Jesus, help me to find real freedom, the freedom to be the person you made me to be. Help me to recognize temptations when they come, and give me the courage to say "no." Amen.

---

1. Quoted in JESUS NOW! Magazine, Issue 1.

# 35 Dog sword-swallower

## Theme
The seriousness of stealing.

## You will need
• a Bible: Proverbs 28:24.

## Presentation
Talk about birthdays and birthday cakes. Have the children ever been tempted to have a bite of their birthday cake before it was cut at the party?

There was a dog with the rather strange name of Apple who lived in New York. His owner had made a birthday cake and left it sitting on a table. It was too much of a temptation for Apple. He bit into the tasty cake, but he was in so much of a hurry to bolt it down that he managed to do a sword-swallowing act with the knife that was being used to cut it!

Fortunately for Apple, the knife went down handle first, or his greed could have been fatal. His owner discovered him with the blade sticking out of his mouth and was able to deliver him from his embarrassing predicament. How's that for being caught red-handed!

**Do animals know the difference between right and wrong?** They certainly know when their owners don't approve of what they do. Both dogs and cats seem to look guilty when caught stealing some food that is not theirs.

**We humans do know that stealing is wrong. But sometimes we try to excuse ourselves by saying it was only something small.**

Listen to what it says in the Bible:

> **Some people rob their fathers or mothers and say, "It's not wrong." Such people are just like those who destroy things.**
> *Proverbs 28:24*

In other words, even taking something small at home without permission – a few coins, or cake or cookies – is as bad as smashing things up. God knows what we are like. The small things we do wrong at home may develop into much bigger things.

Apple got caught in his crime when it went horribly wrong. We may get away with small things most of the time, but there may come a time when it goes horribly wrong. The best way not to get caught like Apple is not to start stealing in the first place.

## Something to do

Children could draw a picture of Apple doing his sword-swallowing act. Underneath they could write a prayer asking God to help them resist temptation.

# 36 Beastly bullfrog

## Theme
A warning against being greedy.

## You will need
• a Bible: Luke 12:15–21.

## Presentation
Have you ever heard the story of Hungry Hagar the beastly bullfrog? Hagar was one of the residents at the Stratford-upon-Avon Butterfly and Jungle Safari centre in England.

One summer staff at the centre noticed that their butterflies were disappearing. Up to twenty of these beautiful and expensive creatures were vanishing every day. Many of them had been specially imported from all over the world.

At first they suspected an iguana, but he turned out to be a vegetarian. Then a watch was kept on a group of cockatoos. For weeks staff were scratching their heads, unable to find the culprit.

Finally one of them spotted Hagar munching one of his cousins, another bullfrog almost as big as himself. For dessert he sprang into the air and snapped up a butterfly in mid-flight.

Catching Hungry Hagar proved almost as difficult as unmasking him. Staff had to wait until the sleepiness of hibernation slowed him down. His punishment? – solitary confinement in a glass case.

"He had an insatiable appetite," said Mr. Lamb, the manager. "He was very fat when we eventually caught him. Now we are feeding him on locusts, which are much cheaper."

## A man who was greedy
Being greedy is very unpleasant. Jesus told a story about a kind of human Hagar. Only this man was greedy for money and things as well as food. Listen to what happened to him.

**Read or tell the story of the Rich Fool in Luke 12:15–21.**

## A reminder

Children could draw a picture of Hungry Hagar for display. Under it they could write Jesus' warning: "Be careful and guard against all kinds of greed."

# 37 AH...AH...AH... TISHOO!

## Theme
A thought for the season of colds and flu: protecting our minds as well as our bodies.

## You will need
• a clean handkerchief.

## Presentation
Start with the most dramatic sneeze you can manage.

**What happens when we sneeze?** We force air explosively from our lungs. The rushing air carries a spray of around 19,000 droplets as much as one meter (one yard). No wonder the old saying warned: Coughs and sneezes spread diseases; catch the germs in your handkerchiefses!

Also, when we sneeze we have to close our eyes. Researchers have discovered that it is impossible to keep your eyes open when you sneeze. This is a good job: the force of the sneeze is great enough to force your eyeballs out of their sockets!

**Why do we sneeze?** For protection. That tickle in the nose or throat might be a harmful foreign body that could be breathed or washed down into the lungs. The sneeze blasts it back out again. It is one of the many ways the body has of protecting itself.

Like many of the body's other defences, it is involuntary. That is to say, we can't make ourselves sneeze, and it is very hard to stop one that is coming. Sneezing is outside the conscious control of our minds.

## Round and round in our heads
But what about our minds? What happens when something possibly harmful gets into them – something frightening or nasty that we see on the television, for example? Once such a picture is in our minds, it can't be sneezed out again. We all know what it is like when something keeps going round and round in our heads and we can't stop it.

That is why we need to be careful about what we watch. It is why some programs can only be shown after nine o'clock in the evening when children should be in bed. It is best not to let harmful things get into our minds in the first place. Sometimes friends or older children or even an adult might want us to watch a video that shows things that are wrong. **To protect ourselves we have to say "no."**

St. Paul puts it more positively like this:

> **Continue to think about the things that are good and worthy of praise. Think about the things that are true and honourable and right and pure and beautiful and respected.**
> *Philippians 4:8*

That is good advice.

Some people like to play jokes with sneezing powder. Others might want you to look at a magazine or video they've got. Protect your mind. Just say no.

## A prayer

**God, we thank you for designing our bodies with lots of ways to protect themselves from harm. Make us aware when something we see or hear might be harmful to our minds. Give us the courage to say no. Amen.**

# 38 1 in 14,000,000

## Theme

A graphic illustration of the chance of winning the lottery jackpot.

## You will need

- a stack of small coins and a marker pen; perhaps a mock giant pay for £10 million.

## Presentation

You might start by asking for a show of hands: how many of the children's (or their friends') families buy lottery tickets each week?... We are going to look at the chances of winning the jackpot.

Show children the small coins and mark one clearly on one face with the marker pen. Tell them that you are going to hide the marked coin somewhere in a stack of coins and you want them to imagine that if they choose the right coin, they will win the lottery jackpot.

(Show the giant pay if you have made one.)

To get the odds right, we are going to need some more coins. The stack will reach the ceiling. Then we'll need a crane to keep building it as high as the Eiffel Tower. After that, it gets a bit difficult. We can perhaps get as high as Ben Nevis in Britain, over 4,000 feet high, but we are still not there. A few more truckloads of coins and we'll reach as high as Mount Everest. After that, we'll have to use a plane to keep adding coins to the top of the stack. Up and up, as high as a jet airliner at 30,000 feet – but we are not even halfway there yet! We need to keep on adding coins until we get a stack over 26,000 meters (84,000 feet) high, or me than 26 kilometers (16 miles).

Now we've got the stack finished, roll up, roll up! Anyone who wants to can pay £1 and choose just one coin out of that pile 26km (16 miles) high. If you choose the right one, you win the jackpot! Any takers?

**Is picking the winning coin out of that pile a realistic dream? That is exactly the same chance as winning the jackpot with a £1 lottery ticket.**

Wise King Solomon once said this:

**Don't wear yourself out trying to get rich. Be wise enough to control yourself.**

*Proverbs 23:4*

A person who spent large amounts of time and money trying to find the one right coin in a pile 26km (16 miles) high would surely wear themselves out for nothing. How much wiser to control ourselves and think through the best way to use our money.

## Something to do

Ask for suggestions of wiser ways to spend £1.

---

NOTE: For four more talks on how Jesus viewed the use of money, see the section MONEY! MONEY! MONEY! in *52 Ideas for Junior Classroom Assemblies* by Chris Chesterton and Pat Gutteridge (Monarch Books).

# It could be you – by 20,000 AD!

*Mathematics is not everyone's strong point, else the national lottery would hardly command the following it does. (But then, Camelot was ever the realm of impossible dreams.) Some children might find this presentation of salient figures gives pause for thought. (But perhaps that too is just wishful thinking?)*

## Theme
The wise use of money.

## You will need
- two large pieces of paper with these figures on: £11,817 and –£5,070.

## Presentation
Ask for two volunteers who would like to help in an experiment by spending a few thousand pounds over the next twenty years. We'll call them Jo and Chris. Stand one on either side of you.

Jo and Chris both get £5 a week pocket money. Jo spends around £3 of hers each week and gets her dad to buy her two lottery tickets with the rest. She is hoping to win the jackpot and become a millionaire.

Chris also spends £3 a week, but would rather save the rest so he has it to use some day. He puts £2 a week into a savings account.

Five years later they both have a bit more spending money – £10 a week. Jo decides to double her lottery tickets. Chris also doubles the amount he saves.

Another five years on and they are both out at work. Jo now spends £8 a week on lottery tickets, and Chris puts £8 a week into his savings account.

Finally, five years later, Jo can afford to spend £16 a week on lottery tickets in the hope of winning the big one, whilst Chris increases his savings to £16 a week.

**Let's see how they are likely to be doing after 20 years.**

Jo has spent £7,800 on lottery tickets. Has she won a million pounds? Almost certainly not. She has probably won smaller prizes totaling around £2,730. So overall she has lost £5,070. (Give "Jo" the minus £5,070 sign.)

Chris has put the same amount, £7,800, into his savings account. With interest it now comes to over £11,800. (Give "Chris" the £11,817 sign.[1]) As the wise King Solomon said,

**He who gathers money little by little makes it grow.**    *Proverbs 13:11*

Minus £5,070 on one side, plus £11,817 on the other – Chris is almost £17,000 better off than Jo.

**What happens if Jo goes on buying lottery tickets in the hope of choosing the six right numbers?**

If she spends at the rate she has done over the past 20 years, it will take her until the year 20,000 (yes, twenty thousand!) to have even a one in two chance of winning the jackpot. That's another 180 centuries. By that time she will have spent over £70 million on tickets.

**Should she continue the experiment? What do you think?**

---

1. This figure is based on a 6% interest rate.

# Warning Signs

# 40 Thank you, God, for pain!

## Theme
Pain is a valuable warning that something is wrong.

We live in a culture that views pain almost as an evil in itself, as bad as the things that cause the pain. The shocked response of children when one suggests that we should thank God for pain is most instructive.

## You will need
- a garden cane and a ruler;
- OR a hammer, nails and a piece of wood.

## Presentation
Make a show of swishing the cane around. Today's children have not met with this as an instrument of punishment (unlike some of us of the older generation!).

Swap the cane for a ruler (less dangerous) and get a volunteer to hit you across the hand with it. (It might need two or three attempts to get them to do more than tap you with it.) Shout "Ow!" and make a fuss about how much it hurt. Then get the volunteer to sit down and say that you have a prayer to say this morning. Your prayer is:

**Thank you, God, for pain.**

**Alternative introduction.** Do a bit of carpentry or hammer in a picture hook and pretend to hit your thumb with the hammer. Then go on to the prayer, as above.

## An encounter with leprosy
Ask the children if they think you are crazy? Why should we thank God for pain? A famous doctor gives us the answer.

As a boy, Paul Brand lived in India. His father was a doctor and a missionary. He vividly remembers the only time in his life he saw his father hesitate to help someone.

He was seven years old at the time. Three men came to the Brands' house one day for medical treatment. As they approached, Paul noticed a difference from the hundreds of others who came. Their skin was thick and mottled, their ears were swollen. They had blood-stained bandages around their feet. Closer still, Paul saw they had fingers missing, and one had no toes.

Paul's mother came out, and her face went pale. She told Paul to run and get his father and then to shut himself inside the house.

Full of curiosity, Paul slipped out of the house and found a hiding place where he could watch. He saw his father put on surgical gloves – this was most unusual. As he watched his father bathing and dressing the men's wounds, he realized that they were not wincing or crying out in pain.

**This was Paul's first encounter with leprosy, the oldest recorded and most dreaded disease in the world!**

When he grew up, Paul became a doctor himself, and a world authority on leprosy. In his studies of leprosy patients in India he discovered that the disease is not like some fungus, eating away at fingers and noses, but that it simply attacks the nerve cells. Gradually the sufferer loses the sense of pain in parts of his body.

So he pinches a finger and doesn't even notice. Or twists an ankle and continues to walk on it. Or his eyelids stop blinking away dust and dirt and he goes blind.

**Pain is the body's alarm system. It tells us that the dish we have just picked up is too hot and that we need to put it down quickly before we get burned. It is our first line of defence against harm.**

None of us like pain – it would not be much good as an alarm system if we did. But without it we would be in serious trouble. Perhaps you can join me now in my strange prayer:

**Thank you, Lord, for pain.**

The story is taken from *Fearfully and Wonderfully Made* by Dr. Paul Brand and Philip Yancey (Hodder and Stoughton, London, 1981), pp. 35–37.

# 41 Tset gnilleps

## Theme
Misunderstanding God's rules for living.

## You will need
- a list for a backwards spelling test, e.g., honey, seven, milk, race, football, thumb, white, mouse, town, school
- a Bible: Mark 3:1–6 and 2:27.

## Presentation
Either ask for volunteers and give them words to be spelled backwards, e.g. honey – y-e-n-o-h, or you spell them backwards and ask for hands up, who can tell you the word.

**Tell the story of Jesus and the man with the shrivelled hand** in Mark 3:1–6. This is a story about people who had gotten things backwards.

If necessary, explain that the synagogue was the place where Jewish people went to worship God and listen to teaching, like a church or a mosque. The Sabbath is Saturday, the Jewish holy day. The Jews had very strict laws about not doing any work on the Sabbath. Many Jews keep similar laws today.

The religious leaders of the time had gotten things backwards. Jesus said,

**The Sabbath was made for man, not man for the Sabbath.**   *Mark 2:27*

In other words, God's rules for living are to help us live fuller, not more restricted, lives. In the Fourth Commandment, God told people "to observe the Sabbath and keep it holy." It is a day for resting from work and remembering how God created the world and himself rested on the seventh day. God did not intend it to be a burden on people in which keeping rules actually stopped them from doing good.

**Would Jesus tell us off for getting things backwards, like he told off the religious leaders then? Perhaps the way in which we have turned "holy days" into "holidays" when we just do what we like and not think about God at all makes Jesus sad. What do you think?**

# A prayer

Lord Jesus, you were angry at the religious leaders, but you also felt sorry for them because they were so stubborn and wrong. Help us to understand God's rules for living right, and not to be stubborn. Amen.

# 42 Lizard muesli

## Theme
Watching what we say.

## You will need
- a bowl of cereal, a spoon, and a prune or large raisin
- a Bible: Mark 7:14–23. (This passage could be split into sections and given to a couple of children to prepare.)

## Presentation
Apologize for being late with your breakfast and start diving into a bowl of cereal. Hold up a spoon with a large raisin or prune in it and tell this story about a teacher from Bristol.

He was eating his breakfast muesli when he found what he thought was a dried prune. Fortunately, he examined it carefully before putting it into his mouth. He discovered that it was a small, dried up lizard! This tree lizard, a black iguanid, had got itself mistaken for a large Californian raisin. (Eat your prune and declare it to be "very tasty.")

The makers and suppliers of that brand of muesli were fined £3,500 each for failing to take enough care about their product. Foreign bodies in food are rare, but some of those that do happen quite turn your stomach over.

**Ask for a show of hands – who likes pizza?...** Would they have liked the variety served up by one Dutch take-out? Its extra special, mouth-watering topping was...horse manure!

Then there were the boxes of porridge oats sold by a supermarket in East London. They were found to contain more than 1,000 beetles and 5,000 grubs, all of them alive.

Not forgetting the well-known brand chocolate slice with the extra, rather chewy ingredient – a cigarette end.

Tales such as that make us feel quite queasy. What goes into our mouths can be pretty worrying, but what comes out of our mouths can be just as bad. (And we are not talking about being sick after hearing the tales above.)

Have children read the prepared Bible passage: Mark 7:14–23.

Jesus is saying that we should be a lot more worried about the words that come out of our mouths than the food that goes into them. What would happen if we got a £3,500 fine today each time we said something bad about someone else or had a nasty thought? Most of us would be very heavily in debt by the end of the day!

## A prayer

Father God, help us to keep nasty things out of our minds, and, most especially, to keep a guard over our mouths so that nasty and hurtful words do not come out of them. Amen.

# 43 BUZZ OFF!

## Theme
A lesson from nature about the dangers of judging others.

## You will need
• a picture of a wasp. Find one in a nature book or copy these onto OHP acetate or get some children to draw their own versions.

## Presentation
Find out how many people have been stung by a wasp this year?... Who's allergic to wasp stings?... Who's frightened of wasps?... Who doesn't mind them buzzing around?

Did you know that there are thousands of different kinds of wasps? The smallest are microscopic, and the largest queen is 4cm (1$^1$/2 inches) long with an 8cm (3 inch) wingspan. Fortunately she lives in the Himalayas so there is not too much chance of meeting her!

**Try a vote. If we could get rid of all wasps from the earth, who would vote for that?...**

Anybody in favour of keeping wasps?... Why?... Can anyone think of any good that wasps might do?

In fact, wasps play a vital ecological role. One of the jobs they do is to pollinate flowers, like bees. They are not quite so important in the ecosystem as bees, but they still do a lot of essential work. Take fig trees, for example. In the world's rainforests figs are the most important source of food for fruit-eating animals. Each of the many different species of fig has its own type of wasp to pollinate it. The fig and the wasp are entirely dependent on each other. Without the wasps the figs would not be

115

pollinated and no fruit would grow. Without the fruit countless animals would die. A large part of the rainforest ecosystem would collapse.

Perhaps even more important is the way they control the numbers of other insect pests. The painful sting that we know is a development of a paralyzing poison that many wasps use. The wasp attacks a spider, a caterpillar or a grub and paralyzes it. Then she takes it to a nest she has made – perhaps a hole in wood or soil, or one made out of mud – and she lays an egg on or in it. When the wasp larva hatches out it feeds on the paralyzed insect or spider.

It sounds horrible! But if the wasps weren't quietly going about feeding their larvae in this way, populations of other pests might explode and upset their ecosystem. People might lose crops or have to use chemical pesticides. The sawfly, a serious pest in North America that was destroying spruce trees, was controlled by introducing wasps.

It's a good job we were not able to really vote wasps out of existence. Just think: we would have killed millions of other animals in the rainforests and wrecked whole ecosystems all over the world!

**Things are rarely as simple as they seem. Perhaps that's why Jesus warned us not to judge each other. Somebody might be a real pest, but there are certainly all kinds of good things about them that we aren't even aware of. Perhaps we should think of the wasp before telling them to buzz off!**

# A prayer

Great Creator God, you designed the world and all the plants and animals in it. You did a good job. You made all the people, too. When I am tempted to judge somebody because I don't like something about them, remind me of the wasp. Amen.

 **Super injustice**

## Theme
Injustice.

## You will need
- a picture, comic or video of Superman.

## Presentation
Ask children to raise their hands if they have heard of Joe Shuster. (If anyone does, ask who they think he is.) Then ask who has heard of Superman. Display a Superman comic or video if you have one. Joe Shuster was the artist who created Superman.

While still at school, aged seventeen, Shuster teamed up with another student, Jerry Siegel. Siegel was the writer, with a special liking for science fiction. Together they began producing comic strips for their school newspaper. They also sent off examples to national newspapers, but all of them were rejected.

It was in 1936 that Siegal and Shuster got their first real break, with two series in a comic called *"More Fun"*. Two years later, Superman made his first appearance in *"Action Comics No 1"*. If you had a mint copy of that in good condition today it would be worth more than £40,000!

Joe Shuster died in 1992. As Superman had starred in at least forty-four comic book series, plus radio, TV, and film series, and four of the world's biggest money-making movies, Joe Shuster should have died a very rich man. But he wasn't.

## Unfair treatment
For many years he had been almost penniless. His eyesight had started failing and he had had to retire early. For many years he was supposed by his wife Joanna, the original model for Lois Lane. He and Jerry Siegel had fought in the courts for a share in the Superman profits for nearly forty years but had got nowhere.

It was only when Warner Brothers was launching the first Superman movie that they agreed to give $20,000 a year each to Siegel and Shuster, hardly over-generous, and Joe did not live many more years to enjoy it.

**How does that story make you feel? Does it make you want to shout words like, "Unfair!"**

Superman was always fighting for justice – that is, treating people right, fairly – yet his creators were treated most unfairly.

Unfair treatment – injustice – is all around us. Sometimes it is much worse than the example we have just heard. (You could mention an example from current news.) Sometimes we are part of it ourselves, perhaps without realizing it, as when people in Third World countries are treated little better than slaves to produce food we eat or clothes we wear.

We may not have super powers, but we ought all to be involved in the fight against injustice. There are some famous words from the Bible we could think about or use as a prayer. This was spoken by the prophet Amos, a man who hated injustice:

**Let justice flow like a river. Let goodness flow like a stream that never stops.**
*Amos 5:24*

## Something to do
Older children might look for stories of injustice in newspapers, cut them out, and make a display. Add the words from Amos 5:24.

# Buried Treasure

# 45 Treasures of darkness 1

## Theme
Treasure from the natural world tells us about a generous God.

## You will need
- a number of items made (or partly made) from plastics e.g., yogurt container, cola bottle, ink pen, radio or cassette-player, piece of polystyrene, article of clothing made of nylon, etc.

## Presentation
Show your collection and ask the children to think how many other things they will use today made of some kind of plastic.

**Does anyone know where all this plastic comes from?**

Does it grow on trees?

Are there genetically mutated cows that have plastic skins instead of leather?

Are there armies of children in Asia working sixteen hours a day pulling wings off flies to make polythene bags?

The answer is: oil, crude oil – or petroleum, to give it its proper name. It's that black stuff we get on us on the beach during the summer break because a tanker of crude oil has had a spillage somewhere.

Petroleum was known in the ancient world because there are places where the sticky, tarry, crude oil seeps out on the surface. They used it to caulk ships and even sometimes to build roads. Those uses were valuable enough, but they could not have dreamed of the riches hidden away inside that sticky black stuff.

Its first main use in the modern world came when it was refined to produce oil to be burned in lamps and replace oil from whales. So one thing it has done is to help save the whale! The first oil well was drilled in the United States in 1859.

## Imagine a world without plastics
Today oil is the major source of power in the world, driving virtually all our cars, trucks and planes. And it is not only plastics that are made from it, but solvents,

paints, asphalt, fibers for clothes, soap, cleansing agents, explosives, fertilizers, and even medicines. Could we imagine a world now without them?

Centuries ago the prophet Isaiah spoke this message from God to Cyrus, king of Persia:

> **I will give you the treasures of darkness, riches stored in secret places, so that you may know that I am the Lord, the God of Israel, who summons you by name.**
> *Isaiah 45:3,* New International Version

When we look at the use we make of the crude oil that comes from deep under the earth or under the North Sea, it seems as if God has said that to the whole human race. He has given us treasures of darkness, riches stored in secret places.

## A prayer

> **Thank you for ink pens and cola bottles, cassettes and CD's, trainers and TV sets. Thank you for the men and women who have discovered the "treasures of darkness" and given us so much to use and enjoy every single day. Amen.**

# 46 Treasures of darkness 2

## Theme
Discovering the treasures inside us.

## You will need
• ask a group of children aged eight or older to make a list of things they can do now which they could not do when they started school. If they are able to identify skills rather than knowledge, so much the better.

## Presentation
Recap on the previous talk about crude oil and what can be made from it.

Through accident or research, people are constantly discovering new resources and riches hidden not just in oil but in countless other things in the natural world around us. New ways of treating and changing and refining substances are being discovered to provide even more materials.

**But you don't have to be a scientist to discover riches hidden in secret places. Every one of us has hidden skills, gifts and understanding.**

Ask the group to come and talk about some of the skills they have discovered since they started going to school.

**Have they enjoyed discovering these things?... Have they "refined" them – that is, improved them?... Are they proud of their achievements?...**

A big part of the excitement of life is discovering and refining the resources buried inside ourselves. Going to school is one part of that process of discovery and refining.

When we look at the world around us, and then look at ourselves, it is as if the whole world is a treasure house. One of the main purposes and joys of life is to discover that treasure, bring it into the light, and use it. And what did the prophet Isaiah say the reason was for all this?

> **So that you may know that I am the Lord, the God of Israel, who summons you by name.**
> *Isaiah 45:3*

# A different kind of prayer

We can give a clap to the people who talked about their discoveries of things they have learned. As we applaud them, we can also applaud God who created us with those resources inside us waiting to be discovered.

# 47 Beauty on the inside

## Theme
A spring-time analogy from nature and a Greek myth shows that our inner gifts are more important than outward appearance.

## You will need
- a bowl or a bunch of daffodils (or, out of season, a daffodil bulb);
- perhaps a mirror.

## Presentation
**Which is more important: how we look on the outside, or what kind of person we are?**

Perhaps a bunch of daffodils can teach us something. They certainly look pretty and cheer us up after the dreary days of winter. But scientists have recently discovered something inside the dull-looking daffodil bulb that could do certain people even more good than admiring the flowers.

Daffodils belong to the narcissus family of plants – some of the daffodil-type flowers you can grow or buy in the shops are called narcissi. There is an old Greek myth about these flowers and their beauty.

There was once a young man named Narcissus. He was extremely handsome, but his mother had been told when he was a baby that he would only live a long life provided he never looked at his own face in a mirror.

A nymph called Echo fell in love with Narcissus, but he rejected her. The gods were angry and decided to punish him. One day Narcissus sat down beside a pool of still, clear water. Looking into it, he saw for the first time the reflection of his own face. Never having seen himself in a mirror, Narcissus was so struck by the beauty of the face looking back at him from the water that he fell in love with it.

Of course, the face only existed while he remained gazing into the water. Whenever Narcissus moved away he lost sight of it. He was so much in love with his own reflection that he stayed on the bank of the pool until he pined away and died. On that very spot, a flower grew. It was named after him: a narcissus.

Even today, people who spend a long time admiring themselves in a mirror are called narcissistic.

# Inside the ugly bulb

The daffodil bulb is quite ugly compared to the flower. It even has an unpleasant means of self-defense. To stop animals eating it, it contains a chemical that makes them feel sick. It doesn't sound as if this could be any use to anybody except the plant itself. But scientists have found that this chemical might help people who suffer from Alzheimer's disease.

Alzheimer's is a very unpleasant disease of the brain. People who suffer from it lose their memory and have difficulty speaking, even though they may not be very old. It is as hard for their families as for the person who has it. There is still no cure for Alzheimer's, and little doctors can do to help the people who get it. If the scientists are right, and the daffodil-bulb extract really does slow down the disease, many people will be extremely grateful.

So some of the fields of daffodils are now growing beautiful flowers above the ground and medicine under the ground.

# A special way to help others

It is not wrong to be proud of the way we look – unless we get like Narcissus and spend too long admiring ourselves in the mirror! But like the daffodil bulb, there is something far more important hidden away inside every one of us – some special way of being able to help others.

**Do you know what special way you have of being able to help others? Maybe it is something you do, or the way you talk to people, or how you feel about things and show that.**

The Bible puts it like this:

> **People look at the outside of a person, but the Lord looks at the heart.**
>
> *1 Samuel 16:7*

It is in "the heart" – our innermost selves – that lies the desire and special way each one of us has of being able to help other people.

# A prayer

In a moment of quiet, each person could ask God to "grow" that special way of being able to help others and to really use it.

# 48 Creepy-crawly or doctor's friend?

*Here's a talk that rates really high for "Yuk!" factor. You can guarantee it will get talked about at home.*

## Theme
An enemy turns out to be a friend.

## You will need
- If you know a fisherman who will supply you with a few maggots, so much the better. No other preparation is needed – apart from practicing a ghoulish horror-movie voice for maximum effect.

## Presentation
Who has seen a fisherman's tin full of wriggling maggots?... Or even a dead bird or animal covered with the repulsive white creatures gorging themselves on the rotting flesh until only the skeleton remains?

Now imagine them crawling over your bare skin! It's the stuff nightmares are made of.

Yet one day you might go to the hospital with an injury and find the doctor saying,

**"Yes, that looks nasty. I think I'm going to prescribe a jarful of hungry young maggots. They'll soon get chomping away at the wound."**

**Yuk!**

No, this isn't an April Fool or a scene from a horror film. It is a very effective way of helping a nasty wound to heal up quickly and to fight infection. It is already being used at some hospitals in Britain and other parts of the world.

This is why. Up to the 1930's, if you were injured in an accident or a battle, there was a serious risk that the wound would become infected. Often the only answer was amputation, otherwise the infection would spread through the body and kill you. Then penicillin was discovered, and other antibiotics followed. We have all grown up in a world where an injection or a week's medicine does the trick and fear of serious infection has almost disappeared.

**Now, though, some bacteria are becoming increasingly resistant to antibiotics!**

Despite drugs and dressings, that wound may not heal up. So doctors are rediscovering a method of treating wounds that was used before antibiotics, especially in the United States.

The maggots are bred from the eggs of a kind of fly, the greenbottle. They are sterilized so that they don't carry infections. Depending on how large the wound is, from half-a-dozen up to a few hundred maggots are placed in it under a special dressing. The patient does not feel anything. The maggots get to work eating dead and diseased tissue in the wound. Usually they are removed after three days. Doctors find that infections disappear and the wound heals quickly.

**One doctor reckons that perhaps 2,000 patients each week around Britain could be suitable for treatment by maggots!**

It may sound revolting, but when you think about it, it is a natural way of promoting healing. Maggots are one of nature's environmental clean-up specialists.

Isn't it strange? We don't like flies such as the greenbottle because they spread disease – and they do. That is why it is important to keep food covered and not let flies land on it. Yet the larval form of the greenbottle, the maggot, is one of nature's ways of fighting disease. A creature that seems at first sight to be an enemy turns out to be a very valuable friend.

# A prayer

**Creator God, you made this world with so many strange and wonderful things in it. Help us to look beyond our first reactions and discover new friends in unexpected places. Amen.**

# 49 Hidden value

## Theme
The unseen treasure of the kingdom of heaven.

## You will need
- some saffron – if you can afford it!
- a flower to show stamens
- perhaps a crocus bulb
- a Bible: Matthew 13:44.

## Presentation
Imagine it is springtime and the crocuses are in bloom. Imagine me showing you a field full of white and purple crocuses and saying, "I'll give you these flowers if you give me everything you own. Your bike, your Sega or Playstation, your Walkman, everything." How many of you would do that swap?

If I tell you that there is treasure in that field, would that help you make up your mind? I might tell you that you are staring right at the treasure, and yet you probably can't see it! If I say that it is worth three times as much as gold, would you believe me?

If I tell you that the treasure that you are staring at is the fluffy yellow bits in the middle of the crocus flower, the stamens (show these on a flower) you will probably think I am a raving nutcase!

But it is true. Crocus stamens are picked, dried and sold as saffron, the most expensive spice in the world. Ten strands – ten of these dried stamens – cost nearly £3 in the shops. That works out at over £4,000 for 100g (a quarter of a pound).

Saffron has been known and used for thousands of years. King Solomon mentioned it in the Bible. Buddhist monks use it to dye their robes golden yellow. Oriental cooks use it to colour and flavour rice and other dishes.

The Romans are said to have slept on saffron-pillows to cure hangovers. At around £10,000 at today's prices that is a highly expensive remedy for a night's over-indulgence!

## A different sort of treasure
Jesus once told a story about a different sort of treasure in a field. Here is his story:

**The kingdom of heaven is like a treasure hidden in a field. One day a man found the treasure, and then he hid it in the field again. The man was very happy to find the treasure. He went and sold everything that he owned to buy that field.**

*Matthew 13:44*

**What is Jesus telling us in this story? What is so valuable that it is worth selling everything else for? Why was the man so happy to find it?**

**Jesus is saying that there is a way of living that is better than any other way.** That way of living is life in what he calls "the kingdom of heaven" or "the kingdom of God." In other places he tells us a lot more about what it means to live that kind of life.

Life in God's kingdom is so much better than any other way of living that, like the treasure in the field, it is worth giving up everything else for. That does not mean that God actually usually asks people to give up everything and go and be a monk or a nun. But he might ask us to give up something which is getting in the way of living life in the best way possible.

You would not have given me all that you own as a swap for a field of crocuses. That is because you did not realize how much they are worth. The treasure was there to see, but you did not recognize it.

**The kingdom of heaven is there to see, but many people do not recognize it. It is only when they discover its true value that they realize it is worth giving anything in order to be able to live life like that.**

Who's going to plant crocuses in their garden for next spring?

# A prayer

If there is treasure to be found, I don't want to miss out on it! Lord God, give me eyes to see the real treasure and the courage to give up anything that is stopping me finding it. Amen.

# 50 Hidden harvest

## Theme
More of nature's treasure-trove.

## You will need
- if possible, collect a few wild fungi – most gardens or a stroll in the local wood should supply some specimens
- try leaving some bread or fruit out a week or two in advance to get a nice crop of mold
- at the very least, buy some mushrooms.

## Presentation
Show the children whatever examples of fungi you have. These are just a few of the thousands of fungi in the world. Some we can eat, while others are deadly poisonous. NEVER eat a wild mushroom without it being first identified by an expert. In France, people take them along to their local chemist's shop for identification!

Some mushrooms or toadstools can have strange effects. There is one called the common ink-cap which often grows in gardens, especially at the base of trees. People who know what they are looking for can eat the ink-cap perfectly safely. But if they drink a glass of beer or wine in the next few days they start to feel sick and sweat a lot and get really bad pins and needles!

If one species of mushroom contains a substance that has that sort of effect, what other good or harmful chemicals might be lurking in fungi?

**Who knows what penicillin is and what it is used for?... Where does penicillin come from?...**

It comes from the common blue or green mold which grows on rotten food. Penicillin made from moldy melons saved countless lives at the end of World War II and afterwards. Some of us here might never have been born if our grandparents lives hadn't been saved by penicillin!

## Chinese mushroom helps hay fever
Who likes Chinese food?... There is a type of mushroom called the Shitake mushroom which is often used in Chinese and Japanese cooking. It has been found to be helpful in treating stomach cancers. It also contains an antihistamine and so can help relieve the symptoms of hay fever.

131

Researchers are looking at more than 200 substances in fungi which have been found to have an effect on cancers. Lots of work remains to be done for any of these to be accepted as reliable medicines without harmful side effects, but it shows what an extraordinary harvest there is hidden inside humble mushrooms, toadstools and molds.

A Jewish songwriter once looked at the natural world and was astounded at all that God had provided in it. He wrote:

> **O Lord, what a variety you have made! And in wisdom you have made them all! The earth is full of your riches.** *Psalm 104:24,* The Living Bible

That long-ago songwriter could never have imagined the skills and techniques modern scientists have for bringing to light the hidden harvest in fungi and plants. But he had grasped the essential truth: in his wisdom God created a world with a bewildering variety of riches waiting to be discovered.

## A prayer

> **Father God, perhaps one day my life might be saved by a medicine made from a fungus. Thank you for the riches that you have stored away for us in this wonderful world. Amen.**

# 51 A nutty question

*This is the first of two talks featuring the humble, but surprising, peanut.*

## Theme
What can come out of a simple question.

## You will need
• a packet of peanuts or a good American peanut butter and jelly sandwich.

## Presentation
Feed some children with peanuts or the peanut butter and jelly sandwich. *(NB – **check they are not allergic to nuts.**)* Tell them they are going to learn some surprising things about peanuts.

Take one child born as a slave, one peanut plant, and one silly question, and you get…millions of people's lives improved! How come?

The child was George Washington Carver, the son of a slave woman in the southern United States of America. The peanut plant and the silly question came later. Carver was born in 1860, and orphaned during the American Civil War. He was interested in the natural world around him, and he also took up drawing, singing, and playing the organ. As a teenager and a young man, he supported himself with a variety of jobs – cook, laundryman, farm worker – while attending different schools and colleges to get an education. By the time he was in his thirties, he had gained a master of science degree.

In later years, he used to tell this story about what happened to him during this period of his life.

## The right sized question
One day while walking out in a field he said to God,

**"Mr. Creator, why did You make this universe?"**

God replied, **"Little man, that question is much too big for you."**

**"Well then, Mr. Creator, why did You make the human race?"**

Again came the answer, **"Little man, even that one's way too big for you."**

133

Carver's eye fell on a peanut plant.

**"All right then, why did You make the peanut?"**

This time God said, **"Little man, that's just about your size. Listen, and I'll tell you."**[1]

And George Washington Carver did listen. It may have sounded like a silly question, but the answer was far from silly. He got a job as the head of the department of agriculture at the Tuskegee Institute in Alabama. Working in his lab, Carver developed some 300 products made from peanuts, things as different and surprising as: cheese, milk, coffee, flour, ink, dyes, plastics, soap, floor-coverings, medicinal oils, and cosmetics. He often referred to God as his co-worker in the laboratory. With the agricultural training they received from him, black people whose parents had been slaves became skilled farmers. The whole economy of the Southern States of America was improved through the peanut industry.

**"Mr. Creator, why did You make the peanut?"**

**How many millions of other questions like that are there waiting for someone to ask them?**

**Have you asked any nutty questions recently?**

## Something to do

Children might like to think up some nutty questions to ask and share them the next time you meet.

---

1. David Seamands, *Living With Your Dreams* (Scripture Press), p. 178.

# 52 Eat a peanut and thank God!

## Theme
Finding hope in bad times.

## You will need
• some peanuts in their shells; a packet of roasted peanuts.

## Presentation

If you want a nutritious snack, you can hardly do better than a packet of peanuts. They contain more protein, minerals and vitamins than liver, more fat than full-cream, and more energy than sugar. They are also just the snack to eat when you are feeling miserable because something has gone wrong – as we will discover in a moment.

Peanuts are not nuts at all. In fact, the "pea" part of their name is more accurate. They grow in a most strange fashion. After the flowers on the small peanut bush fade, a stalk (called a peg) grows down from the base of each one and pushes right into the ground. As much as 10 cm (4 inches) under the surface, a pod starts to develop at the tip of the peg – the familiar peanut shell – and the seeds inside start to swell. To harvest the peanuts, the whole plant is pulled out of the ground and left to dry in the sun. (Show peanuts in their shells.)

There is an odd story about peanuts from the town of Enterprise in Alabama, America, centre of a peanut growing region. In the middle of the town is a unique monument built in the shape of a beetle. It is probably the only statue erected in the honour of a bug in the world! This area used to grow cotton, but in 1915 the crop was almost destroyed by a small beetle, the Mexican boll weevil. 60% of that year's cotton was lost. The desperate farmers turned to other crops, and were surprised at how much they earned growing peanuts. In 1917 they grew more peanuts than any other county in the nation. They were so grateful that in 1919 they erected the beetle statue. Written on it are these words:

> **In profound appreciation of the boll weevil,**
> **And what it has done as the herald of prosperity.**

In 1915 the farmers were cursing the beetle that was ruining them. Four years later they erected a monument in its praise! It reminds us of an old saying that sounds rather past its sell-by date, but which has a certain truth: Every cloud has a silver lining. What seems at the time to be a disaster may push us into thinking afresh

135

about what we are doing, trying out something new, deciding what is important. The farmers of Enterprise discovered that they earned more money growing peanuts than cotton, and improved the soil as a bonus.

## Helping spread the good news

This is a truth that Christians have long known. For example, there is a story in the Bible about how Paul was taken to Rome as a prisoner to be judged by the Emperor. When he got there, he was allowed to live by himself, but chained to a Roman guard twenty-four hours a day. That sounds pretty terrible.

But Paul saw the good side of this. In one of his letters he wrote:

> **Brothers, I want you to know that what has happened to me has helped to spread the Good News. I am in prison because I am a believer in Christ. All the palace guards and everyone else knows this.** *Philippians 1:12–13*

Because different soldiers had spells on duty chained to Paul, they didn't have much choice but to listen to him. The whole of Caesar's crack troops, the palace guard, got to hear the message about Jesus! Paul was very pleased about that. Again and again in his letters as a prisoner he told people to be thankful.

So next time things go wrong, and you are feeling really low, why not buy a packet of peanuts? And while you're munching them, try Paul's recipe for happiness: thank God, and ask him to show you the silver lining in your cloud!

---

The boll weevil monument story is on p. 170 of David Seamands, *Living With Your Dreams* (Scripture Press).

 **53 Hidden treasure**

## Theme
The value of the Bible and the peace it promises.

## You will need
• an old, black Bible and a newer one with a red or colourful cover.

## Presentation
What would you do if you suddenly discovered you owned treasure worth nearly £400 million?... This actually happened to a man in India a few years ago – but eighteen months later he hadn't spent a penny of it! In fact, Mr. Vidyaraj was still living in an old house that he rented for £3.50 a month. All the money he had was the few pounds that his son in America sent him each month.

Mr. Vidyaraj's treasure was precious stones: three of the biggest rubies in the world (the largest weighs 495 grams [just over a pound]!) and the largest known double-star sapphire. They had been in his family for centuries, but they were so black with soot that no one knew what they were. "They just looked like odd-shaped lumps of coal," he said.

One day he got to thinking about them and sent his family off to the cinema. When he cleaned them, he discovered what they were. It took some hard work with hot water and an old toothbrush before red and blue specks started to appear through the grime.

## Treasure on a shelf
Do you think you might have a treasure like that at home? Sounds unlikely, doesn't it, just a nice daydream. But how about one of these? (Show black Bible.) Perhaps you have one of these sitting on a shelf; maybe it has even been handed down in your family. It might never have occurred to you that there could be something very precious under the black cover.

Of course, it does help if the outside looks a bit more attractive. (Show coloured Bible.) And it helps a lot if you can understand the language inside. Some people have thought that what this book contains was so valuable that they gave their lives translating it into their own everyday language.

Mr. Vidyaraj was not too sure about selling his jewels. "I do have the urge for money," he said. "But I would be haunted by so many people – relatives, friends, the taxman, thieves – that my peace of mind would be lost."

**The funny thing is, that's part of the treasure the Bible promises: peace of mind. A lot of grown-ups would give anything for that!**

£400 million or peace of mind? What a choice! But then, most of us don't have that choice. We don't have any odd-shaped pieces of coal sitting on a shelf. Lots of us do have Bibles, though...

## Something to do

Children could use a computer Bible program (or an old-fashioned concordance!) to find what Jesus said about peace. They could choose something to print out.

# 54 Wisdom – worth more than gold

## Theme
Wisdom is the real treasure worth seeking for.

## You will need
- make a model of an Egyptian "diadem" or coronet from card as in the drawing or copy the picture onto OHP acetate or paper.
- a Bible: Proverbs 2:1–5.

## Presentation
Get a volunteer to wear the diadem and introduce her as Queen Mentuhotep, the Great Royal Wife of an Egyptian king.[1]

Queen Mentuhotep lived in the town of Thebes (modern Luxor) some 3,500 years ago. This was roughly a century before Moses led the Israelites out of slavery in Egypt.

When she died, her body was mummified. This gold and silver diadem with two cobra's heads was placed on her bandaged head. She was buried in a tomb near the famous Valley of the Kings.

After that, there are only long centuries of darkness and mystery – until 1995, when two brothers decided to sell some bits and pieces that had belonged to their grandparents. By chance, an expert on ancient Egypt saw the coronet in the sale rooms. He recognized it as being like the only other one known to exist, which is in a museum in The Netherlands.

The brothers were astonished. They knew their grandparents were art historians, but had not realized that the blackened metal band was anything special. All through their childhood, a priceless gold and silver treasure had been sitting in a cabinet in their living room. They had given it no more thought than if it had been a souvenir mug from Disney World.

Who likes watching one of the Antiques shows on TV? Probably most of us have dreamed of finding a treasure like this.

---

1. Okay, so you want to know his name – it's King Sekhemre-sementawy Djehuty. Try pronouncing that in public!

# The king's treasure

Another royal personnage – a king this time, not a queen – was very strong on the idea that treasure was there waiting for anyone who was prepared to really look for it. This king's name was Solomon. King Solomon had gold and silver in plenty, but he knew that there was something even more valuable. This was the advice he gave to young people:

> **My child, believe what I say. And remember what I command you. Listen to wisdom. Try with all your heart to gain understanding. Cry out for wisdom. Beg for understanding. Search for It as you would for silver. Hunt for it like hidden treasure. Then you will understand what it means to respect the Lord. Then you will begin to know God.**
>
> *Proverbs 2:1–5*

Wisdom? Understanding? Respecting the Lord? Knowing God? Some people would say, "Huh! Those are just some blackened old relics that might have interested my grandparents but aren't much use to me!"

There might only be a handful of people who thought it was worth following King Solomon's advice. Just a few who want to search for wisdom as they would for silver, or hunt for understanding like hidden treasure. They could be the ones who discover the real treasure.

# A prayer

Here is a part of a prayer of King Solomon when he was young and God spoke to him in a dream. He realized how hard it was going to be to rule his people well. Anyone who wants to seek "the king's treasure" can echo this prayer.

> **I, your servant, am here among your chosen people. There are too many of them to count. So I ask that you give me wisdom. Then I can rule the people in the right way. Then I will know the difference between right and wrong.** *1 Kings 3:8–9*
> **Amen.**

# True Stories

# 55 A sweet sound in your ear

*This is Catherine Aldridge's own story of how she was healed of partial deafness when she was nine. It was written down in 1993 when she was eighteen and at University.*

## Theme
Healing: a true story.

## You will need
- a bar of chocolate
- a Bible: Mark 7:31–37; a child to read it.

## Presentation
For an attention-grabbing opening, ask for a volunteer who would like to earn, say, a chocolate bar. Have an adult place her hands firmly over the volunteer's ears and say to her in a normal voice, e.g., "I will give you this chocolate bar if you can tell me the name of the President." Play on the volunteer's bafflement a moment or two before allowing her to hear others calling out the answer. Give her the reward, and talk briefly about the problems of deafness.

Have a child read the account of Jesus healing the deaf-mute in Mark 7:31–37. Then tell Catherine's story.

"Until I was nine I was partially deaf in both ears. This caused me many problems, especially in school. The classroom noise made hearing and understanding extremely difficult. As a child I loved to sing but, due to my deafness, I was completely unable to hear tunes or sing them back properly. Countless visits to the doctor didn't help to improve my hearing.

"I used to go to church with my parents. One Sunday we found ourselves at a healing service. Although they knew the stories in the Bible about Jesus healing people, my parents had never thought of taking me for prayer. God had other ideas!

"As people went to the front of the church to be prayed for, the music group was playing songs. They began to sing one which ends, 'let it be a sweet, sweet sound in your ear.' My parents turned to each other, wondering whether to take me forward. At the same time, my eleven-year-old brother was flicking through his Bible. Suddenly he said,

"**Hey, look!**"

His Bible had fallen open to a page with a story about Jesus healing a deaf man. That settled it. We went to the front of the church and someone asked God to heal my deafness.

## My parents were talking

"Later on that day I was playing in our back room. My parents were talking in the kitchen, and they mentioned my name. I jumped up and ran to ask why they were talking about me. There was no way that with my level of deafness I could have heard them. My parents began to be curious.

"The next morning I woke up by myself and was instantly mad that I had been left in bed. I went to tell my parents off for forgetting to wake me, but they were still in bed. It was still ages till our normal getting-up time. I had been woken up by the birds singing. They weren't singing any louder than usual, it was simply that for the first time in my life I could hear them.

"Since then all my hearing tests have recorded perfect hearing in both ears. Singing has become something which I not only enjoy but also have a talent for. In fact, I now help lead the worship in church on Sunday mornings.

"What better way to use my talent than to praise the Lord and thank him for his healing!"

## A song

Sing: *A Sweet Sound in Your Ear* (Songs of Fellowship, no. 49, Book 1, Kingsway Publications, 1981).

# 56 Healed of dyslexia

## Theme
A remarkable true story.

## Presentation
Ask the children if they know what dyslexia is. It is sometimes known as "word-blindness." Children suffering from dyslexia often fall behind at school and their frustration can lead to bad behavior. Talk about the difficulties it causes. Then tell this story of Pat Carlin of Nottingham, England, and the remarkable events which have happened in his life.

When Pat was born, he had spina bifida. There was a lump the size of a tennis ball at the base of his spine. Doctors said he would never walk without braces or crutches.

Spina bifida patients have fluid on the brain. This makes the head swell and an operation is needed to relieve the pressure. At that time a valve was usually put in the head to drain off the fluid, but at the last moment the doctors decided to try a different experimental operation on baby Pat. It was so new that they did not try this operation on anyone else for five or six years.

Every six months Pat had to be taken back to the hospital for check-ups. The operation was clearly a success, as Pat was actually in advance of normal development for children of his age. He was the first child with spina bifida who walked naturally, without braces or other aids.

## Dyslexia diagnosed
The bad news was that Pat was very slow in learning to read. By the time he left elementary school he could only read as well as most six year olds. At middle school they said he was dyslectic and he was sent for special teaching.

When he was twelve, Pat started going to church. He wasn't religious, he just wanted to earn some pocket money! He joined the church choir and was paid to sing in Sunday services. He thought the people in church were off their rockers believing what they did, but he kept going because he wanted the money.

But gradually he began to think there might be something in it after all. When he was seventeen, he prayed in bed one night,

**"Lord, if you are really there, show yourself."**

Pat tells what happened next,

**"I felt a tingling over my whole body. The atmosphere in the room changed. I felt the presence of God."**

A few years later, Pat started going to some big Christian conferences. He heard about people being healed of different illnesses and he wondered if he could be healed of dyslexia. One autumn he went to a special healing service in his local church. It was to turn out to be a remarkable evening.

## Shut up and receive

The guest preacher prayed for several people. He was just about to finish when he said, "Is there anyone here with word-blindness?" Pat was out to the front like a shot. He says,

**"The preacher started praying for me. I was praying too, but he said, 'Shut up, and just receive.' Then he opened a Bible in the middle of the Old Testament, handed it to me, and said, 'Read that.'**

**"I was shocked, because I was able to read it and say it straight out without thinking about it. The preacher said, 'Slow down, you're going too fast!'**

**"I have never had any problems with reading since."**

Pat now works for an engineering company. On Sundays he plays his guitar and helps lead worship at church. Seeing him at work or at church, you would never know that he has struggled with both spina bifida and dyslexia.

# 57 Suffering doesn't stop the joy

## Theme

The true story of a person who has suffered a great deal, but has retained a strong faith in God.

This is one man's personal experience, but it invites children to reflect on questions of suffering, of purpose, of where happiness is to be found, and of how faith can be the central reference point in someone's life.

## Presentation

A suitable introduction might be to ask children how they think they might feel if they knew they were going to be confined to a wheelchair for the rest of their lives. How would they cope with constant pain and the knowledge that the pain was likely to get worse, not better?

One of the many people who has had to face those questions for real is Allan Tibble. Allan had been a miner in a coalfield in England for seven years when the accident happened. He was in an underground train on the way to the coal-face when the train stopped. Another locomotive ran into the back of the stationary train. Allan suffered a whiplash back injury which damaged his spine, nerves and muscles.

After four spells in the hospital he was able to walk with a stick. But the doctors told him that the effects of the injury would get progressively worse. They were right. Within a couple of years, Allan needed a wheelchair to get around. He was – and is – in constant pain. Sometimes the pain gets so intense that he can't get out of the house for several days.

## Church was a kind of club

As a child, Allan had been sent to Sunday school, but he stopped going as a teenager. When he met Christine, his future wife, he started going to church again. He believed in God, but not God as a person, more as an unknown something, a force out there, something in control. He thought being a Christian meant simply doing no one any harm and doing a bit of good. Church was a kind of club where you met nice people. He began to help with the Boys Brigade.

But the pain in his back kept getting worse. He started blaming God.

**"Why me? I don't deserve this. Other people have done much worse things than me."**

He got angry, mad at God, unsure if he was really there.

Gradually Allan realized that there was no point blaming God or anyone else. Instead he started asking God for help. Several times he went to services where people prayed for him to be healed, but nothing happened.

## The big change

Allan tells when the turning point came. In his own words: "The big change came one night. And it was purely God."

"It was a really bad night. I was praying, 'Please, God, take this pain away.' I was making promises I knew I probably couldn't keep. Then it just came into my mind to ask for help to bear it, to face it, to deal with it, not to take it away."

As soon as Allan handed the problem over in this way, the answer came immediately. He felt a kind of warmth all over. The nearest way he can describe it is like being in the physiotherapy pool at the hospital – surrounded and supported on all sides; a gentle, soothing warmth. The pain didn't seem to matter so much.

It was the first time he fully realized that God was personal, real, alive – not a force or a thing. "From then on," says Allan, "he was a friend. And friends can help, especially a friend with that sort of power."

## A very important message

Allan is still in his wheelchair, known to thousands of children in the schools he visits for assemblies in his home town. The fact that he can't walk doesn't prevent him from showing the joy he has inside him that comes from God. Allan believes that just seeing him in his chair gives people a very important message: that suffering doesn't stop the joy.

He firmly believes that whatever is given to God will work out. No matter how bad you feel, it's not possible to be totally miserable. He is quite sure that one day he will be walking again – it might be on earth, or it might be in heaven; it doesn't matter which. But in his own words:

**"I know one day I'm going to be walking alongside Jesus. He won't be pushing the chair – I'll be walking!"**

# Andrew's last words

## Theme

We tend to shy away from talking about death with children, and yet it is vital that it should not be a taboo subject. This account of the last hours and words of Andrew Pickering contains much that is positive and full of hope.

## Presentation

It is always a tragedy when a child dies. Nothing can take away the grief of the family. Thoughts and questions like, "Why?" and "Where was God?" are bound to come.

That was as true of the death of eight-year-old Andrew Pickering as of any other child.

**But Andrew's last words were so strange that they made front-page news and are echoing around the world.**

Andrew was a wonderful character, kind and courageous. He took life seriously, and yet was always full of fun. One of the great loves of his life was buses. He knew all the local buses just by the sound of their engines.

On his eighth birthday, the city bus drivers sent a double-decker to collect Andrew and his friends. They treated them to lunch at one bus depot and tea at another with lots of visits in between.

After his death, a special bus was named in his honour.

It was just before Easter 1994 that Andrew died after a long battle with leukemia. In his last few hours, at home with his parents, Andrew drifted in and out of consciousness many times. He wasn't feeling any pain, and seemed relaxed and happy. At one time he talked about being in a snowstorm. At another, he made noises that sounded like he was enjoying a roller coaster ride.

He finally roused himself and spoke to his father one last time. What he said has made a great impression on many people. He said,

**"Don't blame Jesus, Dad. It's not his fault."**

People often do blame Jesus or God when tragedies happen. They say things like, "Why did God let this happen?" or "If God is all-powerful, why couldn't he stop this?"

**Did Andrew meet Jesus as he was dying? Are his last words a message to the world?**

We can't be sure. But a song was written based on those words. The first verse and chorus goes like this:

> There's a bomb blast in Egypt
> A murder in Leeds
> And a riot in Germany, too
> There's an earthquake in India
> A fire in L.A.
> And what in the world can we do?
>
> Don't blame Jesus
> He suffered violence and shame
> Don't blame Jesus
> It was only for love that he came
> He isn't the one you should blame.

That song became the climax of a musical based on the life of Jesus. When it was performed by 300 school children before audiences of over 4,000 people, Andrew's parents were guests of honour. As the first notes of "Andrew's Song" were played, a deep hush came over the audience. They had read Andrew's last words in the newspaper headline on the anniversary of his death two days before the show. Many people were in tears.

That song has already gone to Africa, Australia, America, Lebanon and other countries. Many children in Britain are learning it as they take part in the musical. Andrew's courage as he faced leukemia impressed many people. The message of his last words is set to impress many more.

# Easter and Pentecost

# 59 Andrew's last words

## Theme
God's love and justice meet in Good Friday.

## You will need
- a few centimeters of milk in a bottle that has been left out a couple of days to go obviously sour.
- an unopened carton of long-life milk.
- 2 glasses
- a cross.

## Presentation
Today we are going to think about a riddle, and how Good Friday is the answer. You meet the riddle when you think about heaven. If someone says about something, "That was heaven!", what do they mean?... It was just perfect.

We may not all believe in heaven, and none of us knows what it is like, but one thing we can probably all agree on is that heaven must be perfect. No crime, no hunger, no injustice, no suffering.

**Now, hands up everyone who is perfect...**
**Who has never told a lie?...**
**Never taken a cookie when mum said not to?...**
**Never been nasty to someone else?...**

Okay, so none of us is perfect. What would that do for heaven if God lets us in?... It would no longer be perfect because we would be in it and we are not perfect!

## A drink of sour milk
Let's think about something entirely different for a moment: milk. Open the carton of long-life milk and offer a drink to a volunteer. Now offer someone else a drink of sour milk. Yuk!

What is the difference? How long will long-life milk keep unopened? Why?... Pasteurising milk kills most of the bacteria, but enough are left to turn the milk sour after a few days. Long-life milk is sterilized to kill all the bacteria.

We have all admitted to being less than perfect. We may not be out and out evil, but we all have the "bacteria" of wrong-doing in us. If God let us into heaven, would it

155

still be perfect? Or would we "infect" it? If I pour this sour milk into this long-life milk, what will happen?... It will all go sour.

**So here is the riddle. It looks as if the situation is this:**

1.  God made us and told us about heaven.
2.  He also gave us the ability to choose between right and wrong.
3.  We all make mistakes and do wrong things. None of us is perfect.
4.  But heaven is perfect – so none of us can go to heaven. Goodbye, get lost!

Does that make you want to shout, "Unfair!"?... Right. But the Bible tells us this about God: he is holy (everything about him is perfect); he is just (he can't stand unfairness); and he is love. Because he is all those things, God provided an answer to the riddle. The answer is Good Friday. (Show the cross.)

# God's goodness poured into us

Christians believe that Jesus was perfect. He was sinless. But listen to how St. Paul explains what happened on Good Friday when Jesus was crucified:

> **For God took the sinless Christ and poured into him our sins. Then, in exchange, he poured God's goodness into us!** *2 Corinthians 5:21,* Living Bible

Jesus was pure, sinless. (Hold up long-life milk.) God poured our sins into him. (Hold up sour milk.) The difference between Jesus and milk is that our "bacteria" did not infect him. Then, having totally cleaned us out, he poured his goodness, his perfection, into us. In his love, he makes us fit for heaven. The riddle is solved at Good Friday.

That is why Christians celebrate the crucifixion of Jesus – and why we all have a holiday.

# A prayer

> **Father God, there are many riddles and puzzles in life. We ask you to show us the answers to the important ones. Amen.**

# 60 Fine paid

## Theme
The meaning of Good Friday.

## You will need
• nothing, unless you want to make a list as a visual aid (see end of sixth paragraph).

## Presentation
Here is a question for the days leading up to Easter:

**Why is a woman who could not pay a fine like Good Friday?**

The woman, Sharon Jones of Ebbw Vale, was expecting a baby one November when she had to go to court. She has six other children. She was sentenced to five days in jail for failing to pay a £55 fine. She broke down in tears when the sentence was passed. She was due to give birth in just two weeks.

One of the people in the court was a solicitor called Carole Anthony. (A solicitor helps people present their case if they have to go to court.) She was so moved by Mrs. Jones' distress that she organized a collection among other solicitors present. Between them they raised the £55 for the fine and so saved Mrs. Jones from having to go to prison.

Mrs. Anthony said, **"Everyone felt sorry for this poor lady, so we very quietly put the money forward for the fine – it just seemed the right thing to do."**

## We owed a debt
So why is that like Good Friday? Well, it says in the Bible that we all owe a fine that is too big for us to pay. St. Paul puts it like this:

> **We owed a debt because we broke God's laws. That debt listed all the rules we failed to follow.**
> *Colossians 2:14a*

The ways we have all broken God's laws include how we treat each other and how we fail to care for the world God created for us. That adds up to a pretty long list for every one of us. (You could have a roll of paper purporting to have a list on it. Hold it up and let it unroll.)

But Paul goes on:

**But God forgave us that debt. He took away that debt and nailed it to the cross.**

*Colossians 2:14b*

The debt we owed, the fine that is too big for us to pay, was nailed to the cross with Jesus. As Paul says,

**(Jesus) paid for our sins, and in him we have forgiveness.**
*Colossians 1:14*

This is why the Friday on which Christians remember the crucifixion of Jesus is called "Good." Every Christian remembers the list of things he or she has done wrong, the debt he cannot pay, to God. He remembers how he has said sorry for those things and admitted that there is no way he can pay the fine. He has asked Jesus to pay it for him.

If you can imagine how Sharon Jones felt when that fine was paid and she was saved from prison, then you can get a sense of what every Christian feels. That is a good reason for calling Good Friday "Good"!

## Something to think about

The children could imagine their list and what might be on it. Have they given that list to Jesus to be nailed to the Cross? Do they want to?

(The story of Sharon Jones appeared in the press on 26 November 1993.)

# 61 An unusual French cross

*In homes and churches in parts of the French Alps you can sometimes see a fascinating cross decorated with symbols representing different parts of the crucifixion story. The drawing is based on one such in a tiny chapel in the hamlet of Les Cours, near the Col du Lautaret (a regular stage of the Tour de France). It is a good teaching aid, and one we can easily copy for either a single talk or a series.*

## Theme
The story of Good Friday.

## You will need
- a copy of the drawing on OHP acetate or start with a bare cross on paper or an OHP and add different elements or a group of children might make their own version out of wood or card and scrap materials.
- a Bible. Most of these elements of the story can be found in John's account of the crucifixion, chapters 18 and 19 of John's Gospel. Other references are given below.

## Presentation
Tell the story pointing to or adding the various elements. Depending on the amount of detail, or the lessons one wants to draw, this could be a single talk or a short series.

The various elements are:

- **a coin** – one of the thirty pieces of silver paid to Judas for betraying Jesus

- **the cock** that crowed when Peter denied knowing Jesus for the third time

- **the whip** used to scourge Jesus

- **a hand** – one of Pilate's when he washed his hands of the guilt of Jesus' death (Matthew 27:24)

- **hammer, nails, ladder and pincers** used for fixing Jesus to the cross and later removing his body

- **INRI sign** – initial letters of Jesus of Nazareth, King of the Jews (Latin: Jesus Nazarenus Rex Judaeorum) which Pilate had fixed to the cross

- **a goblet and sponge on a stick** used to give Jesus a drink of sour wine

159

160

- **dice** used by the soldiers to gamble for Jesus' clothes (Matthew 27:35)

- **sun and moon** – darkness fell from mid-day to mid-afternoon (Matthew 27:45)

- **a spear** used to pierce Jesus' side to check whether he was dead

- **the Ten Commandments** – to symbolize the fact that Jesus' death satisfied the demands of the Law (Romans 8:3–4)

- **the heart** – to symbolize the love of God shown in Jesus' death (1 John 3:16)

# 62 Har-dtor-eco-gni-ze

## Theme
Introducing part of the Easter story, the road to Emmaus.

## You will need
- to prepare some words as in the examples below, taking the ability of the children into account.
- a Bible. Refresh your memory of the story of Jesus on the road to Emmaus in Luke 24:13–35.

## Presentation
On acetates or sheets of paper, write out some words with the letters split into odd groups as in the examples below. Get some volunteers and ask them to read the words aloud. Show them one at a time. See how long it takes to recognize the words.

Examples: **too-thac-he**, **fi-rem-an**, **co-atho-ok**, **cha-ins-aw**, **frig-hte-ni-ng**, **my-sterio-us**.

To make it even more difficult, some might be written like this:

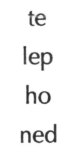

te

lep

ho

ned

Some people will find this very hard. Others might find they do not recognize the word at first, then suddenly they see it.

## The road to Emmaus
There is a well-known Easter story about two friends who took quite a long time to recognize someone they knew very well. Fill in the background: this is the Sunday after Jesus was crucified and buried on the Friday. Tell the story of how Jesus appeared to two disciples on the road from Jerusalem to Emmaus. It is in Luke 24:13–35.

Make the connection with the introduction: a person or a word seen in an unexpected way or place may be hard to recognize at first. In this case they were sure

Jesus was dead. Perhaps he wore a cloak with a hood, or perhaps in some way they were prevented from recognizing him. One translation of verse 32 says,

**And then, they were allowed to recognize Jesus.**

We have had some fun exercising our brains to play a game recognizing words. How much more brain-stretching it was for these friends of Jesus as he told them all the things the Bible taught about him. And how much more exciting when the penny finally dropped and they realized it was Jesus risen from the dead who had been sharing their walk along the Emmaus road.

## Time for reflection

Play some quiet music. The children might like to replay this story in their minds, perhaps imagining themselves as one of the two disciples.

# 63 Victory cup

## Theme
Reminders of victories won; the meaning of the communion cup.

## You will need
- a silver cup or other trophy that has been won by an individual or a team
- a glass of "wine" (grape or blackcurrant juice) or a communion chalice if you can borrow one

## Presentation

Show the cup or trophy and talk about it. This is a reminder – a reminder of a past victory.

Show the glass of "wine" or chalice. This cup is also a reminder of a victory. To Christians it is a reminder of the most important victory of all.

On the night before he was crucified, Jesus shared what is often known as "the last supper" with his friends. During that meal he took a cup of wine and passed it around the table for them all to drink. This is what he said:

> **This cup shows the new agreement from God to his people. This new agreement begins with the blood of my death. When you drink this, do it to remember me.**
>
> *1 Corinthians 11:25*

Later that night he was arrested, tried and crucified. That sounds like a terrible defeat. But Christians believe it was the forces of evil in the world that were defeated, not Jesus. Paul put it like this in a letter:

> **God defeated the spiritual rulers and powers. With the cross God won the victory and defeated them. He showed the world that they were powerless.**
>
> *Colossians 2:15*

Every Sunday all over the world – and often on weekdays, too – Christians do what Jesus told them to and take some bread and wine in the service known as the Mass or the Eucharist or Communion. As they do so, they remember how Jesus died and they celebrate the victory over evil.

This cup [show trophy] is a reminder of a past sports victory. It also encourages those who compete next time to try their hardest to win it. This cup [show wine] reminds people of the victory of Jesus over evil on the cross. It also encourages Christians to try their hardest to live in the way God wants, knowing what he has already done for them.

## Something to do

Can someone print out a picture of the bread and wine and Jesus' words in 1 Corinthians 11:25 on a computer? They could either draw the bread and wine or see if they can find some clip-art.

# 64 The church's birthday

## Theme
Pentecost is the time to celebrate the church's birthday.

## You will need
- a birthday cake, some candles, matches, and a taper if possible
- a Bible: Acts 2:1–4.

## Presentation
**Show the cake.** Today (or next Sunday) is someone's – or rather, something's – birthday. Anyone know whose? A clue: it is around 1970 years old. Answer: the church. Not our church or the one down the road, but the church made up of all the followers of Jesus.

When we have a birthday cake, it is often brought in with the candles alight. Then the birthday person has to take a deep breath and blow them all out. The church started with a strong breath and flames, but it was sort of the other way around.

**Describe the coming of the Holy Spirit** in Acts 2:1–4. Let the candles represent the followers of Jesus. Light a match or taper and bring it down onto the candles so that each one has a flame on its "head".

The flames of the Spirit were not blown out. Briefly describe the rest of the events of that day, culminating in three thousand people being baptized (Acts 2:41). The church has gone on growing down the centuries. There are around one billion Christians in the world today. That's a lot of people to join in celebrating the church's birthday!

## Something to enjoy
With a small group, the cake can be cut and eaten. A church might decide to ask members to bring "birthday" cakes to share after the service. If this message is used for a school assembly, take the cake to be eaten with coffee in the staffroom at break. This will ensure that it is a very popular assembly with the staff!

# 65 Breath and spirit

## Theme
The surprising effect of the Spirit of God.

## You will need
- two table-tennis balls, some thread, sticky tape, and a broom handle. Stick thread to two table-tennis balls with sticky tape and suspend them from a broom-handle across two chairs as in the illustration. Make the gap between the balls 6–7 cm (2$\frac{1}{2}$ inches). Raise high enough for your audience to see.
- a Bible. Prepare the two stories of Peter in Luke 22:54–62 (his denial of Jesus) and Acts 4:1–22 (Peter stands up fearlessly to the authorities) or arrange for a group of children to read these sections in *The Dramatised Bible* (published by Marshall Pickering / The Bible Society).

## Presentation
**Show the "apparatus" you have prepared** for a small experiment. If you blow on one of the table-tennis balls, will it move towards you or away?... Obviously, away.

If you blow between the two balls, will they move away from each other or towards each other?... Demonstrate. They move towards each other. Why?... Air moving over a curved surface drops in pressure, creating "lift." This is what keeps a plane up in the sky: air moving over the curved upper surface of the wing pulls it – and the plane – upwards. Air moving over the table-tennis balls pulls them towards the side over which your breath is blowing.

**Refer to the story of Pentecost** and the sound like rushing wind (Acts 2:1–2). The Spirit of God came on the followers of Jesus in power. The word for "spirit" in the original language is the same as the word for "breath."

**When you breathe – or the wind blows – you can't see the air moving, but you can see its effects.** The table-tennis balls experiment is one example. It is the same with the Spirit of God. You can't see him (although the disciples saw something that looked like fire), but you can see the effect he has in people's lives. Just as with the table-tennis balls, that effect can often be quite surprising.

Briefly tell the "before and after" stories of Peter in Luke 22:54–62 and Acts 4:1–22. Draw attention to Acts 4:8 – Peter was "filled with the Holy Spirit" – and v. 13 – "they saw the courage of Peter and...were astonished."

## A prayer

**Holy Spirit, come and breathe on us. Change us like you changed Peter. Do things in our lives that will astonish people. Amen.**

# 66 Pentecost rap

## Theme
Re-telling the story of the day of Pentecost in a modern idiom.

## You will need
- copies of the text. This is best performed by a group of children. When reading or reciting this rap, emphasize the rhythm. It can be accompanied by finger-snapping 4 beats to the line. Insert a line of finger-snapping between stanzas, or get a percussionist to play a link.
- copy or photocopy the illustrations of Art Simple onto acetate – there is one to accompany each stanza. Get someone to practice showing the correct ones to accompany the rap.

  OR designate one of the group as Art to mime responses.

## Presentation
The Jews celebrate the feast of Pentecost, also known as the Feast of Weeks, seven weeks after Passover. It is the time for celebrating the grain harvest. For Christians, the day is also very important because of what happened after the first Easter. Here is the story of the events told in a rap with the help of a character called Art Simple.

Now get your mind in gear and don't wander or get lost,
Here's a real solid tale about the day of Pentecost.
To keep us on the line, please meet a guy called Art,
He wants you all to listen and he says, "That's real smart."

You'll know about this Jesus who those Romans crucified,
But he gave his friends instructions just the night before he died,
Said, "Wait here in Jerus'lem, there's a gift got to be given;
He's the Spirit of the Living God, an' he's coming down from heaven!"

The disciples got together and they all
   began to pray.
One hundred and a-twenty were just
   waiting for that day.
Then suddenly one morning, with a
   shriek and with a wail,
A violent wind from heaven filled the whole house with
   a gale!

There was fire in the air and the glow began to spread
Until each of the disciples had a flame
   upon his head.
They all began to laugh and shout, for
   not a soul was burnt,
But each could speak a language that
   none of them had learnt!

Well the people heard the racket and thousands came a-running,
But to hear their own language spoke now that was really stunning!
Then Peter took the lead and said, "This ain't no drunken rave,
The Son of God was crucified, but he's risen from the grave!

You people are just full of sin, your
   lives need a new start,
Let Jesus sort the mess out, he's got
   power to change your heart."
Three thousand got the message
   then, three thousand all believed,
Three thousand got baptized that day, and
   new life they received.

Now you may have heard some rappin' and some laughing and some clapping
Caught the rhyming and the rhythm till your fingers started snapping
But until the Holy Spirit comes and sets your heart on fire
There's no power in all the earth that'll ever take you higher.
Said, no power in all the earth that'll ever take you higher.

Thanks to Rev. Ian Blake of St Christopher's, Sneinton, Nottingham, for the original idea.

# 67 Jesus or Barabbas?

## Theme

A theme for Easter: the choice between the way of violence and the way of peace.

## You will need

• some details of a conflict situation in the news.

## Presentation

Talk about a war or terrorist situation that is in the news. The children might be asked if they know about other violent conflicts that are going on.

Disagreement, argument and conflict are bound to happen. We all disagree with other people, usually several times a day. When an argument becomes very heated, there may come a moment when one of the sides chooses to become violent. In every war we read about or see on the TV news, such a choice has been made.

## The Palm Sunday coup

The Easter story gives us a dramatic account of some people making a choice like that. Jesus arrived in Jerusalem on Palm Sunday. The people welcomed him like a king. He went to the temple and threw out the money-changers. Crowds flocked to hear him in the temple precincts during that week.

In a sense, Jesus took over the temple. He showed that the rulers of Jerusalem and the temple had lost the right to be moral and spiritual leaders. But he did it non-violently. On Palm Sunday, Jesus deliberately chose to enter the city on a humble donkey. This fulfilled the words that the prophet Zechariah had spoken more than 500 years earlier:

> **See, your king comes to you, gentle and riding on a donkey.**
>
> *Zechariah 9:9* and *Matthew 21:5*

The way he came was gentle, non-violent.

Now listen to what happened on the night of Thursday of that week when Jesus was arrested and brought before Pilate, the Roman governor.

Read or have children present **Matthew 27:15–26**.

This crowd was given a choice. They could choose Jesus, the man of peace, or Barabbas, the man of violence. These two men offered two different kinds of revolution. Jesus offered a new quality of life and a new way of living: the kingdom of heaven. Barabbas offered the way of armed rebellion against the Roman empire. The crowd made their choice – they chose freedom for the man of violence, and a violent death for the man of peace.

## Horrific bloodbath

We can learn a lot from what happened later. Some groups continued to rebel against Rome. Around 40 years after the death of Jesus, Rome sent an army to put an end to the rebellions. The temple itself was destroyed in a horrific bloodbath as the Roman legions defeated the rebels.

Meanwhile, some people continued to follow the way of the man of peace, Jesus. These early Christians began to spread throughout the Roman empire. Sometime after 310 AD the Roman Emperor himself became a Christian. Now, nearly 20 centuries after that first Easter, followers of Jesus are counted in billions all over the globe. Which was more successful, the way of violence or the way of peace?

## Something to think about

Sometime this week, perhaps today, we might get into an argument with someone. As we get more and more angry, we might be tempted to hit out – and hitting out can be with words as much as with fists. But before it gets too heated, we still have a choice. Which will we choose: the way of violence or the way of peace?

# 68 Who wants the lot?

## Theme
A lively auction leads to thinking about why Jesus was prepared to pay the ultimate price on Good Friday.

## You will need
- items to auction, suitable for your group (which could include stuff belonging to leaders that the children might regard as trophies); plenty of pennies; a suitable auctioneer's mallet, for example, a large inflatable one.

This should be fun, but it could also raise money for a cause you support. Tell the group in advance what you are planning. Bids only go up in pennies. Have a good supply of pennies and run a bureau de change before you start. Give some pennies to children who come unprepared so that they are not left out.

## Presentation
Get a good, loud extrovert as the auctioneer and make it fast and noisy.

When the auction is in full swing, one of the leaders starts making extravagant bids for popular lots so that the children have no chance of getting them. After this has happened a few times, step in, drag the leader to the front, and ask the children what they think of him. Greedy? Selfish?

The auction could be finished with the greedy leader generally behaving but once or twice giving way to the temptation to outbid the children – and probably being shouted down for doing so.

Calm things down, perhaps with a song.

## No limit
Now let's imagine an auction in which one bidder is determined to get everything. He outbids everyone else, no matter how high the bidding goes. He seems prepared to pay anything, no limit. We would probably want to know why. Does he have a special reason for wanting everything on sale? Is he just a rich nutcase? Or is there an interesting story that explains his strange behaviour?

Let's look at a case where something like this actually happened.

Probably the most famous verse in the New Testament says,

**For God loved the world so much that he gave his only Son. God gave his Son so that whoever believes in him may not be lost, but have eternal life.** *John 3:16*

God wants the lot. He wants every single person on the face of the planet. He was prepared to pay whatever it cost. So he sent Jesus, the Son, God in a human being. And Jesus ends up dying a terrible death on a Roman cross!

So what's the story that explains God's strange behaviour?

# Funny creatures

It's the story of a Creator who made a universe of a hunded trillion stars so that one planet could exist with some funny two-legged creatures: human beings. It's a story of how he loved the creatures he made so much that he wanted them to live for ever, to live with him in a place beyond their dreams.

So that they could share that eternal life with him, he made the funny two-legged creatures a lot like himself. He gave them imagination and creativity and free choice. But some of the things they imagined, and some of the things they created, and some of the things they chose were destructive and evil. Every single one of the creatures was tainted, spoilt. They were unfit for the eternal life the Creator had planned for them. They were lost.

So what did he decide to do? Say it was all a mistake? Scrap the lot? Begin again? What would you do?

# He wants the lot

Because he loved them so much, God found a way for his creatures to begin again – but without scrapping them. What was the way he found? **"God gave his Son so that whoever believes in him may not be lost, but have eternal life."** He sent Jesus. And Jesus paid the highest possible price for the funny two-legged creatures: he gave his life when he was crucified.

Was that greedy? No, just the opposite. It's the most generous thing imaginable. Jesus paid for our freedom, the freedom from our own mistakes and wrong choices. The freedom to live with him for ever in that place beyond our dreams. Satan may have had a claim on us. But Jesus outbid him. God does not want to lose even one of his funny creatures. He wants the lot.

 **Road to Emmaus**

## Theme

The Easter story of the disciples meeting Jesus on the road to Emmaus.

## You will need

- some jelly babies, three clean yoghurt pots or plastic cups, and an OHP.

## Presentation

Explain that you are going to demonstrate to the audience a trick which they can show to their family or friends. You need one volunteer.

Place three different coloured jelly babies on the OHP. (They won't need an OHP to do this at home; you are using it so everyone can see.) Cover them with the yoghurt pots.

Ask the volunteer to choose one of the pots, lift it up, and eat the jelly baby. Replace the pot where it was. Repeat with the other two jelly babies, keeping up suitable "patter", e.g. "You do realize these are *magic* jelly babies. I hope they don't turn you into a frog. Still, your friends probably couldn't tell the difference." "Do you want to check under that pot just to make sure the jelly baby has really gone?" etc.

Now ask the volunteer to choose one of the pots – but not to tell you which one yet – and concentrate really hard. In a moment everyone is going to see that the chosen pot is over all three jelly babies!

Ask the volunteer to point to her chosen pot. Make a bit of play about asking if she wouldn't rather have this other one; then give in, lift it up and *hold it on her head*. The pot is now over the three jelly babies! (Laughter all round – we hope!)

Ask for a round of applause for the volunteer.

## Taken by surprise

Tell the audience that they were expecting one thing to happen, but something different happened instead. At the end, we were all taken by surprise, although what happened was quite obvious when we saw it. Sorry though, there was no magic!

There is a story about the first Easter in which two people had certain expectations about what was happening but got taken completely by surprise. In this story it looked as if there really was magic at the end, but it was something far more wonderful.

Tell the Emmaus Road story from **Luke 24:13–35**.

As you tell it, emphasize the elements which echo and contrast with the introduction:

- the expectations of the two which, in part, prevented them from realizing whom they had met. (It was also true that there was something "different" about Jesus after his resurrection.)

- the surprise of the revelation when they realized who had been talking to them.

- but this was no trick or magic: "The Lord really has risen from death!" The risen Jesus was able to appear and disappear at will. He appeared several times to his followers. Once, the Bible tells us, 500 people saw him at one time.

An unexpected ending to a trick can make us laugh. The unexpected ending to this story – and to the whole Easter story – excited the disciples so much that they devoted the rest of their lives to telling other people. It was a story that changed the world.

# Advent and
# Christmas

# 70 CHRISTMAS FAITH 1
## F is for Father

*This is the first of a series of six talks explaining the meaning of the word faith in the context of Christmas. The first five are based on words beginning with the letters of FAITH and the last sums up the whole series and invites a response. Each is accompanied by the appropriate carol.*

## Theme
Faith is in a person, God the Father.

## You will need

- five large boxes wrapped in Christmas paper with cut-outs of one of the letters F A I T H on each.
- a Bible. Prepare to briefly retell the story of Lazarus in John 11:17–45.
- music for "O Come All Ye Faithful," or a recording.

## Presentation

Play or sing the first verse of "O Come All Ye Faithful." This famous carol invites people who are faithful to come and worship the baby Jesus. Faithful means "full of faith," but what is faith?

Show your Christmas boxes with the letters on them.

**For Christians, faith is always in someone, in a person. That someone is God.**

Jesus always talked about God as his Father, so on this first box the F stands for Father.

Jesus had an earthly father, Joseph. He was a good man, but even the best earthly fathers can let us down. Jesus knew that his heavenly Father would never let him down.

Let's look at an example from his later life of how Jesus had faith in his heavenly Father. Retell the story of the raising of Lazarus from John 11:17–45. Focus on verses 41–42:

**Then Jesus looked up and said, "Father, I thank you that you heard me. I know that you always hear me. But I said these things because of the people here around me. I want them to believe that you sent me."**

If we have a friend we know really well, we might be sure they will not let us down. Jesus knew his heavenly Father so well that he could say, "I know that you always hear me." That is faith. And Jesus wanted the people around him to have that same faith in God as their heavenly Father.

## A song
"O Come All Ye Faithful".

# 71 CHRISTMAS FAITH 2
# T is for Trust

## Theme
A vital element of faith is trust.

## You will need
- the five F A I T H Christmas present boxes
- a bottle of coloured water (use food colouring) with a label saying "MEDICINE" and a spoon.
- a Bible: Luke 1:26–45. This could be given to a group of children to prepare as a dramatized reading.
- music for "Once in Royal David's City".

## Presentation
**Show the box with the T on it.** T stands for Trust, one of the most important parts of faith.

**Ask for a volunteer** who has been to the doctor's recently. Show her the bottle of medicine.

**If the doctor had asked her to take a spoonful of something like this, would she have taken it?… If a stranger had come up to her in the street and said the same thing, would she have taken it then?…**

**What is the difference? – Trust.**

**Retell or present as a dramatized reading** Luke 1:26–45, the story of the angel Gabriel's message to Mary.

Bring out Mary's fear and lack of understanding. Despite this, Mary trusted – verse 36.

**Show the box with the F on it.** Last time we said that the important thing is that it is faith in a person. Who is that person? – God the Father. Because it was God (through an angel) who spoke to her, Mary was able to trust that he would not let her down.

**Can we trust him like Mary did?**

## A song
"Once in Royal David's City".

# 72 CHRISTMAS FAITH 3
## A is for Action

## Theme
In James' words, "Faith by itself, if it is not accompanied by action, is dead."

## You will need
- the five F A I T H Christmas present boxes
- a milk bottle full of water and a piece of card a little larger than the mouth of the bottle. See the text below and try the demonstration at home first to convince yourself that it works.
- a towel in case of disasters!
- a Bible: Matthew 2:1–12
- music for "As With Gladness" or "The First Noel".

## Presentation
**Show the box with the A on it.** A stands for Action. Last time we looked at T for Trust. Now we are going to see if someone trusts enough to put their trust into action.

**Fill a milk bottle with water** leaving no more than a few millimeters airspace. Place a fresh, flat piece of card over the top. Tell children that if you turn the bottle upside-down the card will stay in place and no water will come out (except possibly the odd drop). This is not a trick, just simple science. It is the effect of air pressure. Who believes you?… Who is prepared to put that trust into action by standing underneath the bottle as you turn it upside-down?…

**Choose a volunteer**, hold the card in place as you turn the bottle upside-down, count to three and release the card. The water remains in the bottle. (Well, this series is about faith!)

**Read, retell or get children to read** Matthew 2:1–12, the visit of the wise men or scholars. These men put their faith into action in at least three ways. One: they said, "We saw his star in the east and have come to worship him." Two: they had come prepared with gifts. Three: they acted on the warning dream at the end of the story.

**See how when the wise men acted in faith, the proof came afterwards.**

**Faith may be a step into the unknown, but once the step is taken it can be seen to be right.**

The wise men not only saw the Christ-child, they were "overjoyed" (v. 10). If they hadn't put their belief into action they would have missed out on the proof that they were right. And they would have missed out on the excitement and the joy.

## A song
"As With Gladness" or "The First Noel".

# 73 CHRISTMAS FAITH 4
## I is for Incarnation

## Theme
At Christmas we meet God "in the flesh."

NOTE Although we try to avoid using jargon, especially when talking to children, it is good practice to introduce longer or harder words like "incarnation" from time to time.

## You will need
- the five F A I T H Christmas present boxes
- a Bible: Luke 2:8–20
- somebody who can talk about a famous person they met or a couple of people to prepare a spoof interview with a famous person or photos from a pop-music or sports magazine.
- music for "Hark the Herald Angels Sing" or "Love Came Down at Christmas".

## Presentation
**Show the box with the I on it.** I stands for Incarnation. It is a long word. What does it mean?

**Introduce the person who has met somebody famous,** or the sketch, or show the pop-idol or sports photos and ask the children if they have ever met one of their heroes. We talk about meeting somebody "in the flesh." It is very different – and exciting – meeting someone you've only known on a TV screen "in the flesh."

That is exactly what the word "incarnation" means: "in the flesh" or "in a human body."

People like Mary and the wise men knew God and trusted in him even though they had never seen him. The great excitement of the first Christmas was that they met him for the first time "in the flesh," in a human body.

**Read or retell** or have children read the story of the shepherds in Luke 2:8–20.

Stress verses 11–12. This is "a Savior...Christ the Lord"; the angel Gabriel had told Mary he was "the Son of God", and yet he had come as a baby. This is what Christians call "the incarnation", God come into the world in the flesh, in a human body.

From this moment on, faith for those who would later be called Christians was not just faith in God the Father, it was – and still is – faith in God the Son, God in a human body!

## A song
"Hark the Herald Angels Sing" or "Love Came Down at Christmas".

# 74 CHRISTMAS FAITH 5
## H is for Holy

## Theme
Holiness is to be experienced.

## You will need
• the five F A I T H Christmas present boxes
• candles and matches
• music for "Silent Night".

## Presentation

**Show the box with the H on it.** H stands for Holy. It's a word that comes up a lot in the Christmas story and in Christmas carols: "Silent night, holy night."

**Play the music of "Silent Night".** (It would be very effective to continue playing the music quietly in the background while talking about aspects of experiencing holiness.)

When the angel Gabriel comes to Mary, he tells her about "the holy one to be born." When Mary sings a song of praise to God she says, "for the Mighty One has done great things for me – holy is his name."

**What does "holy" mean?**

You can't really explain what "holy" means, you can only experience it. Perhaps the best way is to imagine ourselves at the first Christmas with Mary and Joseph, the angels, the shepherds and the wise men. When we sing carols, especially at a candlelit carol service, it can help us imagine what it felt like to be there.

**One of the things people feel is that this is a very special moment,** perhaps the most special moment you will ever know in your whole life. The wise men were clever scholars, but the Bible says that they "bowed down and worshiped" this baby of a poor family. They knew this baby came from God. It is only God who is holy, or things or people that belong to God.

**Another thing people feel and know without being told is that they are in the presence of someone pure and completely good.** This goodness is so perfect that it can only come from God. Would you swear or quarrel or lie if you came to see Jesus in the manger? No, you would just feel that that would be utterly wrong.

**A third thing people feel is that they are in the presence of a mystery.** They feel that there is something which is bigger than human understanding. We can't fully understand God incarnate, God in a human body. We can't fully grasp how or why. We can only marvel. After the shepherds left the Bible says that "Mary treasured up all these things and pondered them in her heart." She pondered them; they were a mystery.

**People who have been in the presence of holiness feel tremendously privileged and very humble. They are filled with deep peace and joy.**

**This was the experience of all those who came into the presence of the baby Jesus at that first Christmas.**

It was the faith of the shepherds and the wise men and Mary and Joseph that led them to this place. And being close to "the holy one" made their faith far, far deeper. When people have an experience like this, they remember it all their lives and it becomes a very important part of them.

## A song
Light some candles and sing "Silent Night".

Children might be informed of a candlelit carol service they could attend.

# 75 CHRISTMAS FAITH 6
## A Gift

## Theme
Summing up: faith is a gift.

## You will need
- the five F A I T H Christmas present boxes
- music for "O Little Town of Bethlehem."

## Presentation

**Play or sing** a verse of "O Little Town of Bethlehem".

**Display the five boxes.** Remind children of the aspects of faith these letters stand for. F is for God the Father in whom Christians put their faith. A is for the Action that shows that faith is genuine. I is for Incarnation, God in a human body, Jesus in whom Christians also put their faith. T is for Trust, the trust in God that leads to action. H is for Holy, the holiness that people may experience as a result of their faith – and which leads to even deeper faith.

The first lines of the third verse of "O Little Town of Bethlehem" read: "How silently, how silently, The wondrous gift is given!" The gift the carol speaks of is the gift of Jesus, the Christ, to the world.

**These boxes wrapped in Christmas paper remind us that faith is also a gift. This gift is given quietly to those who want to receive it. There are many people in the world who would say it is the most precious gift they have ever received.**

Mother Teresa puts it like this:

**"In India I was asked by some government people, 'Don't you want to make us all Christians?'**

**"I said, 'Naturally, I would like to give the treasure I have to you, but I cannot. I can only pray for you to have the courage to receive it.'**

**"Faith is a gift from God."**[1]

---

1. Mother Teresa, *Loving Jesus*, Fount (London, 1991), p. 100.

As people all over the world sing "O Little Town of Bethlehem" this Christmas, many of them will use the last verse as a prayer, asking God to renew and deepen their faith once again:

> **O holy child of Bethlehem,**
> **Descend to us we pray;**
> **Cast out our sin and enter in;**
> **Be born in us today.**

That prayer is open for anyone to pray if they wish.

## A song
Sing "O Little Town of Bethlehem".

# 76 Christmas present from afar

## Theme
God's goodness in sending Jesus into the world.

## You will need
- two Christmas stockings, an old-fashioned one with nuts, an orange and a small toy, and one with some electronic wizardry from Japan such as a personal stereo or game cartridge.

## Presentation

**Show your old-fashioned stocking.** Talk about the contents and how an orange would have been an exotic treat for a previous generation.

**Ask what children are hoping for this Christmas.** Some will want Playstations, Sega, etc, or new games for their existing sets. Display the contents of your second stocking. Point out how popular items come from Japan, thousands of miles away around the world.

A return flight to Japan costs between £500 and £1,000. If parents had to go to Japan to buy these presents, how many children think they would be getting them for Christmas? Not many! Isn't it a good job importers bring them over for us at a fraction of that cost!

For thousands of years, people all over the world have believed that the most important thing in life is to know the Creator of the universe and to be right with him. But if he is the Creator, he is "outside", "beyond" the universe he made. How do we find out what he is like? We might make some good guesses, but how do we really know? Traveling to Japan for Christmas presents is too much for most parents. Going "outside" the universe is too much for anyone!

But the Christmas story tells us we don't have to. The Christmas story says that God came to us. One of the names given to Jesus was "Immanuel". It means, "God with us."

There is a line in the well-loved carol, "Once In Royal David's City" – "He came down to earth from heaven Who is God and Lord of all."

From heaven to earth: that is an infinite distance, impossible for people to cross. But God loves us so much he sent Jesus to earth as his Christmas present to the world!

## A song
"Once In Royal David's City".

# 77 The Christmas watchers 1

## Theme
This Christmas mini-series takes three groups of people who were watching and waiting – the shepherds, the Magi, and the worshippers at the temple – and asks questions about whom God speaks to and how he speaks.

## You will need
• a wall display or OHP transparency as below. The two top lines are filled in ready; the other boxes can be written in or have prepared words stuck on at the appropriate moments. Decorate the chart to make it attractive.

| THE CHRISTMAS WATCHERS | | |
|---|---|---|
| Who were they? | What were they doing? | How did they hear God? |
| Men on the night shift | Working and wondering | Through a mega sound-and-light angel show |
| | | |
| | | |
| | | |

• For further visual impact, have a small group of children dressed as shepherds.
• A picture of the shepherds is available at *www.77talks.co.uk* in both full colour and outline (for children to colour themselves). This can be printed onto thin card for children to take home and stand on the mantelpiece or window ledge. Or they can find it on the website and print it themselves. The other two groups of watchers can be added in subsequent weeks.

## Presentation
Ask the children how much time they spend on an average day watching – watching TV, watching sport, or watching a teacher showing them something . . . Watching is one way of learning.

The first Christmas was a time when a few people who were quietly watching found themselves caught up in the most amazing events. There were three groups of watchers who were all very different kinds of people and who heard God speak to them in very different ways.

The first group of watchers were just ordinary working men – the shepherds.

If you have a dressed-up group, bring them out. Ask the children who the shepherds were… Fill in the first box: Men on the night shift.

Near to Bethlehem was a tower on the road to Jerusalem. It was called Migdal Eder, "the watch-tower of the flock". This was where shepherds who were taking their flocks of sheep for the sacrifices in the temple at Jerusalem spent the night.

## Big questions about life

If you are outside under the stars at night, what sort of mood do you get into? [Sadly, many children will not have experienced this, but you may still get some very interesting answers.] . . . People often go quiet. They feel small under the big night sky, but they may also feel close to something important. It's a time when people think about big questions about life and God and themselves.

The shepherds would have thought they were very humble people – not like the priests in the temple in Jerusalem where they were taking the sheep – but perhaps they were wondering whether God would ever use or talk to ordinary people like them.

On the chart, we put in the second box that they were working – because they were doing their daily task – but also that they were wondering.

What happened next? [Get the rest of the story from the children.]… This bunch of men who had never seen more than an oil-lamp or a fire at night were suddenly treated to 50 megawatts of angel power and a full heavenly sound-system! [Fill in the third column on the chart.] And they became the very first to see the Christ, the Messiah, the Saviour.

The Bible doesn't spell out exactly what they did then, but it is very likely that they finished their job by taking the sheep to Jerusalem – and telling everyone who would listen about the extraordinary things they had seen and heard.

> **…all who heard it were amazed at what the shepherds said to them.**
> *Luke 2:18,* New International Version

Probably some people thought that they had had too much to drink. But there was another group of watchers at the temple, and they would certainly have pricked up their ears with interest.

The Bible says,

> **The shepherds returned, glorifying and praising God for all the things they had heard and seen, which were just as they had been told.**
> *Luke 2:20,* New International Version

And the watchers at the temple? We'll find out about them next time.

# 78 The Christmas watchers 2

## Theme
For some reason Simeon and Anna (Luke 2:22–38) are almost invariably omitted from nativity plays. (Is it because they are less picturesque than the shepherds and wise men? Or is it ageism?) Yet they play a vital role in the story of the welcoming of the Messiah into the world.

## You will need
• stage two of the Christmas watchers chart:

| THE CHRISTMAS WATCHERS | | |
|---|---|---|
| Who were they? | What were they doing? | How did they hear God? |
| Men on the night shift | Working and wondering | Through a mega sound-and-light angel show |
| Senior citizens | Waiting and worshipping | Through listening to other people and to the inner voice of the Holy Spirit |
|  |  |  |
|  |  |  |

• You could print a photo of the Temple Mount in Jerusalem onto OHP transparency from the *www.77talks.co.uk* website.
• You could have two senior citizens dressed as Simeon and Anna. They might be prepared to talk about themselves in character and you could adapt the talk accordingly.
• A picture of Simeon and Anna for children is available at *www.77talks.co.uk*.

## Presentation
Use the chart to recap briefly on the first group of watchers, the shepherds. Ask the children if they can remember where the shepherds may have taken their flocks after seeing the baby Jesus…the Temple Mount in Jerusalem.

Show a picture of the Temple Mount if you have one. It was an amazing piece of engineering. King Herod extended it to the size of 32 football pitches and built the temple on it. (Today there is a mosque there, and the Dome of the Rock – a very holy place for Muslims.)

There were other watchers who came regularly to the Temple Mount. One of them was called Simeon and another was Anna. Anna was 84 and Simeon was an old man who knew he was nearing the end of his life.

[Fill in the first box: Senior citizens – or other appropriate term: the authors would say they were like themselves – wrinklies!]

Simeon and Anna were both Jews who were hoping to see the coming of the promised Messiah. In fact, the Holy Spirit had shown Simeon that he would see the Messiah before he died. For years they had waited for that day to arrive and had come regularly to the temple to worship God. [Fill in the second box.]

# Only waiting

If we were to see a couple of old people slipping into a church on our way to school, we probably wouldn't think they were doing anything very important. But even though Simeon and Anna were only waiting and worshipping, God had plans that would make sure their names were remembered until the end of time.

God used a big "angel spectacular" to speak to the shepherds. But he used a completely different way to speak to Simeon and Anna, a way that he often uses to speak to people. We have already heard that the Holy Spirit had shown Simeon that he would see the Messiah. How had the Holy Spirit shown him that? Perhaps it was just a quiet inner voice.

Then there may have been something else as well. They may have heard the story of the baby in a manger that the shepherds told when they came to Jerusalem. If so, they would certainly have listened with excitement. They would have asked themselves, "Is this the time that God promised? Is this what we have been waiting for?" This is the kind of way God often works, using other people to confirm what the Holy Spirit has said to those who are watching and listening. [Complete the third box.]

Then the Holy Spirit spoke to Simeon again, or not so much spoke as gave him a nudge to go to the temple.

Imagine that huge area on the Temple Mount with hundreds of people milling around. There were priests, there were money-changers, there were traders selling animals for sacrifice, there were worshippers, there were scholars and teachers, there were beggars, and there were plenty of people with nothing much else to do but to hang around the place where all the action was.

And in the middle of all that bustle, there was a couple with a baby. They were just an ordinary couple, like many others who had brought their babies at 33 days old to present to the Lord God at the temple. It was just an ordinary baby, too, probably with a turned-up nose and a little black hair poking out of the cloths he was wrapped in. At least, he looked like an ordinary baby on the outside.

If this were a film, the camera would zoom in and focus on that little family, singling them out from the crowd. But there was no camera, just the Holy Spirit focussing the eyes of old Simeon on a man and a young woman and a baby – a family from up north, like the shepherds had talked about. It was Mary and Joseph and the month-old baby Jesus.

## Die in peace

Simeon took the baby in his arms. With tears in his eyes, he thanked God that the promise had been kept. He had seen the Messiah, the Saviour. He could die in peace.

And as he was speaking to Mary and Joseph, someone else happened on the scene: 84-year-old Anna. She was just as excited, eager to tell all her friends who were hoping and praying the Messiah would come that this baby was him, the one the prophets had spoken about.

If our imaginary camera were to zoom slowly out again, we would see a little knot of people talking excitedly and beckoning others to join them. As we took in more of the scene, we would see that all over the rest of the Temple Mount it was just business as usual. The priests, the scholars, the traders, the beggars – they all had far more important things to do than to bother about a few doddering old wrinklies making a fuss about a couple of poor northerners and a baby. Funny how people can be so busy living that they miss what life is all about.

But for those who had watched for years, and waited for years, and worshipped for years, this was the most wonderful moment of their lives. They knew they were part of the biggest thing that had ever happened in the history of the world.

What they didn't know was that another group of watchers from far away was following a sign in the sky that was leading them to Jerusalem, too. You can probably guess who they are, but if not, we'll find out next time.

# 79 The Christmas watchers 3

## Theme
The story of the Magi (Matthew 2:1–12) completes this Christmas mini-series and underlines how God speaks to all kinds of different people in different ways – if only we have our eyes and ears open expectantly.

## You will need
• stage three of the Christmas watchers chart:

| THE CHRISTMAS WATCHERS | | |
|---|---|---|
| Who were they? | What were they doing? | How did they hear God? |
| Men on the night shift | Working and wondering | Through a mega sound-and-light angel show |
| Senior citizens | Waiting and worshipping | Through listening to other people and to the inner voice of the Holy Spirit |
| Researchers | Watching and working out | Through observations and enquiries |

• As in talks 1 and 2 of the series, people could be dressed as the Magi.
• A picture of the Magi for children is available at *www.77talks.co.uk* to complete the set of Christmas watchers.

## Presentation
Use the chart to recap briefly on the first two groups of watchers and how they heard God speaking to them.

Away to the east was another group of watchers who, like the shepherds, spent time out under the night sky. In a sense, it was their work too, except that what they were watching was not sheep but the sky itself. They watched the stars because they believed that the positions of the moving stars – what we now know to be the planets – could point to important events that were happening in the world.

Today, people like these who like old books and knowledge and trying to understand the world would be university professors or researchers. In those days they were known as Magi – "wise men". [Fill in the first box.]

As these men watched the sky, they may have seen some of the brightest stars – planets – coming close together. This is called a conjunction. From their books they worked out what it meant – that a new king of the Jews had been born. [Fill in the second box.] And then there was the moving star – a comet, perhaps? – that was to help them find where this new king had been born.

## Old books tell the truth

What happened next? [Get the rest of the story from the children.]… These men were surprised not to find the new king of the Jews in the palace at Jerusalem. But they made enquiries, and King Herod's own wise men got out their old books which said that the Messiah would be born in Bethlehem. The star they had been following confirmed what the books said and left them in no doubt that this Jewish baby was the king they were seeking. No ordinary king, either. This was the long-promised Messiah. They bowed down and worshipped him.

So, quite differently from the shepherds at Bethlehem and the senior citizens in Jerusalem, these "wise men" heard God speak to them through their observations of the natural world and through the enquiries they made. [Fill in the final box.]

As we have been filling in our Christmas watchers chart, we have been doing some research of our own. And we have used an old book, too – the Bible. Our research shows us some interesting things. It shows us that God speaks to all kinds of different people: people doing ordinary jobs, people of all ages, people trying to understand the world. It shows us that they can be doing all sorts of different things: working, worshipping, watching, working out – even just waiting patiently. And it shows us that God can speak to us in all sorts of different ways: through angel messengers, or very quietly inside us, or through other people, or through books. The lovely carol "O Little Town of Bethlehem" says:

> How silently, how silently
> The wondrous gift is given!
> So God imparts to human hearts
> The blessings of his heaven.

There were lots of people at that time hoping the Messiah, the Saviour, would come. There were many people at the temple who could have seen him in the arms of Mary and Joseph, but most of them were too busy to stop and wonder and ask questions – too busy living to find out what life is about. It was those who were quietly waiting and watching who discovered **"the wondrous gift"**. Will we be too busy this Christmas? Or will we be watching, hoping that God will speak to us, show us Jesus, and impart to our watching hearts the blessings of his heaven?

# 80 Inside-out Christmas

## Theme

The way we retell the Christmas story, even in church, all too often brings it perilously close to a fairy story and obscures the reality of the God who identifies with the poor of the earth.

## You will need

- to wear a couple of items of clothing you can take off, for example, a jacket and sweater or waistcoat. This works best if you are dressed smartly. Alternatively, appear with all your clothes on inside-out already.

## Presentation

Silently take off the jacket. Hand it to a member of the "audience". Take off the waistcoat or sweater, turn it inside-out, and put it back on again. Do the same with the jacket. Dressed like this, present the message:

What a stupid thing to do – wear clothes inside-out! We've done the same with the Christmas story: turned it inside out. Like jackets, real-life events have an inside and an outside. The inside of events is the private things that happen, the thoughts people have, their feelings inside. The outside is what the neighbours see or what gets printed in the papers.

The Christmas story is like any other: it has an inside and an outside. But we've turned it all outside-in.

The *inside* of the story was that this baby was the Saviour whom people had been waiting for, for centuries. Men who listened to God had predicted where he was to be born, plus hundreds of things about his life and death. He was a very remarkable baby. But you couldn't see that from the outside.

And you wouldn't have seen the angels. At least, most people didn't. The heavenly choir chose to appear to a handful of men in the dead of night, well away from the big city. When was the last time you spent the night out of doors, sitting in a field?

## Sugar icing

What we have done is to take those amazing but unseen parts of the story and lay them all over the outside, like sugar icing on a cake. That's why we decorate everything and make it colourful and glittery. It makes the whole thing look like a fairy story.

The real *outside* of the story, what most people would actually have seen, was very different.

You would have seen a very ordinary couple from a poor village where children often went hungry and many people were crippled or blinded from various diseases.

Then you would have seen the soldiers, because the country was occupied by a foreign army. And if you were around for any length of time, you would have seen the resistance fighters who had been caught, dying slow, agonizing deaths on crosses beside the roads.

And this couple had to make a long journey to another village for a census. She was pregnant. But you don't argue with the soldiers of an occupying power. When they got there, if they had had enough money, or weapons like the soldiers, they could have got a room. But they had neither weapons nor money.

The usual inside-out story shows them in a clean, rather attractive stable. Have you ever been in a real, old-fashioned cow shed? It is filthy and it stinks.

## No place for a baby

Actually, the Bible doesn't even mention a stable. It only talks about a feeding-trough, a manger. It was probably in a dark cave. What a place to have a baby!

And that reminds me of babies who are born on the streets and in shanty towns all over the Third World. Some of them spend all their lives on the street and die in the gutter.

That's why this story is so important: because Jesus knows what it is like to be a baby born in poverty. He was one of them. He knows what it's like to be one of the poor in a country occupied by foreign troops. He was one of them. He knows what it's like to be a refugee. He was one of them.

Which version of the story do you prefer? The pretty-pretty, sugar-coated, inside-out version for people who don't want to think too much?

Or the rough and dirty right-side-out version that says that God cares so much for the poor of the earth that he sent his own Son to be one of them?

*Walk away quietly, having ensured in advance that whoever takes over at this point leaves a few moments of silence.*

# 81 Santa can't but God can

## Theme
A Christmas message that puts Santa Claus in his place. For use with older children, partly because of the content, but also because of the reactions of some parents to people tampering with childhood illusions.

## You will need
- a Santa hat.
- You could use the cartoon at *www.77talks.co.uk*.

## Presentation
Put on a Santa hat and tell the group that spoilsport scientists have brought poor old Santa Claus down to earth with a bump. Apparently someone at the Massachusetts Institute of Technology decided to put Santa's claims to the test. Then they spilled the beans by publishing the results on the Internet.

They worked out that Santa has to visit more than 90 million homes worldwide (not counting Muslims, Hindus and people of other faiths, because they have their own festivals). Racing round the world before the sun rises, Santa has just 1 thousandth of a second to climb down each chimney, fill stockings, and consume whatever mince pies and glasses of sherry have been left for him.

Although that is going to put him rapidly over the limit – can you be charged with drunk-driving a sleigh? – it's unlikely any police vehicle is going to be fast enough to catch and breathalyze him. Santa's sleigh is moving at 1,000 kilometres (625 miles) per second, or 3,000 times the speed of sound!

## Super-strength reindeer
Then there is the problem of the weight of all those presents. With no more than one kilo (two pounds) for each child, that amounts to over 300,000 tonnes. Of course, Santa's reindeer are specially selected for the job, but even with super-reindeer ten times as strong as normal, it needs 214,200 of them to pull the sleigh.

This is where Santa gets into real difficulties. Including the weight of the reindeer, there are some 350,000 tonnes flying through the atmosphere at 1,000 kilometres (625 miles) per second. In the song, some people say Rudolf's nose glows bright red. This quickly comes true, as with the immense friction his nose rapidly changes from merely red to white-hot, and then poor Rudolf himself bursts into flame and vapourizes with a tremendous sonic boom. In less than 5 thousandths of a second, reindeer, sleigh, presents and Santa are no more than a fantastic fireworks display. This is as bad as the asteroid that put an end to the dinosaurs, so most of the people on earth are wiped out by the fireball and its global effects. Happy Christmas, everyone!

## Impossible task?

In the past 150 years or so, Santa Claus has become an indispensable part of the celebrations of the birth of Jesus. But if Santa's task has been proved to be impossible, what about some of the claims for God and Jesus made in the Bible? For instance, what have scientists got to say about the claim that millions of people can talk to God – pray – all at the same time, and that God can listen to them all? That sounds very much like Santa's impossible task.

For this one, we have to go to what some scientists are saying about the very beginning of the universe. According to one idea – known as string theory – in the first tiny fraction of a second of its existence the universe was expanding in ten dimensions. But almost immediately, six of those dimensions stopped expanding and remained incredibly tightly rolled up. That left us with the three dimensions of space and one time dimension which we live in now. If you haven't a clue what all this is about, don't worry. You need to be a physicist to understand it properly!

A Creator – a God who caused this universe to come into being – would have to exist in at least one more dimension than the universe he created. So if string theory is right and the universe began in ten dimensions, then God must live and operate in at least eleven dimensions.

This gives God unimaginable power. He would only need two dimensions of time to be able to listen to any number of people all praying to him at once. It would be no harder for him to move from one person to another in two-dimension time, listening carefully to each one, than for us to move from one film to another in the video or DVD shop, reading the labels on each one as we go.

## 1 trillion times greater

In fact, living in even just one dimension more than us gives God at least 1 trillion times greater power and ability than we have.

Lots of the things in the Bible that people find hard to understand or believe – things like God being three in one, or Jesus walking on water and some of his other miracles – are easily solved when we realize that God operates in more dimensions than we do.

The biggest question we are left with is not *how* God can do things that seem impossible to us, but *why* he should choose to restrict himself to our four dimensions and be born on earth as a baby at Christmas. That, as they say, is another story.

But at least now we know one thing: **Santa can't, but God can.**

# Parables from Cyberspace and Deep Space

New ways of picturing truths for all time

# 82 Cataclysmic love

## Theme
The origins of gold in colliding stars speaks to us of the power of God's unfailing love.

## You will need
- gold jewellery, especially a wedding ring. If using this in a church, ask people in advance to bring something made of gold with them. You can then get them to hold it for the climax of the message.

## Presentation
Show some jewellery and talk about it, especially any presents. The children may be able to tell you about something they have.

For some people, the most precious thing they have is their wedding ring. Wedding rings are nearly always made of gold. They symbolize the love two people have for each other and their promises to stick with each other through thick and thin for the rest of their lives.

Gold has always been much sought after and, for centuries, alchemists tried to discover how to turn base metals, such as lead or copper, into gold. They could never suspect that it would take a furnace heated to a billion degrees and the risk of being sucked into a black hole!

A physicist at the University of Leicester, Stephen Rosswog, solved the mystery of how gold is created with the use of a tool the old alchemists could not have dreamed of – a supercomputer. The theory is that all it needs is a couple of neutron stars colliding. A neutron star is the core of a burned-out star that was once like our sun, but which has collapsed into an incredibly dense state. A mass a million times heavier than the earth is squeezed into a ball just 20 kilometres (12.4 miles) across!

## Iron into gold
If two neutron stars are close enough to attract each other by their powerful gravity, they spiral ever closer together until there is a cataclysmic collision releasing vast amounts of energy. The extraordinary forces involved change elements such as iron into gold and platinum. Huge amounts of these precious metals are thrown into space and become part of the dust clouds which in future eons will be the birthplace of new stars – and planets such as ours.

Who would have thought that the gold in a wedding ring – a symbol of peace, harmony and love – should have been created in a furnace of such unbelievable forces?

Perhaps we can see in that a picture of our whole world. Here we are on a piece of rock whirling through space. A few miles above us is the cold and vacuum of space that would kill us instantly. Seven light-minutes away is a nuclear furnace – our sun – with temperatures of 15 million degrees Celsius at its centre and a million degrees in the corona that surrounds it.

## Temporary place

Our world is really only a fragile biosphere that is just a thin envelope stretched around the planet. The world seems huge to us, but in the vastness of space it is incredibly tiny. As far as we know, it may be the only place that can support life in the whole universe.

The nature of the Creator who made this is love. The Bible puts it very simply: "**God is love**" (1 John 4:16). That love is seen and demonstrated most wonderfully in Jesus. In love God used all the massive and violent forces of nature to create a fragile and temporary place for us to live in – the earth. A place not just to live, but to grow and think and discover – and learn to love ourselves. As that same part of the Bible goes on to say, "**We love because he first loved us**" (1 John 4:19).

Of course, human love is not perfect, and sometimes, sadly, it fails. But the love of God never fails.

## Something to think about

If you have arranged for the group to bring something made of gold with them, get them to hold it now. Otherwise, get one child to come and hold something you have brought. Play some appropriate music and lead a quiet reflection like this:

When you hold a gold necklace, or chain, or ring that someone has given you because they love you, you can say to yourself,

**This gold was formed in a billion degree furnace as stars collided, before the earth and sun even existed. It speaks to me of the immense power of the Creator who made all things. And the love of the person who gave it to me reminds me of the eternal love of that same incredible God who first loved us. Just as this gold will never rust, never tarnish, so God's perfect love will never fail me.**

# 83 Playing God with E-Dog

## Theme
A lesson on God's care for us from an electronic pet.

## You will need
- to get a child to bring an electronic or cyber pet (the appearance and sophistication of these is developing all the time), especially one that complains when it gets hungry and can get sick or "die" if not cared for properly.
- Alternatively, use the picture of Pootch from www.77talks.co.uk.

## Presentation
Get the children to talk about any electronic pets they have and what they have to do to look after them. Some of the children may have quite expensive toys, others pocket games or a "pet" that lives in a computer.

What can you learn from looking after a cyber pet? Well, it could teach you a lot about caring, for instance, that caring is not a quick one-off. Caring for a pet – or a person – is a long-term commitment.

Caring is not something you do when you want to do it, but when the pet – or person – needs it. If your pet gets sick and you neglect him, he'll die.

Caring means being responsible. You have to be there yourself or else arrange with someone else to take over when you can't be there.

Caring means doing unpleasant things sometimes, like cleaning up the mess.

## Rewarding but sad
Caring isn't just being soft. Sometimes you have to say that something is wrong and reinforce that with discipline.

Caring can be very rewarding, but it can also be sad. People have been known to get genuinely upset and cry when they see a digital gravestone on a computer screen.

## Something to think about
If you learn those lessons, you can learn something else, too. When you learn what it means to care, you can turn it round and appreciate God's love and care for you. Talking to parents one day, Jesus put it like this:

If your child asks for bread, do you trick him with sawdust? If he asks for fish, do you scare him with a live snake on his plate? As bad as you are, you wouldn't think of doing such a thing. You're at least decent to your own children. So don't you think the God who conceived you in love will be even better?

*Matthew 7:9–11,* The Message

If Jesus were around today, perhaps he would say something like this:

"Learn a lesson from your electronic pet. If you take such good care of a virtual pet who only 'lives' in a computer chip, how much more does God care for you, his real, live, flesh-and-blood creation!"

# 84 CD-ROM

## Theme
CD-ROMs and their contents give insights into Jesus' statement that he is "the light of the world".

## You will need
- a spare or old CD-ROM or DVD.
- If you have several, you could write the letters L I G H T on them and hang them up as a mobile.

## Presentation
We all know what this is – a CD-ROM. But imagine you knew nothing about computers and had never seen one before. Would you have any idea what to do with it? Use it as a mirror, perhaps? Or a bird-scarer?

You know that this has an amazing amount of information stored on it. It could be music, or photos, or a whole encyclopaedia, or a computer game.

Can anyone tell us how all that information is stored on this disc and how the computer reads it?…

Digital information is stored in the form of tiny pits on a layer of the disk. The CD-ROM drive on your computer uses a low-power laser beam to read the data. A laser emits a beam of a special kind of light, light of a single colour in which the light waves are all in step with each other. Laser light provides a very powerful and fast means of reading and transferring data.

One time, Jesus was speaking to people and he said,

> **I am the light of the world. The person who follows me will never live in darkness. He will have the light that gives life.**
> *John 8:12*

The **"light that gives life"** must be a very special sort of light. It must have a very special sort of power. How can we understand it? Does thinking about a CD-ROM give us any clues? Maybe it does.

My CD-ROM may contain pictures. The laser allows me to view them. Jesus was constantly putting pictures into the minds of his followers. Things like: **"A man was digging up a field when he found some treasure…"** or, **"A foolish man built his**

**house on sand."** These pictures stick in people's memories. They help us understand what the world is really like, especially the way God sees it. So Jesus was taking data from God – information about the world and people as God created them – and transferring it to our minds in a way we can easily understand, just as we quickly take in the information in a picture when it comes up on the computer screen.

## A glimpse of heaven

My CD may have songs or music on it. As far as we know, Jesus didn't write music. But all through the centuries ever since, his life has been the most amazing source of inspiration to musicians. Countless thousands of songs and hymns, as well as some of the greatest pieces of music ever written, were inspired by Jesus. This music can have the power to lift people out of their everyday lives and give them a glimpse of heaven.

My CD-ROM may contain fascinating and useful information about something I am interested in. It can teach me something I would like to learn. The teaching of Jesus has helped millions of people to live in a way that is right and good. It has inspired countless people to strive to make the world a better place.

What about computer games? Lots of computer games involve some sort of fighting. Surely Jesus wasn't into that! Well, playing is about preparing for real-life situations. And Jesus was quite clear that we are in a real-life battle – a battle between good and evil. From time to time he talked about the enemy – the devil, or Satan. Parts of the last book in the Bible, Revelation, almost read like the script for a computer game involving the defeat of Satan! Learning God's way of fighting that battle is one of the most important things we can do.

## Something to think about

Some people learn a little about Jesus, but they don't understand what the fuss is about and the light just scares them away. Others look more closely. They discover that the more they know about Jesus, the more they understand and appreciate the world and themselves. They find that Jesus truly is **"the light that gives life"**.

# 85 Text test

## Theme
We can see God in Jesus – when we learn to read the message.

## You will need
- at least two mobile phones per team, so ask your group in advance to bring them.
- identical sets of four or five cards with Bible texts on them for each team.

## Presentation
Divide your group into two or more teams and split each team into two halves. Get the team halves to swap phone numbers. Send one half of each team to the opposite end of the hall or to a different room. (It can be fun to have an adults-only team. They will be hopeless!) The aim is for the "home" group to send a Bible text (given to them on a card) as a text message to the "away" half of their team who must then write it down in full. (Minor spelling errors permitted!) The away group sends the message back to the leader in old-fashioned style – on paper carried by a runner. If the wording is correct, the next card is given to the home group. One of the verses to be sent is, **"Anyone who has seen me has seen the Father"** (John 14:9).

Award a prize to the team that completes the task in the shortest time.

Bring the groups back together and get one or two children to show how they condensed the Bible texts into mobile "text" to send them quickly. (This could be an educational experience for the adults.)

God wanted to send a message to the world to show people what he was like. But God is infinitely great. It is a bit like you trying to explain what and who you are to an ant. Impossible! So how could God do it? He sent Jesus. Jesus is God "condensed" into human form. But Jesus said, **"Anyone who has seen me has seen the Father."** Of course, it takes a bit of practice to see the all-powerful God, Creator of the universe, in Jesus, just as many adults have a job getting the message if you text it to them. You have to take the time to get to know Jesus so that you can see God in him. But it is worth the effort.

**"Anyone who has seen me has seen the Father."** Get the message?

## A prayer
You could ask the group – or one or two in advance – to write prayers in text message format. These might be read from an overhead projector (OHP).

## NOTE

If you can't run this as a team game (e.g. if you have a large group or are in school) try it as a game with one or two people at the front communicating to one or two at the back. Two messages will be enough.

# 86 Dangerous attachments

## Theme
Exercising caution before we take someone as our hero or role model.

## You will need
- two people to prepare a mime as follows:
  - Number one mimes getting into a car, driving, parking, getting out, putting a coin into a supermarket trolley, collecting goods, paying, taking the goods back to the car, and driving off.
  - Number two mimes getting into a car, driving, parking, getting out, putting a credit-card into a lock to force entry into a house, collecting items and putting them into a bag, exiting via a window, getting back into the car and driving off.

## Presentation
Ask the group to watch the two mimes. Then ask them to guess what was happening in each. Give clues as necessary and perhaps re-run the mimes or parts of them.

One of the main ways we learn is by watching and copying. Much of what a baby learns comes from watching and listening to its parents – and brothers and sisters – and copying them. As we get older we discover that there are some things it is better not to copy, as when we see someone get into trouble for what they did.

We may also have a hero, or a role model – someone we look up to and want to be like.

As in the two mimes, it is not always easy at first to know whether someone is a good model to follow. Will they help us to learn new things, to grow up, to become wiser – or will they lead us into things that may be harmful? How do we know?

In the famous "Sermon on the Mount", Jesus gave a warning about people who set themselves up as leaders and role models but who were actually quite dangerous people to follow. He said, **"By their fruit you will recognize them"** (Matthew 7:16, *New International Version*). What did he mean?

If Jesus was talking to people today, he might put it something like this:

**"Suppose you get an e-mail from someone with an attachment with a fun-sounding title. But when you open it, it contains a virus which crashes your**

215

computer. You know then that that person is not to be trusted. You have recognized the kind of person they are by the things that they do."

## Sound advice

So Jesus was giving some sound advice in the Sermon on the Mount. Be cautious, he was saying. Don't rush into trusting someone and following them before you have found out what they are really like. Look for the "fruit" – or the e-mail attachments – the effect they actually have in the world and on the people around them. Then you will know whether they are worth copying or not.

Sometimes it is the people who seem to be the most successful and have the most friends who are actually quite dangerous. They are usually very good at conning people. Every so often there is a story about someone like that in the news – a Robert Maxwell or a Jeffrey Archer. They end up disgraced or in prison – or even committing suicide. Jesus put it like this:

> **Every tree that does not bear good fruit is cut down and thrown into the fire.**
> *Matthew 7:19*

They come to a sticky end.

When that happens to someone famous, his or her friends and followers feel pretty stupid. Everyone can see that they got taken in. They want to crawl away and hide under a stone.

So take your time in deciding who you can trust, which is a good gang to belong to, who is a hero worth following. It's better not to be one of the in-crowd now than end up with egg on your face later.

## A prayer

**Our Father in heaven, we've learned to be cautious about opening e-mail attachments without checking first. Teach us to be cautious about following other people. You know what every person is really like inside. When we meet someone who could be a dangerous person to get close to, speak to our spirits and help us to listen to that still, small voice inside. Amen.**

# 87 One touch is all you need

## Theme
Jesus used touch as a way of demonstrating the message of God's love.

## You will need
- a digital watch if you have one.

## Presentation
We are going to fast-forward to a morning in school a few years in the future. I am the teacher. You have done your homework – I hope! – and I am going to collect it in. If you people on the front row would just hold a finger up in the air like this...and I'll collect in your work. [Look at your watch – press a button on it if it is a digital watch – then touch each person's finger for one second.] Yes...thank you. Next...thank you...etc.

Now I'll take your work to my office and transfer it to my computer ready for marking. I set my wrist-unit...then place my finger on a touch-sensitive pad for a few seconds...That's it: a whole set of homework waiting to be marked!

How does it work? A research team at IBM in California calls this a Personal Area Network – or PAN for short. It allows information to be passed from one person to another simply by touch.

## Transfer via bald spot
If you were wearing a PAN transmitter it would create a tiny electrical current over the surface of your skin – just 1 billionth of an amp. All you need to do is to touch my finger – or my nose – or even my bald spot! – and your essay, drawing, or whatever else you have prepared on your home computer, will be transferred to my PAN receiver.

It is absolutely safe; even combing your hair creates an electrical field 1,000 times greater. Handing in your homework will be completely painless! (Of course, teachers might get a shock if certain people handed in their homework on time!)

That might be a few years away, but touch is now – and always has been – a vital way of people communicating with each other. Touch gives us messages we all need to hear, things like: acceptance, friendship, sympathy, and love.

217

Shaking hands when we first meet someone gives the message, "I accept you as a friend."

A kiss on the cheek or a hug means, "You are a close friend or a member of my family, someone I care for. You are important to me."

And when something dreadful happens, what we need most of all is someone to hold us tight.

When we read the stories of Jesus, we see how important touch was to him. Although he could heal someone without even being near them, again and again he chose to reach out a hand and touch the sick and the needy. He touched an untouchable leper; he put his fingers in a deaf man's ears; he held a dead girl by the hand and raised her to life.

You could expand this here by telling one of these stories. See **Mark 1:40–42**; **Mark 7:31–37**; **Mark 5:21–24, 35–43**.

## Something to do

God made us in such a way that we all need touch – a kiss from Mum, a hug from a grandparent, a friend's hand on the shoulder. These things tell us that people love us. Jesus used touch to show God's love to those who needed it most.

We can share a bit of that love around: give someone a hug today!

# 88 God's glory on tour

## Theme
Photos of comets can draw gasps of awe and wonder from children (and adults). Use them to share something of the splendours of God's creation.

NASA's Stardust mission is due to pass through the tail of comet Wild 2 in 2004 and bring back samples of interstellar dust in 2006. And on 4 July 2005, the Deep Impact mission plans to blast a hole in a comet and analyze the resulting debris. Media reports at these times could give special opportunities to use this talk.

## You will need
- pictures of comets from books or from NASA's superb Astronomy Picture of the Day site. You can find these at *www.77talks.co.uk*.
- Alternatively, go to http://antwrp.gsfc.nasa.gov/apod/. At this site, click on Archive (near the bottom of the page) which brings up a list of past photos, organized by their dates. Suggested pictures are of comet Hale-Bopp at 1997 April 16, and a sungrazer comet at 2000 May 20. For more photos and information about comets, click on Search at the NASA site and enter "comets".

## Presentation
Ideally, begin with the photo of comet Hale-Bopp. Some children will be old enough to remember having seen this comet in 1997. It was exceptionally bright and we will be lucky to see another comet as bright as this in our lifetimes.

A comet has been described as "a dirty snowball". It is made of ice and dust. A comet itself is far too small to see – Hale-Bopp was just 40 kilometres (25 miles) across. But as it approaches the sun, it warms up and gives off gas and dust. That is the round "head" that we can see. Hale-Bopp's corona of dust and gas was some 100,000 kilometres (60,000 miles) wide.

This gas and dust is then blown straight out by the "solar wind" – hot plasma that streams out continuously from the sun's surface. That creates the tail of a comet. Hale-Bopp actually had two tails – a blue ionized gas tail and a white dust tail. The tails stretched millions of kilometres into space.

Comets orbit the sun in a strange way. Their orbit is a giant ellipse that takes them way out into deep space and then swinging back close to the sun. Hale-Bopp came closest to the sun on 1 April 1997 – 153 million kilometres (96 million miles) from the sun's north pole. (Earth is 150 million kilometres or 93 million miles from the sun.) Since then, it has begun a journey that will take it far away from the sun and the planets, not to return for another 4,000 years.

## Spectacular sungrazers

Some comets come even closer to the sun. They are known as sungrazers. (Show the photo if you have it.) By using a disc to block out the sun, SOHO, the space-based SOlar and Heliospheric Observatory, has been able to take photos of these comets as they dive to within 50,000 kilometres (31,000 miles) of the sun. Not surprisingly, many sungrazers do not survive their encounter with the sun.

Comets have always fascinated people. The star of the Christmas story which led the wise men from the East to go in search of the baby king of the Jews may have been a comet.

Many centuries ago, David the shepherd boy spent some of his nights under the stars watching over the family's sheep. The first part of one of the songs he wrote goes like this:

Read **Psalm 19:1–4a**.

One writer translates the opening words as: **"God's glory is on tour in the skies."**[1] We don't know if David had a comet in his sight at the time, but that would be a pretty good description of one!

## Something to think about

This song, Psalm 19, is a poet's response as he looks up at the sky, the sun, the moon and the stars. He is filled with wonder as he thinks that there is no place on earth where people can't just look up at any time of the day or night and see a reflection of God's power and splendour. People may have no Bible, no religious education, no scientific understanding, but something of the truth of the Creator is there for anyone with eyes to see.

Many of us who spend our days and nights under artificial light rarely turn our eyes to the skies. When a comet appears it encourages people to get away from their TV screens and gaze up at the wonders of the night sky. But we don't have to wait for a comet. Every clear night, the stars and planets are on show. Perhaps if we take time to gaze into the wonders of the night sky, our hearts will also respond to the revelation of **"God's glory...on tour in the skies"**.

---

1. Eugene H. Peterson, *The Message* (Colorado Springs: Navpress, 1994). You might like to use Peterson's version for the whole of the reading.

# 89 10,000 trillion stars

## Theme

More gasp-inducing photographs lead to humbling reflections on the power of the Creator and the reasons why he made the universe.

## You will need

- The Hubble Space Telescope has given us amazing pictures of stars and galaxies. Some of these have been published in books or you can find them at the NASA Astronomy Picture of the Day site. For this talk you need at least Whirlpool Galaxy (2001 April 27) and the Milky Way (2000 January 30). These pictures have been copied to our own site: www.77talks.co.uk or you can find them at the NASA site, below.

## Presentation

Show the photo of the Whirlpool Galaxy on the OHP. (If you can darken the room, so much the better.)

A galaxy is a kind of city of stars. It is a great swirl of dust, gas and stars slowly rotating in space. Astronomers believe that at the centre of most – maybe all – galaxies is a supergiant black hole.

The Whirlpool Galaxy is 30 million light-years away from earth. That means that it has taken the light from these stars 30 million years to reach us. The Whirlpool Galaxy is 60,000 light-years from side to side. It is one of the brightest and most beautiful galaxies in the sky, although you would need a telescope to see it.

Each of the stars in the galaxy is a sun like ours, some of them much bigger. Does anyone know how many stars there are in a galaxy like this?…100 billion!

In **Psalm 147** in the Bible it says, God

> **determines the number of the stars and calls them each by name. Great is our Lord and mighty in power; his understanding has no limit.**
>
> *Psalm 147:4–5,* New International Version

A God who can create a galaxy of 100 billion stars is certainly "mighty in power"! But this isn't the only galaxy by a long way. We live in another galaxy. Does anyone know what our home galaxy is called?… The Milky Way.

Show picture.

# 100 billion neighbours

The Milky Way is a spiral galaxy that looks rather like the Whirlpool Galaxy. But because we are on one side of it we see it edge on. So this is a photo of our sun's 100 billion nearest neighbours!

That's just two galaxies. Would anyone like to guess how many galaxies there are in the whole universe?…100 billion – the same number as there are stars in one galaxy.

So if there are 100 billion galaxies, each with 100 billion stars – that adds up to 10,000 trillion (1022) stars in the universe!

The writer of that psalm says, **"He determines the number of stars."** If he determines the number of stars, why did he make 10,000 trillion of them? Surely that's going a bit over the top! After all, we only need one, our sun, to give us all the light and warmth we need on planet earth.

In recent years scientists have begun to tell us a different story. Apparently planet earth wouldn't be here at all if there weren't all those 10,000 trillion stars. The mass of the universe has to be exactly right. If the mass of the universe was either slightly larger or slightly smaller it would be impossible for earth – or any other planet like it – to exist. It seems that God wasn't going over the top in creating 100 billion galaxies. If you want to have one small planet that can support life – and human beings – you have to design a universe that big to start with. God knew what he was doing.

And he knew why he was doing it. Take a look at the person sitting next to you. If there weren't 10,000 trillion stars he or she would not be sitting there. And neither would you. You must be pretty important for God to go to all that trouble!

Surely the songwriter was right when he said, **"Great is our Lord and mighty in power; his understanding has no limit."**

# New Life Starts Here

There's no technology that can change the human heart

# 90 Be refreshed

## Theme
Inviting Jesus to clean us up and give us a new start brings life with a sparkle.

## You will need
- a bottle of a well-known cola (preferably brought ice-cold in a cool-box) with two empty glasses; another glass of cola that has been left out a day or longer with one or two foreign bodies added, especially a dead fly or wasp; some cola-bottle sweets from the pocket-money counter; a bowl of water to wash a glass, and a cloth to dry it.

## Presentation
Ask for a volunteer who fancies a glass of cola and pour them one, emphasizing how cool and refreshing it is. Ask for a second thirsty person and offer them the stale cola, complete with dead fly. Tell them how long it has been poured out and what it is likely to have in it. Will they drink it?… Will anyone?… It is good for nothing except to be thrown away.

Thank your volunteers. A big "Aaah!" for the second one who remains thirsty – and a cola-bottle sweet as a consolation!

Pour and hold up a second glass of fresh cola. This is how God intended life to be – full of sparkle, zest, joy. But the reality for a lot of people – especially many grown-ups – is that life has gone stale and flat. There may even be unpleasant things floating around in it that they would rather not talk about. Or perhaps they had big hopes and dreams, but what they have ended up with is – hold up another cola-bottle sweet – a big disappointment.

Jesus said,

**I came to give life – life in all its fullness.** *John 10:10*

"Life in all its fullness" – that could be a good advertising slogan for cola! It is certainly the real thing, not a cheap imitation or a stale left-over.

So if life is like this – the stale cola – how do we get it back to the way it was meant to be, like this – the sparkling cola? Let's see if we can find out from the beginning of Mark's story of Jesus.

225

# Ducked in the river

Straight away in chapter 1 we find this rather strange man who wore designer clothes – well, he designed them himself from camel's hair! His name was John and his big thing was ducking people in the river. You might think he would get himself arrested for doing that – and he did later – but at this time loads of people were coming to see him. He told people that they needed to repent, which means to turn around and make a fresh start. Lots of people knew their lives were like stale cola with dead things floating around in it – the wrong things they had done and the mistakes they had made – so they were quite ready to repent and get rid of the mess of sin in their lives. [Empty the stale cola out of the glass.] Perhaps more people would do that today if they knew what was on offer.

Then John ducked them in the river. [Plunge the glass in the bowl, wash and dry it.] This was a sign that they were being cleaned up inside. It was called "baptizing", and the camel-hair shirt man got the nickname, John the Baptizer. Today we might call him John the Plunger or John the Ducker.

John the Baptizer also told people that someone far more important than him was coming, someone who would soak people not with water but with the Holy Spirit. And guess who came along? – Jesus.

Jesus asked John to baptize him – not that he needed to be cleaned up – and the Spirit of God came down on him in a way that was kind of visible. Some people said it looked like a dove.

# A new sparkle

A few weeks later, John did get thrown in prison, but by then he had done his job. Now it was Jesus' turn to tell people some good news. Not only could they get cleaned up inside, but a whole new way of living was open to them – God's kingdom. [Pour a little fresh cola in the cleaned glass.] God's kingdom is where living is exciting and challenging, because God is in charge.

Then, to show this was not just words, Jesus started doing amazing things like healing people. Loads of people's lives got a new sparkle then. [Add some more cola to the glass.] You can find all this in just the first chapter of Mark's story of Jesus.

If you go on to read other parts of the story of Jesus, you will find that what John the Baptizer said about him came true. Jesus did soak people in the Holy Spirit, or fill them with the Spirit. Then their lives really started sparkling! [Fill the glass to the top.]

Ever since then, all down the centuries, people have been finding that it really works. I don't mean religion. Religion is just an unsatisfying substitute. I mean the real thing: **"life in all its fullness"**. Cheers! [Drink cola.]

# Finding treasure

## Theme
The contrast between the remote possibility of winning the lottery and the certainty of the treasure of God's kingdom.

## You will need
- a box containing a lottery ticket, a black marker pen, a treasure map (see *www.77talks.co.uk*), a blindfold, a crown (made out of card). Extra items if possible: a magnifying glass; a metal detector – or broom as a substitute (not in the box – hide it).

## Presentation
Place the box on a table where it will be clearly visible. Show the objects one at a time and place them in view on the table. When all the objects are displayed, ask the children what they think the talk is going to be about… It is going to be about treasure.

One way lots of people think they can get treasure is by playing the national lottery. I wonder how likely they are to win the jackpot? Let's see if we can find out. We're going to give one person the same chance of finding something as of winning the first prize in the lottery.

Ask for a volunteer who doesn't mind being blindfolded – *Henry*. Now you need ten more volunteers who all have fair hair, if possible. Line them up at the front.

What we are going to do is choose one of these people and then choose one hair on their head. Then we'll mark that hair with a marker pen. But first we'll blindfold *Henry*.

Choose one of the ten, separate out a single hair, hold it against a piece of white card or paper, and mark the end few centimetres with the marker pen.

Do you know how many hairs you have on your head? Blond-haired people have around 145,000 hairs, dark-haired people around 120,000, and red-heads 90,000.

## One hair on ten heads
Now here's the test for *Henry*. He has to see if he can find the hair with the black mark on it among these ten people. Ask *Henry* to choose a number between one and ten, place him behind the chosen person in the line, and get him to single out one hair. He might need a bit of help. Then take off his blindfold and hand him a

227

magnifying glass, holding a piece of paper behind the chosen hair. Is it the right one?!

What chance did *Henry* have of finding the right hair? There are ten people here, each with around 145,000 hairs. How many hairs is that?…1,450,000. *Henry* had one chance in nearly 1.5 million of finding the right hair. I said this was going to be like the chance of winning the first prize on the lottery! To do that properly we would have needed 100 people in the line, not ten. Getting the right six numbers to win the lottery is the same as finding the one right hair from the heads of 100 people.

Thank the volunteers and ask them to sit down.

Playing the lottery looks like just about the worst possible way you could choose of finding treasure. Let's see what we've got here that might be more helpful. This treasure map, for example. It has some words written round the outside. Get a child to read it:

> **The kingdom of heaven is like treasure hidden in a field. One day a man found the treasure. The man was very happy to find the treasure. He went and sold everything he owned to buy that field.** *Matthew 13:44*

Jesus was telling a story about someone finding treasure. If it was today, they would probably use a metal detector. (This is the place for a bit of action with your broom/ metal detector.)

Imagine the excitement of discovering a whole chest full of gold and silver coins! The trouble was, the field didn't belong to the man in the story. What could he do? He hadn't got enough money to buy the field. There was only one thing for it – bury the treasure again and sell everything he had to raise enough money. Car, TV, clothes, even his metal detector – everything had to go to raise the money to buy the field.

## A guaranteed winner

Buying the field cost a lot more than buying a lottery ticket. But see the difference. When a person buys a lottery ticket they only have one chance in 14 million of winning the big prize – the same as finding the right hair on 100 people's heads. But when this man bought the field he **knew** he'd won the jackpot. He already knew the treasure was there. He was a guaranteed winner!

But hold on. What is the treasure Jesus is talking about? Is it a chest of gold coins, or something else? There's a clue on the map. Lets read it again: "**The kingdom of heaven is like treasure hidden in a field.**" The kingdom of heaven – I wonder what that is? Is there a clue in the things that came out of the box? What haven't we used yet?… The crown. A kingdom needs a king, and a king wears a crown. Who do you think is the king of the kingdom of heaven?… Jesus, or God. The kingdom of heaven is God's kingdom. It's where everything happens the way he wants it to happen.

Just think about what it would be like in a place where Jesus was king. Do you think there would be people hurting each other or fighting?... Do you think there would be some people starving because other people were greedy and selfish?... Do you think things would be spoiled by waste and pollution?... Do you think people would be bored or miserable?... Do you think there would be anyone there who didn't have exciting things to do?... No.

People hope to win the lottery because they think they will be able to buy lots of things to make them happy. But in God's kingdom of heaven people have already got all they need to make them happy. Just being there is the treasure. The man in the story was bursting with happiness and excitement when he found it.

[Hold up the crown and the lottery ticket for everyone to see.]

I wonder which you think is the best way of finding treasure?

## A prayer

**Father God, please help me not to waste my time looking for the wrong kind of treasure or looking for treasure in the wrong place. Please show me what is the real treasure in this life, and how I can find it. Amen.**

# 92 The fear of death

## Theme
How to have a life that cannot be destroyed.

## You will need
• a glass of water.
• a sari or some sari material if possible.

## Presentation
Drink the glass of water.

If I'd drunk that water in Britain in the 19th century – or if I drank it in Bangladesh now – I might be dead in 24 hours. I might die because the water could be contaminated with one of the world's deadliest diseases – cholera. Just imagine living with the fear that your next drink could kill you or a member of your family!

The cholera bacteria cause severe diarrhoea and vomiting within four to twelve hours, which leads to severe dehydration (loss of fluid in the body). More than half the people who catch cholera and are not treated die, sometimes within 18 hours of the first symptoms. Antibiotics are no use in treating cholera, and vaccination is not very much help.

How have we managed to get rid of the fear of cholera in the Western world almost completely? By a huge investment in sewerage systems in the 19th century. This kept polluted water – the water and waste from toilets – separate from fresh water.

## No money for sewers
Many parts of the world do not have such sewerage systems, or the money to build them. Even the wood to boil water to kill the bacteria is too scarce in Bangladesh.

But scientists have found a remarkably simple way to filter the cholera bacteria out of water. It is the sari – and every woman in Bangladesh has one.

The breakthrough came when a team of scientists discovered that the cholera bacteria live inside the guts of tiny organisms in the water. Although the bacteria themselves are too small to be filtered out, the carrier organisms are trapped very efficiently in four layers of sari material, and 99% are removed. Simply hanging the sari out to dry in the sun is enough to kill the trapped bacteria and sterilize the cloth – for free!

If this proves to work long-term in everyday life, many lives will be spared and many people saved from a potent fear of death.

## Something to think about

Because of the efforts of our great-great-grandparents in building sewerage systems, we can drink water without fear of death. But we can never get rid of the fear of death altogether. After all, we are all going to die one day! Christians believe this is why Jesus came. It says in the Bible that people were like slaves all their lives because of the fear of death (Hebrews 2:15). The message of Easter is that death need no longer be feared. Paul wrote:

> **Our Saviour Christ Jesus...destroyed death, and through the Good News he showed us the way to have life that cannot be destroyed.** *2 Timothy 1:10*

For many families in Bangladesh it must be worth finding out how to use their everyday clothing to protect themselves from cholera. Christians believe it is worth anybody's time to find out about **"the way to have life that cannot be destroyed"**.

# 93 I tell you the truth

## Theme
Jesus is the truth-teller, and his truth leads to the prize of eternal life.

## You will need
- a list of true or false statements (there is one provided on the *www.77talks.co.uk* website); possibly a large dice.
- three or four boxes, one containing enough sweets as prizes for one team.

## Presentation
Divide the children into two or three teams and run a "true or false" quiz. Scoring can be with a giant dice to add an element of chance and bigger scores.

When the quiz is finished, show the boxes. The prize for the winning team is in one of them. You will tell them which one. The problem is, you may not be telling the truth, so they will have to decide between themselves whether to believe you and take the box you have indicated or to choose another one! Whether to believe you or not leads to some interesting – and possibly heated! – discussions.

If the winning team chooses wrongly, then the second-placed team have a chance, again with you telling them which one it is. (With three teams you could have four boxes, so that there is always a chance for any team – or none – to get the prize.)

## Hoax death threats
Not knowing whether someone is telling the truth or not is very frustrating. It can lead to doubts, arguments, indecision, bad choices. Imagine the problem faced by the police when they get a phone call saying there is a bomb in a public place. If it is a hoax and they clear the street or railway station or whatever, then there is terrific disruption for nothing. If the call is genuine but they choose not to believe it, lives may be lost. No wonder the police and the courts come down very hard on people who make hoax bomb threats.

No less than 78 times in the gospel records Jesus says, "I tell you the truth…" Sometimes Jesus is talking about life and death situations. For example, in John 5:24 Jesus says,

> **I tell you the truth. Whoever hears what I say and believes in the One who sent me has eternal life. He will not be judged guilty. He has already left death and has entered into life.**

232

Was Jesus a hoaxer, a liar who led people up the garden path? It is an important question because, as Jesus himself made plain, it is a life and death question. If he was a liar, then he was one of the worst men who has ever lived, because hundreds of millions of people have been taken in by him for more than 20 centuries.

But the things that he did, and the way he lived and taught others to live – do these seem like the life and teaching of a liar and a cheat? Even many who don't call themselves Christians would never call him a bad man; they respect him as a great man and teacher.

## The most brilliant mind

But if Jesus was not a liar, then the things he said were the most important things anyone has ever said in the history of the world. He is the man with the most brilliant mind, the man with the greatest understanding, the most gifted teacher, and the most caring and compassionate person who has ever lived. He is the only man who has ever truly known the mysteries of life and death.

To hold a Bible, and to read as Jesus says, **"I tell you the truth,"** or even simply, **"I tell you,"** is to hold in your hands everything you need to know about this life or the life to come.

When Jesus says, **"I tell you the truth,"** you know you are going to find the prize. And the prize is eternal life.

# 94 Bags of goods

## Theme
What we are on the inside can match how we appear on the outside if we let Jesus remake us.

## You will need
- a selection of shopping bags from stores in your area. (If you explain what you want them for, shops will be pleased to let you have one.)
- items to go inside the bags, some appropriate, some not.
- a dustbin liner with a hole cut in the bottom for a child's head to go through.

## Presentation
Get some volunteers to guess what is inside your different shopping bags. Some can be appropriate items, some decidely not – like a pair of smelly socks in a bag from an expensive store. You may even find one or two punning examples, such as a jar of balti paste in a Curry's bag.

You could have one or more bags where the child who correctly guesses the contents gets to keep it.

Unless we are really snobbish and carry around a bag from an expensive store just to be seen with it, what really matters is the contents of the bag, not what it says on the outside. God is looking for people who don't just look good on the outside, but who are right on the inside.

Jesus had a word for people who looked better than they really were – hypocrites. One time, he even said such people were like tombs in a graveyard – painted to look nice on the outside, but full of bones and rotting things inside. That's a lot worse than a posh bag with smelly socks inside. Jesus could be pretty rude about hypocrites!

There is another kind of bagful that Jesus does not want any of us to be.

[Get a volunteer and put the dustbin liner over them, so that their head pokes through the hole.]

Jesus does not think that any of us is like this, a bag full of rubbish to be thrown away. He made us. He loves us. We are precious to him. St Paul says, **"You were bought at a price"** (1 Corinthians 6:20). That price was the death of Jesus on the cross. Nobody ever paid a price greater than that.

Whatever rubbish there is inside us, Jesus doesn't want us to pretend it isn't there, like the hypocrites do. He wants us to invite him into our lives, to clean us up, to make us the wonderful person he designed us to be.

## Proud of our purchases

We go to the shops and buy something, perhaps something we have been wanting for a long time. We take it home and get it out of the bag. We are pleased. We are proud. We want to show it off to our friends. Jesus wants something like that, too. He paid the price for us. He wants one day to take us home to the place he has prepared for us. What we are on the outside won't be needed any more. It can be thrown away, like a plastic shopping bag. The real us, the person we are on the inside, will then be clearly seen.

No one would want to be a hypocrite on that day, to be seen to be just old, rotting bones, to be seen to have wasted his or her life. But those who have invited Jesus into their lives will be seen to be perfect, wonderful, precious, of everlasting worth. That's the way Jesus will have made them.

## Something to do

If the situation is appropriate, listeners may be given the opportunity to invite Jesus into their lives. Or it could be suggested that they explore this further themselves by visiting the Narrow Gate pages of the *www.jubilee-kids.org* website.

# 95 Light from behind bars

## Theme

The remarkable true story of David Lant, a criminal serving a life sentence for murdering another prisoner, and how his life has been radically changed. He cannot ever undo the damage he has done, but today he spends his time helping others, producing Braille to enable blind people to read.

## You will need

- a sample of Braille, if possible. (Try your local library.)
- the codebreaker and translation of Luke 4:18 on page 72 or from the *www.77talks.co.uk* website. This could be photocopied and used as a follow-up, or printed onto acetate to show on the OHP.

## Presentation

David Lant was once one of the most dangerous men in British prisons. He made his first appearance in the juvenile court when he was eight years old. Then he spent 20 years locked up in approved schools and special hospitals. Finally, he was sentenced to life imprisonment for murdering another patient at Broadmoor Hospital. So what made an ordinary boy turn into a violent criminal?

David had an older brother, John. But one day David learned from a stranger that John was not his brother at all. And his mum was not his real mother. He was adopted, and his adopted family had decided not to tell him. (That was quite normal in those days.)

Even now, he still remembers how painful this discovery was: "I had loved, adored, idolized John. Now I felt that he had betrayed me – and in the worst possible way – to a stranger. From that moment my world crumbled around me. My love for John turned instantly to deep hatred towards him and towards everyone in general." The only outlet for this hatred that David could find was violence. He turned to crime.

He was sent to a special kind of school for young people who had committed crimes, and later to prison. Every time he was released, he would slip back into bad ways: "Nothing seemed to stop me. I just continued running away and committing more crimes." And so it went on, until eventually David found himself sentenced to life imprisonment for taking part in the murder of another prisoner.

After he was given the life sentence, he concentrated on learning how to beat the prison system: "Whenever I thought that I had been unjustly treated, I noted it down in what I called my 'box of hatred'. I would have died rather than let that 'box of hatred' out of my sight."

## Letters

After many years in prison, David was filmed for a television documentary called *Lifer*. Some people who saw the programme started writing to him. One of them was a Christian woman called Margaret. She told him she was praying for him. David didn't believe in God, and took no notice of what she said in her letter.

However, he did notice a change in Peter, one of the lads on his wing. It turned out that Peter had become a Christian. He said he was also praying that David would meet Jesus. At that time, David was still not interested in God: "Not in a thousand years will I become a Christian!" There was no way you would catch *him* going all "religious" like that.

Soon after this, David was in his cell one night when he suddenly realized that he did not like the person that he had become. He didn't want to go on hurting and hating others. He wanted to change, like Peter had done, but he knew he needed help, special help. So David found himself kneeling on the floor, apologizing to God for everything he had done and asking God to help him to change into a better person.

## The vilest offender

A couple of weeks later, David woke up in the middle of the night and started whistling a tune. It stayed with him all through the next morning. At dinner-time Peter asked him, "Do you know the words to that tune?" David said he didn't; Peter got out a hymn book and began to read these words:

> **The vilest offender who truly believes,**
> **That moment from Jesus a pardon receives.**

David said: "I knew that Jesus had spoken to me. I was that 'vilest offender'. I had received a pardon for every one of my horrendous sins because I truly believed in him."

Today, David is a very different person. He is still in prison, and like the rest of us he still gets it wrong sometimes, but it is hard to believe such a caring person could ever have got his kicks out of hurting others. Instead, he has committed his life to helping people in difficulty. He translates books from English (and other languages) into Braille, so that blind and visually impaired people are able to read them. He has even won an award for his services to people suffering from blindness throughout the world.

He is also happily married to a woman called Christine whom he met through his work, and is looking forward to the time when he finishes his sentence and they can be together. He is living proof of the fact that no matter how bad our lives may be, we all have the chance to begin again.

# Something to do

Give out copies of the Braille text – or show it on the OHP – and see if the children can translate it into something Jesus said.

## BRAILLE ALPHABET

| 1 | 2 | 3 | 4 | 5 | 6 | 7 | 8 | 9 | 0 |
|---|---|---|---|---|---|---|---|---|---|
| a | b | c | d | e | f | g | h | i | j | k | l | m | n | o | p | q | r | s |

t u v w x y z  . : ; ? ! *

opening quotation    closing quotation    numeral sign

*Can you decipher this?*

*(Luke 4:18)*

---

Condensed from David Lant's own testimony, *Adopted!*

David's Braille ministry operates under LIGHTWING PROJECTS, Registered Charity no. 1016529. For further details visit the website at http://www.wyrecompute.oaktree.co.uk/lightwing.

# I saw a star fall

## Theme
Comets or meteors may wipe out human life on the earth, but the big decision remains the same: Whose side are you on?

## You will need
- a picture of an asteroid, printed onto an OHP transparency if possible. You will find some pictures at *www.77talks.co.uk* and a link to the NASA Astronomy Picture of the Day website.
- a Bible: Revelation 8:6–9:2.

## Presentation
Show a picture of an asteroid, or ask who has seen a shooting star.

Pieces of rock from space hit the earth every day. As they enter the atmosphere they burn up, creating the brief flash of a shooting star. Some are large enough for bits to land on earth. About once every 1,000 years a rock nearly 100 metres (300 feet) in diameter strikes our planet, big enough to cause a tidal wave if it lands in the sea.

But what would happen if a really large meteor was on collision course with the earth?

Actually, it is not a matter of *if* but *when*. The last time it happened was maybe less than 4,400 years ago, around 2350 BC, a mere eye-blink in cosmic time. At that time there seems to have been a great environmental catastrophe, and civilizations collapsed. Mud-brick buildings in northern Syria appear to have been destroyed by what is described as a "blast from the sky".

## The K-T event
So could it happen again? The bad news is, yes, it could. The good news is that a collision with a massive asteroid, over 1km across, is more rare, happening only once in millions of years. But an asteroid that size would create a global catastrophe, wiping out many species of plants and animals.

Is that what killed the dinosaurs? Around 65 million years ago they disappeared, together with about 70% of all species then living on earth. This is known as the K-T event (the Cretaceous-Tertiary Mass Extinction event). Could it have been caused by an asteroid or comet hitting the earth? In 1990 came evidence that it was. A 65 million-year-old crater, 180 kilometres (112 miles) wide, was discovered under layers of sediment in the Yucatan Peninsula region of Mexico. It would have taken an asteroid ten kilometres (6.5 miles) wide to make this crater – big enough to cause massive global disruption.

The last book in the Bible, the book of Revelation, describes some great environmental catastrophes, including what sounds like a description of the earth being struck, perhaps by a chain of comet pieces like those that spectacularly hit Jupiter in 1994.

Read **Revelation 8:6 – 9:2**.

It's a pretty terrifying picture. Christians have different ideas about what it means. Some think it is a prediction of what will actually happen in the future. Some think it is using coded picture language to describe the persecution suffered by Christians in the Roman empire.

# Great war

But everyone agrees in general what the book of Revelation is about: there is a great war going on between the powers of good and evil. In the end, God will deal once and for all with evil. But each person must decide for themselves which side they are on. Many people would prefer not to think about that decision. They bury themselves in their work, or fill their lives with TV and music and entertainment so that they don't have to think. But just doing nothing allows the evil around us to grow.

For each one of us personally, it makes no difference whether we are hit by a twelve-mile-wide asteroid or a number 11 bus! One thing is for sure: we will each meet our own personal end sometime within the next 100 years (a lot sooner for some of us!).

If a big asteroid is headed in our direction, we won't be able to duck it. We can't duck the big question either: **Whose side are you on?**


**NOTE**

This could be expanded – or followed up – by asking the question, **Who will save us?** In Hollywood blockbusters the current megastar gets to nuke the offending asteroid and save the earth. In the real-life war between good and evil...well, most readers of this book know the answer to that one!

# 97 Only the scars tell the story

## Theme
Young Frenchman Franck Fama survived a serious motor cycle accident and experienced a recovery his surgeon described as "miraculous". Here is his story to tell or to use as an illustration.

## You will need
• A photo of Franck can be found at *www.77talks.co.uk* if you wish to use it.

## Presentation
It was a hot June night in 1989 when three friends came out of a disco in the Ardeche region in southern France. 22-year-old Franck swung his 600cc Suzuki onto a dirt track and joined his friends in racing to a point where they could join the road.

On the road, Franck found himself alone. The other two had shot ahead. He leaned left into a bend, hugging the middle of the road. Suddenly he saw the car. It was taking the bend wide, straddling the white line. All he remembers of the next moment is the loud crack as his left arm hit the front of the car.

## Thirteen months in hospital
Lying beside the road, he regained consciousness to find one of his friends kneeling over him, crying. *Am I dying?* he thought. *Am I cut in two? Is that why he's crying?* Then, *I want to sleep. I want to sleep.* And he lost consciousness again.

At the hospital, doctors worked to piece together his broken bones. His right leg was almost severed. A long metal pin holding the bone together from a previous motor bike accident just six months before probably saved it from amputation. There were four breaks in his left leg, and his left arm was very badly smashed. It was the beginning of a thirteen-month stay in hospital.

Coming that close to death makes anyone think about the meaning of life. As a young teenager, Franck had decided he wanted to be free of the things he had learned in his local Catholic church as a child. But the way his life was going now didn't seem to be of much use to him; he decided to give it all to God. He even wrote his decision down on a piece of paper. He felt peaceful, although nothing much more seemed to change at the time.

# Nerve grafts

Six months after the accident, his left arm was paralyzed. He could expect to regain a little movement, but some of the nerves had been completely cut. The surgeon decided to try a kind of operation that was new in France. It involved taking sections of nerves from his legs. These were several centimetres long but not much thicker than a piece of thread.

Then they cut through the muscles at the top of his chest to graft the nerve sections into his left shoulder and arm. After that it was a matter of patience. Would the nerves grow and join up again? Would the muscles in his arm start responding to messages from his brain once more?

During the long months in hospital Franck bought a Bible and started to read it right through. Reading the stories of Jesus and his disciples, he thought, *That's the truth; that's the right way to live. But why don't we see that now? Why aren't there any Christians like that today?*

As he read the Bible, two things started happening. He began to look at life much more positively. And he began to get movement back into his left arm. It progressed so quickly that his surgeon could hardly believe it. "A miracle," was his verdict. The physiotherapist, too, thought it was unbelievable.

Of seven young men on the ward with paralyzed arms, Franck was the only one to recover. He even took to keeping it still in front of the others, in order not to upset them!

He was allowed out of hospital for a few weeks, but then it was back in for a further six months. This time the doctors were going to break both his legs again and reset the bones straighter.

Every morning, he was wheeled down to spend half an hour with a blind physiotherapist who was working with him on his left arm. The physio was a Christian. They spent the time talking about the Bible, and each day, the physio gave Franck a couple of Bible verses he had learned by heart.

# It's all too simple!

What Franck found difficult to understand was how the Bible stories seemed to be so real and so relevant to the physio. It all seemed too simple!

When the time came for him to leave hospital, the physio invited him to an adult baptism in a large church in Lyon. They arrived late to find some 400 people praising God. It was very lively, and different from anything Franck had known of church before. "This is strange," he said to himself, "but there is something in this praise that is really powerful."

He started going to another branch of the same church and realized he had found what he had read about in the Bible – a faith that people really lived out in their everyday lives. There *were* Christians today like those he had read about after all! He felt he had found what he had been looking for all those years. He was baptized himself on 18 April 1993.

## Unexpected bonuses

Seeing Franck today climbing mountains or jumping off ten metre cliffs into the Ardeche river, you would never know how close he came to losing a leg or the use of an arm. Only the scars tell the story.

And there are two other unexpected bonuses. Before the accident he was a jeweller, but he really wanted to do something to help other people. Now he works as a nurse. He sees that as a real blessing.

And the second bonus? Three months after he was baptized, he went to a Christian conference. There he met an English girl – and it was love at first sight! Franck and Rebecca were married four years later and baby Esther was born to them in 2001.

# 98 Just a crowd of silly sheep?

## Theme
Jesus lays down his life for his followers and opens the way to eternal life.

## You will need
• You could use the cartoon *Silly sheep* on the *www.77talks.co.uk* website.

## Presentation
Who has been for a walk in the country and knows what a cattle grid is?

A cattle grid is a series of bars set over a hole in the road. Cars can cross it easily, and people with care, but animals are put off because their feet might slip through and they could injure themselves. Cattle grids are often used on roads in the country and at farm entrances because it saves people having to stop and get out of their cars twice in order to open and close a gate.

But cunning sheep in a village in the New Forest in southern England have learned a new trick for getting to the lush grass on the other side – or to the flowers in people's gardens.

They seem to choose one of their number to lie down on the grid, while the others scramble across her body. [Show the picture.]

## Commando technique
It's the same kind of technique as that which commandos use for getting across barbed wire. The commandos select one unfortunate to lie on his rifle across the barbed wire, and the others walk across him. Ouch!

In one village, people had to install extra protection for their gardens – electric fences in some cases. The church had to put up barriers to stop the sheep eating the flowers off the graves.

Who said sheep were silly? Perhaps this is what you get when you leave sheep to their own devices instead of having a full-time shepherd to watch over them, as in the old days.

Jesus once talked about himself being like a shepherd. In those days there were no cattle grids, but there was a far greater danger – wolves.

This is what Jesus said:

> **I am the good shepherd. The good shepherd gives his life for the sheep. The worker who is paid to keep the sheep is different from the shepherd who owns them. So when the worker sees a wolf coming, he runs away and leaves the sheep alone. Then the wolf attacks the sheep and scatters them. The man runs away because he is only a paid worker. He does not really care for the sheep. I am the good shepherd. I know my sheep as my Father knows me... I give my life for the sheep.**
>
> *John 10:11–15*

Another translation puts that last line, **"I lay down my life for the sheep."**

A New Forest sheep may lay down her body for others to walk across, but we can't imagine her laying down her life for her friends. The Bible teaches that Jesus did just that on Good Friday. He allowed himself to be taken prisoner, to be tried and crucified. He chose to lay down his life.

By laying down his life like this, Jesus provided a way over for his "sheep" (his followers) – a way into heaven. The sheep get across the cattle grid to the fresh green grass they know they like. People sometimes think of heaven like that: more of the life they know on earth, only nicer. But the Bible teaches that heaven is unimaginably wonderful, beyond the bounds of space and time, beyond the power of human words to describe.

## Something to do

We don't know if one sheep can feel grateful to another for lying down and letting her walk over her. Certainly, commandos must feel grateful when one of their friends lies down on the barbed wire to let them cross unharmed. It's not surprising that Christians want to meet regularly and sing songs of praise because Jesus was prepared to lay down his life for them.

Sing a suitable praise song known to the group.

# 99 Robots don't win prizes

## Theme
God gave us freedom, and if we freely choose to be guided by him we will win the greatest prize of all.

## You will need
- an assistant dressed as a robot (the simplest costume to use is an all-in-one protective garment as sold in car-accessory shops) with a duster, brush, etc; a TV remote control.
- a suitable prize hidden well out of sight in the hall you are using.

## Presentation
Inform the group that you are tired of housework and have acquired some cutting-edge home-help technology – a robot. Press a button on the TV remote and your assistant enters.

Give a series of instructions so that the robot goes round cleaning up – including dusting some of the audience. Extol the virtues of this robot that never gets tired, never breaks anything while washing up, never complains. Try the robot on double speed for an extra fast clean-up job. Eventually its batteries start to run down and you have to send it off – very slowly and jerkily – for a recharge. (Or it could even break down altogether and have to be carried off by two previously primed volunteers.)

God could have made robots if he had wanted to. In fact, he has made all kinds of things, from atoms to galaxies, that run as he programmed them to. (God's programmes are what we call the laws of physics.)

But imagine living alone with a robot and never seeing another living person, never having a friend to talk to or share things with. What a deadly existence! There is something so different, so wonderful, about a living person.

The very reason God created the universe was so that we could exist, living beings, each one of us different. He made people. But when he made us, he took the risk of making us free – unlike robots – free to go and do whatever we want to do and be whatever we want to be.

## Happy to choose
Now I would like a volunteer who is not like a robot, someone who is happy to choose to do what I am going to ask. It could be doing some cleaning up – or it could be something nicer.

When you have a volunteer, explain that you are going to ask them to find something hidden in the room. In the time-honoured fashion, you help them by saying, "cold" – "warm" – "hot" etc. Guide them to find the prize, which they show to the others and keep.

There is all the difference in the world between a robot which only follows instructions and a person who freely chooses to be guided by God. You would never think of giving your video recorder a prize or treating your washing machine. They are just robots who follow your instructions blindly. But God rewards those who listen to his voice and follow his guidance in their lives.

The prophet Isaiah knew this. He talked about people who live as God wants them to live, people who are just and generous. Then he said,

> **The Lord will guide you always; he will satisfy your needs in a sun-scorched land and will strengthen your frame.**
> *Isaiah 58:11*

We may not live in a sun-scorched land – although we might wish we did sometimes! – but the promise is good for wherever we live: God will guide us, care for us and meet our needs, even in difficult circumstances. And his reward goes far beyond that. It includes all the wonderful things that Jesus said he is going to prepare for us in his Father's house.

And why? Because we are not robots. Because we are free living beings, able to respond to God's love and choose to follow his guiding voice. Robots don't win prizes, but God rewards those who choose to love and listen to him.

# 100 Some adults never live

## Theme
Sooner or later we all face the challenge of playing it safe or answering the call of Jesus and being a risk-taker.

## You will need
• Nothing needed.

## Presentation
A girl was in hospital. She had leukemia. One of the hospital chaplains came to visit her. **"I'm going to die,"** said the girl. **"But I don't mind. Because I've really lived. Some adults never live. Why don't they?"**

"Some adults never live." You might ask the children if they think this is true and, if so, why? (Be prepared for some interesting and challenging answers!)

Is it because some adults are scared of taking risks, always wanting to play it safe? A radiotherapist who treats cancer patients said that some people only really start living when they get cancer. Perhaps that is because they know they cannot play safe any longer; they've got nothing to lose – they are going to die anyway.

What kind of adult do you think you are going to be?

Let's try the fishing test. Imagine you are a few years older, say, just turned 20. Although you are still young, you've got a small business with a couple of people working for you. You are never going to be rich or famous, but you can be pretty sure of living comfortably for the rest of your life.

But you also reckon that the world could be a better place than it is now, and you are looking for some answers to what life is all about. One day, you meet a man who is like nobody you've ever met before. And he does seem to have some answers – lots of answers. You start to spend some time with him. Wherever he goes, amazing things happen, things that nobody can explain. He really seems to change people's lives for the better. Everyone is talking about him.

Then one day, he comes along when you're working and says, **"Drop what you are doing and come and work with me. There's no money in it, but you are going to change people's lives."**

What do you do? Play it safe and stick with your job? Or take a risk, not knowing where it might lead you?

You might like to see if a couple of the children will tell you what they would do, and why.

## Not foolish risk-takers

We said that this was the "fishing test". That is because, when something like this actually happened, there were three young men and their business was fishing. Their names were Peter, James and John. The man who challenged them to leave their fishing business and go with him was Jesus. They accepted the challenge.

Peter, James and John were risk-takers. But they weren't foolish risk-takers. For a start, these young men had their holy book – what we now call the Old Testament of the Bible. They knew that God had promised to send a Saviour, a Messiah. Because they knew something of what God was like, they had an idea of what the Messiah would be like. So they were not going to be easily taken in. Then they spent enough time with Jesus and saw enough of what he did, to know that he was an extraordinary man with extraordinary power. They also saw that he had the kind of goodness they would expect of someone truly sent by God. So they took the risk.

Did they regret it? Absolutely not. Years later, Peter wrote:

> **Through his glory and goodness, [Jesus] gave us the very great and rich gifts he promised us. With those gifts you can share in being like God.** *2 Peter 1:4*

And John wrote:

> **He who gives life was shown to us. We saw him, and we can give proof about it... We write this to you so that you can be full of joy with us.** *1 John 1:2a, 4*

Clearly, these men thought that leaving their fishing business to go with Jesus was the best decision they ever took. It may have started out as a risk, but they ended up with proof that Jesus was the one they believed him to be, the Son of God.

"Some adults never live. Why don't they?" Peter, James and John lived life to the full. Both James and Peter were eventually executed, but they had discovered that a life following Jesus was worth any risk. They knew by heart something that Jesus had often said:

> **Whoever wants to save his life will lose it. And whoever gives his life for me will save it.** *Luke 9:24*

"Some adults never live." Perhaps they are so scared that they might lose their security or their reputation or their pension that they miss out on the real meaning and adventure of life. In trying to make themselves safe and secure they actually run the biggest risk of all: **"Whoever wants to save his life will lose it,"** said Jesus.

Sooner or later, everyone faces a version of the fishing test that is designed just for them. You can tell how a lot of adults have answered their test by what is important to them. Maybe they'll get another chance. Maybe they won't. What about you? What will you do when your "fishing test" comes?

# Live Today Supernaturally

With God's life within us, the possibilities are endless

# 101 The 160km crawl

## Theme
With God's power working in us, he can achieve in us far more than we can imagine.

## You will need
- a piece of string or ribbon six metres long and a ballooon.
- a road atlas, to find a place approximately 160 kilometres (100 miles) from your town.

## Presentation
Ask a child to crawl out to the front. Can they remember crawling as a baby? Can they guess how far they crawled before they were two years old?… The average baby crawls 160 kilometres (100 miles) by the age of two. That's as far as from here to [insert appropriate place-name]. How ever did our knees survive!

Ask for another volunteer who has a reputation as a chatterbox. Can they tell you a new word they have learned in the past day?… How many new words do the children think they learn each day?… After the age of two, we all learn a new word on average every two hours for the next ten years. That's getting on for 4,500 new words every year, mostly without ever realizing that we are learning them. No wonder some people never seem to stop talking!

Get another child to blow up a balloon. If all the air they breathed out filled balloons, how many would they fill by the time they got to 22 years old?… 3.5 million. That's almost as much hot air as politicians produce in an average week!

## 50 years' hair growth
Get another child with long hair to tell you how long it has taken her to grow her hair that long. If she didn't cut it for 50 years, how long would it be?… Ask the child to hold one end of the piece of string on her head and stretch out the rest down the hall – six metres (20 feet). She would need a couple of full-time bridesmaids to follow her around carrying it!

Actually, hair usually stops growing and drops out by the time it gets to 90 centimetres (three feet) long. (So, did John have a 90cm ponytail where his bald spot is now?)

Did you know that was what your mind and body were capable of? And lots more beside, of course. Unless you are an extremely big-headed person, you can do far more than you think you can.

If you can grow twelve centimetres (five inches) of hair a year, or learn twelve new words a day without thinking about it, how much can the all-powerful God do in you and through you?

Here is what Paul said in one of his letters:

> **With God's power working in us, God can do much, much more that anything we can ask or think of. To him be glory in the church and in Christ Jesus for all time, for ever and ever. Amen.**
> *Ephesians 3:20–21*

No doubt Paul never dreamed that the letters he was writing would be read in churches and homes all over the world 2,000 years later and would transform the lives of millions of people.

At this point, you might want to refer to a story you have told recently about someone God used to bring about real change in the lives of others.

## Something to think about

When God's power works in us, it isn't something for us to be proud of, any more than we should be proud because we crawled 160km (100 miles) before we were two. The glory goes to God – in the church and in Jesus. But we can be pleased. And we can ask God to fill us with his love so that his power can work through us and make the world a better place.

# 102 In-body navigation aid

## Theme
The Bible and the Holy Spirit together provide the ultimate aid to travelling life's journey.

## You will need
- a road atlas.
- If you are doing this in church, you could have some simple plans of the church and two or three sets of instructions for getting from the church door to different significant points in the church.

## Presentation
Talk about an incident when you or someone known to you got lost and could have done with a map (or the ability to read the one they had!).

If using the church plans, this is an opportunity to get some of the children moving around – and learning the names of different parts of the church as they do it.

These days it is helpful to have more than just a road atlas when you are travelling in a car. You may know exactly where you are going, but a traffic jam on a motorway can delay you far more than getting lost. For information on the road conditions ahead and how to avoid trouble spots, an in-car navigation system is very helpful.

Ask if anyone or their parents has one and can tell you about it.

We often talk about life being a journey. The Bible is a brilliant aid to travelling this journey. It not only maps out where we have come from, but where we are going to. It gives loads of advice on how to travel, things to avoid on the way, and good companions to share the journey with. It is also full of travellers' tales – the stories of other people's journeys, the times they stupidly took a wrong turning and got lost, how they got back on the right road, and lots more. Reading these travellers' tales – the stories of Abraham, David, Paul and many, many more – really helps us get the most out of our own journey.

## Instant messaging service
But as you read these stories, you discover something else. Although these travellers lived centuries ago, they all had a kind of in-car navigation. (Except in those days it was probably in-camel navigation!) They had an instant messaging service. Sometimes it warned them of trouble ahead; sometimes it gave them advice on the

best road to take; sometimes it showed them how to get back on the road when they had taken a wrong turn. What was it? How did it work?

It was the Spirit of God, the Holy Spirit. God has given us this amazing road atlas and guidebook, the Bible. But because the road you travel is never exactly the same as anyone else's, and because the conditions on your journey are changing from minute to minute, God gives us his Spirit as the ultimate in-body navigation aid. More far-seeing than any human information system could possibly be, more powerful than any computer, wiser than all the world's experts put together, the Holy Spirit speaks quietly to our spirit to guide us in the best possible way.

Jesus explained this to his disciples on the night before he was crucified. He put it like this:

> **If you love me, you will do the things I command. I will ask the Father, and he will give you another Helper. He will give you this Helper to be with you for ever. The Helper is the Spirit of truth. The world cannot accept him because it does not see him or know him. But you know him. He lives with you and will be in you.**
> *John 14:15–17*

He is the "Spirit of truth" – so he never makes a mistake and sends you in the wrong direction. (Sometimes, though, he sends you down some roads that seem pretty strange until you get to the end of them.) He "will be in you" and "will be with you for ever" – he is always installed; you can't lose him or forget and leave him behind. "The world...does not see him or know him" – many people have little idea about spiritual things so they can't understand the Holy Spirit. But the followers of Jesus will understand.

And this in-body navigation "helper" is free. In fact, he is provided by the Boss. To all who love Jesus and want to live as his followers, Jesus promised: "**I will ask the Father, and he will give you another Helper.**"

Can you travel your journey of life without him?

# 103 The gourd seed

## Theme
Growth and fruit in the Christian life come from being rooted in Jesus. This lesson begins in the spring and continues to harvest. Cyberspace kids need the experience of growing plants to understand the many biblical metaphors drawn from the natural world.

## You will need
- enough gourd seeds and plant pots for each child; compost (preferably peat-free); cling film; dust sheets to protect table and floor as necessary.
- card to make growth records.

## Presentation
Have a seed-sowing session, giving the children as much explanation as necessary. Moisten the compost and cover the pot with cling film. Tell the children to take the pots home and keep them in a warm room – but not too hot – with a piece of paper over the top. Check every day. When the green sprout shows, remove the film and paper, and place the pot on a window ledge. When the plant is established and all danger of frost has passed, they can plant it out in the garden in a sunny spot. Keep well watered.

The seed that they have planted is able to grow as much as six metres (20 feet) in a year, bearing beautiful fruits that are all kinds of shapes and colours. Some look like pears, or apples, or cucumbers, or melons – and they have a wonderful texture. On one occasion a plant grew from beneath a child's window on the ground, right up past his bedroom window, growing just short of eight metres (25 feet) high.

## Good fruit
The intention is to report week by week on its growth, and to point out that if the plant is well watered and well fed, it will grow longer and stronger and have more fruit, just like us. The Bible says that good fruit comes from good trees, and good trees need deep roots. When Paul wrote to the Christians in a town called Colosse, he told them:

> **As you received Christ Jesus the Lord, so continue to live in him. Keep your roots deep in him and have your lives built on him.** *Colossians 2:6–7a*

Paul is using the idea of a growing plant as a picture to encourage us to stay close to Jesus day by day.

Encourage the children to measure their plants week by week, and report back. The children can make a card with the verse above written on it, and a grid to record weekly growth. In the autumn they can bring all their fruit and create an autumn display at Harvest Festival. It is something for the children to look forward to, a lesson to be learned right throughout the year, and one that they can be reminded about at the Harvest Festival service.

## Follow-up ideas

### Training

If it is just allowed to grow where it likes, the gourd vine can get into places where it should not be, perhaps where it can get damaged. With stakes, string or trellis it can be trained. Draw the parallel with the prodigal son when he went off wherever he wanted. Discipline helps us get more out of life.

### Care

Regular watering is essential in dry weather. Feeding helps produce more fruit. Use the children's successes and failures to draw out the lessons. See if they can make the link themselves between regular care for their plant and regular attendance at their Christian group.

# 104 Open your presents

## Theme
Paul's list of gifts that are a blessing to others in Romans 12.

## You will need
- to spend an hour in a store and buy lots of small things to wrap as parcels to give out. (Because this works well with adults present and you need a gift for every child, this is best in a church service or, for example, an all-age party. It could be used at Christmas.)

## Presentation
Greet people at the door and give out the parcels, asking people not to unwrap them yet. Know your parcels, so that, for example, a bald man gets one containing a comb or a duster.

Come the time for your talk, you could first check if it is anyone's birthday and ask them about their presents.

Now today, you want lots of people to have presents even when it isn't their birthday. Get people to open their presents one at a time and show everybody what they have received. Some mischievous thought in advance (as in the comb for the bald man or bird-seed for the choir "canary") can create some laughter here. Where possible, have the recipients use the gifts straight away. Ask them not to screw up the wrapping paper but to keep it, as you are going to use it later.

Read **Romans 12:6–8**. Better, have a group of children prepare it so that different voices come in for each of the sentences beginning, **"If one has the gift of…"**

Draw the distinction between the presents you have given out – things – and the gifts Paul is talking about – abilities, qualities, the kind of person we are. And these are not the sort of things we learn in school. You don't get a GCSE in prophecy or an A-level in encouraging others. You can be totally useless at maths but absolutely brilliant at showing kindness to others. Which rates most highly in God's eyes?

Paul emphasizes that whatever gifts we have, it is vital to use them, to practise them. Ask for a child who learns a musical instrument or a particular sport, and find out how much time they practise each week.

## Something to do

Ask people to think about their own gifts, which may or may not be included in this list of Paul's. To help them think, reread Romans 12:6–8.

Get people to take a small piece of wrapping paper and imagine they are wrapping their gift in it. It only makes a tiny, flat parcel, but it is actually much bigger than anything we might get for birthday or Christmas. If it is used, it will go on blessing people – making them happy, thankful, joyful – for as long as you live.

Ask people to hold their tiny parcel in their hand and to pray a quiet prayer thanking God for it and promising to use it.

## NOTE

Whatever you do, don't follow the example of a certain vicar who collected the gifts from the children at the end of the service so they could be used another time!

# 105 Fruitful or poisonous?

## Theme

We often talk about the fruit of the Spirit but ignore the contrasting list of destructive attitudes that Paul gives us just before in Galatians chapter five. Here we underline the fact that you can't have the one without first dealing with the other.

## You will need

- a selection of fresh fruits; one or two tins of fruit with the labels removed; paper to wrap them each in; tin-opener, spoons and blindfolds.
- nine cards, each with an example of the "fruit of the Spirit" written on them, as listed in **Galatians 5:22–23**.

## Presentation

Produce the wrapped fruits one at a time and ask some children to guess what each one is by feeling it. A banana is obvious, but an apple and an orange can be confused. As for the tins, that is sheer guesswork! When unwrapped, they are still a mystery, as the labels have been removed.

Have one or two children blindfolded and see if they can guess the contents of a tin by taste. If one contains something like lychees this can be quite a test.

We normally do not have a problem recognizing common types of fruit when we see them. If we can't see them it can be more difficult. They still taste good, though! (Well, maybe lychees aren't to everyone's taste.) And they certainly do us good. People who eat a lot of fruit tend to live longer than those who don't.

St Paul wrote about a different kind of fruit, the fruit of the Spirit. Have nine children come out and hold the prepared cards with the blank side to the audience. Like the fruit wrapped in paper or hidden in tins, these types of fruit can't be seen. They are hidden inside people.

See how many of them the children know. Turn each one round as it is remembered or guessed.

Although they are hidden inside people, that doesn't mean to say we can't recognize them quite easily. We just need to be around people long enough to see whether they have patience or kindness or self-control. (The children with the cards can now sit down.)

# A poisonous sort of person

Just a bit before this, Paul gives another list. It contains things like: hating, making trouble, being jealous, being angry, being selfish, making people angry with each other. Someone like that would be a pretty poisonous sort of person. Would you like to spend time around a person who was like that inside? Would you like to be a person who was like that?

St Paul tells us how we get from being that kind of poisonous person to being someone who has the wonderful fruit of the Spirit growing in them:

> **Those who belong to Christ Jesus have crucified their own sinful selves. They have given up their old selfish feelings and the evil things they wanted to do. We get our new life from the Spirit. So we should follow the Spirit.** *Galatians 5:24–25*

If we have a bush in the garden that grows poisonous fruit, the only thing to do is to dig it up and throw it in the bin. It is dangerous to have around. If we look inside ourselves and see things like hating, making trouble, being jealous, being angry, or being selfish, the only thing to do is to say: "The 'me' that does those poisonous things has got to go. I don't want to be like that any more. I am a danger to myself and others."

# A prayer

Then we need the courage to pray like this:

> **Lord Jesus, you died on the cross to deal with poisonous stuff like that. So please deal with that sinful me. Let it be crucified with you. Help me to give up the old selfish feelings. And Lord Jesus, give me a new life from the Spirit. Change me from the inside so that the good fruit, the wonderful fruit, grows in me. Amen.**

Have a time of quiet reflection and give the opportunity for anyone who prayed like that, or would like to pray like that, to talk to a leader.

## NOTE

A wonderful illustration of this is the story of David Lant in "Light from behind bars", p. 69. It would make a good follow-up.

# 106 Unimaginable power

## Theme
The incredible power of God's kingdom is right at hand.

## You will need
- a battery; some electrically powered items; some balloons.

## Presentation
If working with families, ask a father to pick up a child and vice versa. With children only, get one child first to pick up something light, then to try something impossibly heavy. (Make sure it really is too heavy, not something the child might attempt to pick up and strain himself.)

Why can't *John* pick up *his dad*?… Because he's too heavy. In other words, because of gravity. The force of gravity is what keeps us all stuck to the ground. It's what makes sure that when our ice-cream falls out of the cornet it hits the ground, not a pigeon flying overhead!

I want to tell you about another force. It's not a million times stronger than gravity. It's not a billion times stronger. It's a billion billion billion billion times stronger! Pow! That sounds like dangerous stuff! It is – and yet it is what is holding you together right now. It's the glue that holds every atom in your body together – it's called the electrical force. It keeps the electrons buzzing around the nucleus in every atom.

Let's see what happens when we knock a few electrons off something. We've all done this.

Rub a balloon on a sweater and stick it to a wall. Hold another near a child's face so she can feel the hairs being attracted by the balloon.

## One in a billion billion
What we've done here is to knock off a few electrons from the surface of the balloon. Just one in a billion billion electrons releases enough force to make this balloon defy gravity. If you find a way of knocking more electrons off, then you can do something really useful. For example, you can use chemicals and make a battery. And that battery can power a torch, or an electronic game, or a mobile phone.

The power company Powergen does it differently. They use huge generators to create mains electricity, which powers our lights, vacuum cleaner, TV, etc.

If you went home today and had no electricity, what couldn't you do?… Imagine life without it! Yet for most of human history, people didn't even know it existed. Only in 1752 did Benjamin Franklin fly a kite in a thunderstorm and demonstrate the existence of electricity. (Don't try it – you could kill yourself.) And it was much later that electricity companies started to connect houses. Some people didn't want to be connected. They preferred to stick to candles and gas-lights. Imagine!

But this isn't supposed to be a science lesson. So what's it got to do with God? Well, when Jesus started going round preaching his message was:

**Good news! Turn around. The kingdom of the heavens is very close to you.**

*Cf. Matthew 4:17, Mark 1:15*

"The kingdom of the heavens" – or God's kingdom – what's that? Where is it?

# Plugged into reality

Well, it's something like this. [Hold up the battery.] We can't see the electrons, but we know that when we connect the battery up, something happens. The kingdom of the heavens is like that. Only it's fantastically more powerful than even the electrical force. Jesus started to show people what he was talking about. He says a word and: Pow! – a blind man sees… Pow! – a lame man walks… Pow! – a picnic lunch feeds a huge crowd… Pow! – a leper is healed… Pow! – tax-collectors give up cheating people… That's the power of the kingdom of the heavens. It's a new way of living. It's a way of plugging into real truth, real goodness, real love.

It's like the electrical force – but it's personal. You get plugged in by knowing God as your Father through Jesus.

It's like the electrical force – but it's trillions of times stronger. This is the power that created the whole universe! You can't get any bigger than that. And yet it's close. So close you can touch it. It's as close as believing in Jesus and saying, "Yes, I want to swap my old life for this new kingdom life."

You can't see the kingdom of the heavens? No, but you can see schools and hospitals and care for children and a thousand things that were started by people who were plugged into the kingdom. Lots of people in the world don't want to get connected to God's kingdom? OK, but some people didn't want to connect their houses up to the electric power lines, either. Some people just don't know a good thing when they see it!

# A prayer

Lord God, King of all creation, teach us more about the wonders and the power of your kingdom. We often pray, "Your kingdom come" – please show us how the power of your kingdom can make that true in our lives and in the world around us. Amen.

# 107 Power in action

## Theme

The story of the poor widow giving all she had is an example of kingdom power in action. This talk follows on from "Unimaginable power"; the two can be presented as one longer all-age message.

## You will need

- a power tool; two small coins; a bag of coins or a cheque for a large amount; enough smallest denomination coins to give two to each person.

## Presentation

Ask the children questions to review the teaching in "Unimaginable power".

People who have learned about living in the kingdom of the heavens are different. Jesus pointed out one of them just a few days before he was crucified.

Tell the story in **Mark 12:41–44** of the poor widow putting all she had into the temple offering box. Use the coins and cheque to illustrate the story. Tell the children that there were no benefits or social security, so that as a widow this woman would have no income.

Jesus said:

> **This poor woman has put more into the collection than all the others.**

More than all the others? What did Jesus mean? How can these two tiny coins be worth more than this bag of silver/cheque?

Well, we might say, she put in all she had, so in proportion to what she owned she gave more than the others. Is that what Jesus means? Maybe. But Jesus said,

> **she really gave more than all those rich people.**

Could what she gave really be worth more than the large sums the rich people put in? How?

Think about what we have learned about God's power, the power of the kingdom of the heavens. This woman's heart attitude shows that she was plugged into God's kingdom. So her giving was like pressing the switch.

## A tiny action

Demonstrate with a power tool. A tiny action pressing the switch releases power that enables a handyman to drill holes in concrete or saw through thick planks of wood. (Be sure to unplug the power tool as soon as you finish using it and put it out of reach of small hands.)

If the attitude of the heart is right, what may seem to be only a very small thing releases kingdom power, the power of God. We don't know what happened as a result of the faith and generosity of that widow, except that it was recorded in the Bible and countless millions of people have heard the story and been affected by it.

This story shows us that kingdom power is not for people who want to show off by the miracles they perform. It is for those who are humble and trusting and faithful. And you need the eyes of Jesus to see that power being switched on and to see what it achieves.

## Something to do

Give everyone two small coins. Ask them to keep the coins in their pocket as a reminder of this story. Suggest that as the children feel the coins from time to time, they ask God to show them some small act of kindness or generosity that they can do. This is not to boast about or to show what nice people we are, but we pray it can come out of a loving and trusting heart.

**NOTE**

Alternatively, you can give the coins out at the start. This creates a bit of intrigue and the children can have them in their hands as you are telling the story.

# Ingredients for a Healthy Lifestyle

Listen to the Creator to get the best out of life

# 108 Proof of the pudding

## Theme

The most important ingredients of a good life are in Paul's list of the fruit of the Spirit.

## You will need

- a microwave cooker, extension lead if needed, apron, mixing bowl, wooden spoon, 1.2 litre (2 pint) pudding basin, enough teaspoons for large-scale tasting.
- ingredients for a recipe, e.g. 75g (3oz) plain Fair Trade chocolate, 30ml (2tbsp) milk, 175g (6oz) light muscovado sugar, 175g (6oz) margarine, 2 eggs, 175g (6oz) fresh white breadcrumbs, 30ml (2tbsp) cocoa powder.
  a. Melt the chocolate with the milk on High power for 1 minute and mix until smooth.
  b. Mix the sugar and margarine together, then add the cooled chocolate and eggs.
  c. Mix in the breadcrumbs and cocoa powder thoroughly.
  d. Spoon the mixture into the basin. Cook on High power for 6–7 minutes. Leave to stand for 5 minutes before tasting.

## Presentation

Get a child to come and help you make a chocolate pudding. Dress him or her in an apron and a chef's hat if you can get hold of one. (Hotels sometimes use paper ones and will let you have one if you ask.) You could stage this like a current TV cooking programme for extra topicality.

Get the child to mix the ingredients and keep up a running commentary. Place in the microwave and leave to cook. Thank the child – with a promise that he or she can come back and have the first taste when it is ready.

Cooking is fun, but you need to have the right ingredients. Of course, when you get a bit knowledgeable about cooking, you can experiment. Keeping the basic recipe, we could have made a pudding with currants in instead of chocolate. Does anyone have any other suggestions?...

Life needs the right ingredients, too. St Paul gives a list of wonderful ingredients in his letter to the churches in Galatia (modern Turkey): love, joy, peace, patience, kindness, goodness, faithfulness, gentleness, self-control (Galatians 5:22). There is no way a life with these ingredients could be a disaster!

There are many other possible ingredients and, because each one of us is a unique and special person, every life will be different. You can add your love of painting, or your knowledge of technology, or your ability to swim 50 lengths. The important thing is to get the basic ingredients right. Where do you get them?

## A litre of patience?

You can't buy a kilo of love, or a tin of peace, or a litre of patience. So where do they come from? St Paul said, **"The Spirit gives love, joy, peace,"** and all the rest. That is, the Spirit of God, the Holy Spirit. When someone lives a life close to God, open to God, then the Spirit of God comes to live within that person. And the Spirit just naturally and freely gives you these wonderful ingredients. It is his delight to give them to you.

In fact, Paul even said in another letter that people like this begin to smell good, just like this pudding does! (See 2 Corinthians 2:14–16.) It really pleases God to have people made to this "recipe".

So take a big bowl full of love, joy and peace. Stir in the sweetness of patience, kindness and goodness. Add the finishing touches of faithfulness, gentleness and self-control. And what do you have? A recipe for a life that will fully satisfy you – and be a joy to loads of people you meet in your journey of life.

If the pinger hasn't gone on the microwave yet, then it's time for a song. Be ready with plenty of spoons at the close so that everyone can test out the old adage about the proof of the pudding!

# 109 The unwinnable prize

## Theme
The best prizes in life are things that cannot be won; they can only be received as gifts.

## You will need
- questions and props to emulate whatever happens to be the popular quiz show of the moment; cheques (make or print them from the *www.77talks.co.uk* website); sweets.

## Presentation
Run your quiz and give cheques as prizes. The first – lower value – cheques can be swapped for simple prizes, e.g. sweets.

After a few rounds, announce that you are now getting to the big-value prizes. The successful contestant at this point is given a cheque with the word PEACE[1] on it. Your contestant will probably be disappointed, or at least puzzled. Ask why… Is peace not far more valuable than sweets? Wouldn't people in some parts of the world – or those in mental turmoil – give anything for peace?

The child may be smart enough to see the flaw in your argument. If not, help him or her out. Peace is, of course, of far greater value than sweets, but you cannot win peace. Award your contestant a prize in lieu and return the child to the audience.

Produce another cheque, either a giant one that everyone can see, or one drawn on an OHP transparency. It carries these words: **"My peace I give you."**

## Right signature
Peace is a gift. You can't win it. But it can be given to you – provided the right signature is on the cheque. Who said this? Jesus. Write *Jesus* on the signature line.

The question is: How much do we believe that signature is worth? How far can we trust it?

Does anyone know when Jesus said this?… It was the night before he was crucified, as he shared his last meal with his disciples. They had trusted him enough to give up their jobs and follow him. In the next few hours he was going to be arrested and crucified. As he died a cruel death on a Roman cross it was going to seem that their

---

1. Other words and appropriate biblical texts can be used to fit in with a particular theme if you wish.

trust had been in vain. All their hopes would be shattered. How can you have peace in those kind of circumstances?

Yet just 48 hours later, Jesus was going to come back to them. Suddenly, behind locked doors, he would appear. And his very first words? **"Peace be with you!"** (John 20:21) Their trust would be proved right. The gift of peace was real.

Now, who wants to receive this cheque…?

# 110 Fore! thought

## Theme
Keeping our eyes fixed on Jesus.

This talk works best with an all-age group.

## You will need
- a set of golf clubs, a golf ball, a table tennis ball, a "hole" (one of the golf aids that is used on a carpet, or create one).
- enough golf tees for everyone to have one (optional, but worthwhile).

## Presentation
Talk about how much you enjoy golf and want to get in a bit of practice. Show the golf ball and bounce it very forcibly on the floor, while palming the table tennis ball in your hand. Then place the table tennis ball right out at the front of the hall or church. With care, people will not see that you have swapped balls. Tee up and strike it as straight and hard as you can, keeping your eye very much on the ball and your head still. The congregation will dive for cover before realizing what you have done!

It is probably best not to hack it back out from the pews into the aisle, but rather to ask for the shot to be dropped. You might like to get a child to help with the putting.

As you complete the "hole", stress the importance of two things: knowing exactly where we want to end up – in the hole – and keeping our eye on the ball as we hit it. The first is obvious, but non-golfers are unlikely to be aware of the second.

## Many hazards
On the way, there are all sorts of hazards: bunkers, water, trees, even going out of bounds. But if we keep our eye on the ball and keep our mind on what we are doing, we shall get there in the end. Practise enough and you might even become a world-class golfer!

In life we need to have a clear idea of where we want to end up – in that amazing existence called heaven. And the way to get there is to keep our eyes on Jesus. He will always take us through the obstacles and hazards. We may fall into them, but his everlasting arms will be there to lift us out and set us back on the fairway again.

The big difference from golf is that the winner of a round of golf is the one who has the lowest score. On the fairway to heaven, everyone who keeps their eyes fixed on

Jesus is a guaranteed winner. There are no losers, and it doesn't matter how long it takes you.

## Something to do

Give everyone a golf tee. The golf tee is a reminder that every hole in golf has a beginning and that it has a clear end in view. Get them to hold it while repeating Hebrews 12:2,

> **Let us keep our eyes fixed on Jesus, on whom our faith depends from beginning to end.**
> Good News Bible

Ask people to keep the golf tee in their pocket during the week. Every time they feel it, it will be a reminder to look to Jesus.

# 111 Going for gold

## Theme
Picturing a heavenly "medal ceremony" helps motivate us to be the best that we can be.

## You will need
- to make three medals or rosettes – gold, silver and bronze – fixing £1, 50p and 2p coins in the centre of the appropriate medals.
- items for a race or competition of some kind.

## Presentation
Invite all the children to take part in a race, or some of them to take part in another competition depending on the facilities available. This will be more fun if they are competing against you or other leaders, especially if the sport is chosen to ensure that children will win.

Hold a medal ceremony. If you can play this up with anthems and flowers, so much the better. The winners can remove and keep the coins.

Athletes who aim for the top get into serious training. Cyclocross champion, Rob Dane, for example, the number two in the world, cycles 50–65,000 kilometres (30–40,000 miles) every year in training. Today's Olympic games continue a tradition that goes back to ancient Greece. At the time when Paul was writing the letters we have in the New Testament, the Isthmian games were held in Corinth every three years. Athletes would go into ten months of strict training to prepare for the games.

## Your life's ambition
Very few of us have what it takes physically or mentally to reach the highest level in sport. But that doesn't mean that we can't "go for gold". Imagine for a moment a vast stadium, a stadium so big that it can hold the entire population of the world. The whole place is bathed in a wonderful golden light. Imagine that there is a podium in the middle of that arena and that you are standing on it. A shimmering figure approaches and you bend forward to receive, not a medal, but a gold crown. The whole stadium erupts in cheering and clapping. You lift your hands to acknowledge the cheers, feeling both very big and very small at the same time. Your eyes fill with tears of joy, knowing you have achieved your life's ambition.

Fantasy? Not for Paul and other New Testament writers who used images like this to give us a glimpse of the future. Writing about life to people in Corinth (where the Isthmian games were held), Paul said,

**Run to win! All those who compete in the games use strict training. They do this so that they can win a crown. That crown is an earthly thing [actually a pine wreath] that lasts only a short time. But our crown will continue for ever.**

*1 Corinthians 9:25*

What does it take to fulfill that dream and win a crown that lasts for ever? Simple: be yourself! Be the person that God created you to be, but be that to the best you can possibly be.

A phone company put out a TV ad that showed a vast stadium like the one we have been imagining – created inside a computer, of course. In the ad, different people stand in the arena to talk about their ideas or dreams or inventions. A young mum holds her baby and says she sometimes feels overwhelmed by the responsibility and scared that she won't be able to cope. She asks if anyone else ever feels like that.

# Being real

The camera turns to a section of the crowd full of mums and babies. One by one they nod and begin to stand. A wave ripples up the stadium as thousands of mums rise to show they all feel like that at times. The mum in the middle was being real, being honest, being herself. And the viewer watching the ad knows that she will find it easier to cope because now she knows she is not alone. All young mums feel overwhelmed by the responsibility of that young life in their arms.

At times in our lives, running to win simply means being as good a mum or as good a dad as we can be – with God's help. Or as good a student, or as good a friend as we can be – with God's help. At times we may be involved in, say, a project to help people in need. We can give our best to that – with God's help. At other times in our lives, we may get a sense of being called to do something or be something special. Paul was called by God to take the good news of Jesus to dozens of towns like Corinth in the Roman empire. But God has as many different things for people to do as there are people.

Going for gold – doing things to the best of our possibilities – is tough at times. A mum knows she cannot take a day off and just leave her baby in the cot. Athletes know that you can't let up on the training. Paul talked about training like a boxer – even hitting his own body and giving himself a black eye! (1 Corinthians 9:26–27) – as a picture of his determination to spread the amazing story of Jesus and his resurrection round the world.

# Something to do

Close your eyes and think of something you are involved in at the moment – a situation with a friend or within your family, a skill you are learning, a project or an adventure you are planning, a difficult challenge you are facing. Thank God for the resources you have to face this challenge and ask him to help you see it through. Ask him to make you tough – the kind of person who doesn't give up and give in. And imagine that scene in the stadium again. Imagine yourself on the podium, receiving that everlasting gold crown. Imagine how good that feels. Go for it!

**NOTE**

During this meditation it would be good to play some music in the background, eg a piece associated with a major sporting event being broadcast on television.

# 112 Curried grapefruit

## Theme

We may look very different and act differently, but we are all one in Jesus, the bread of life.

## You will need

- to make up some sandwiches with odd fillings, e.g. chicken and banana, beetroot and jelly beans, curried grapefruit (made with spicy chutney), liquorice and sardines, or whatever unlikely combinations you can come up with. Alternatively, do the same with pizza toppings.

## Presentation

Find out who eats sandwiches and what their favourite fillings are (or pizzas and favourite toppings).

Now you need some adventurous characters who are willing to taste samples of a new range which you think could go down really big.

Give your volunteers your prepared concoctions and ask them if they can say what the fillings are. Provide a basin to spit into, and water for those who need to wash the taste away!

The followers of Jesus come in all sorts of shapes, sizes and weird combinations. His first disciples were a pretty motley bunch. They wore what many of us would think of as strange clothes; at least one was a tax-collector – a traitor working for the enemy – and several of them probably smelled rather strongly of fish!

## Some were barbarians

As belief in Jesus spread, all kinds of people began to discover this new life, a life with the power and love of Jesus in them. They spoke different languages, ate different kinds of food, had different customs. In those early days, some were free citizens of the Roman empire and some were slaves. Some were highly educated and civilized; some were barbarians. But it wasn't the differences that mattered any longer; it was what they all shared.

In one of his letters, Paul reminded people about this,

**In the new life there is no difference between Greeks and Jews. There is no difference between those who are circumcised and those who are not**

**circumcised, or people that are foreigners, or Scythians [the most barbarous barbarians]. There is no difference between slaves and free people. But Christ is in all believers. And Christ is all that is important.**                    *Colossians 3:11*

It's not the filling that matters. It's the bread. And Jesus once called himself **"the bread of life"** (John 6:35).

Get one child to stand on a chair and look down on the others.

One of the easiest temptations to give way to is to look down on other people because they are different. Whether it's the clothes they wear or the food they eat or the music they like, we can kid ourselves into thinking that they are inferior and we are superior.

# A new kind of life
But Jesus brought a new kind of life. And people who get into this new life discover that they are on the same level as everyone else. (Get the child to sit down again.)

At least, they *should* discover that. Sadly, some Christians don't get the message and even think that they are superior because their church is better than other churches!

Differences can be fun. (We can learn to laugh at ourselves.) Differences can be interesting. Differences can teach us things we didn't know and help us discover new experiences. But the really important thing is what we share: Jesus, the bread of life.

# A prayer
In the same bit of that letter Paul said,

> **In your new life you are being made new. You are becoming like the One who made you.**
>                    *Colossians 3:10*

It doesn't happen all at once. We are being changed bit by bit to become more like Jesus. So perhaps we can pray something like this:

> **Lord Jesus, when we start to feel superior, may your Holy Spirit give us a nudge and remind us that in your sight we are all equal. And when we feel inferior, remind us that you are in us, the bread of life, and that nobody can look down on you. Amen.**

# 113 Trousers three times as risky as skirts

## Theme
Home accident statistics lead into considering the risks Jesus pointed out in the parable of the house built on sand.

## You will need
- a box, a lump of cheese, a pair of socks, a sandwich, a slipper, a magazine.
- if possible, a hard-hat, goggles and gloves.
- other items from the talk as desired.

## Presentation
This is a good introduction for ham actors! Announce that today you are going to be thinking about safety education and you have brought in some dangerous items. Put on protective clothing if you have it, then gingerly produce items as above from the box.

All these items landed people in hospital, according to government figures on safety in the home. Every year, the government produces a report based on people who end up in the Accident and Emergency unit at 18 of the country's largest hospitals.[1] Multiplying the numbers from those hospitals to give us a picture of the whole country, it looks like in one year, no less than 957 people were injured by cheese, while sandwiches accounted for 4,472 cases needing a doctor's attention!

Slippers turn out to be nearly 14 times as dangerous as wellington boots. So if you know someone who puts on slippers when they get home from work, warn them of the risks and tell them to wear wellies round the house instead. Better to be safe than sorry! And as for trainers, 27,752 accidents were caused by them. As only 234 injuries were caused by clogs, quite clearly people who go out for an early morning jog should run in clogs. (Does anyone know if Reebok does a line in high-tech clogs?)

As for the 8,593 injuries caused by socks or tights, the mind boggles! How do you injure yourself on a pair of socks? Is it possible that some people's socks smell so strongly that they pass out when getting undressed, hitting their heads on the dressing table as they fall?

One of the most enlightening categories is injuries caused by office and school equipment. You might think that sharp-pointed compasses or dividers posed the

---

1. All information taken from the Department of Trade and Industry's *Home Accident Surveillance System* (HASS data) for 1998.

worst threat. But no. In fact, they only accounted for 20 accidents, far fewer than the 488 caused by seemingly harmless crayons. The really dangerous school items turn out to be *pens, pencils, paper and books* – running up a worrying 11,054 injuries between them!

Does this mean there ought to be a nationwide schoolkids' strike, demanding the banning of books, pens and paper in schools? All in the interests of safety, of course! (But before anyone gets too tempted, you ought to know that far more injuries were caused by footballs.)

All this goes to show that you never know when disaster may strike. It's not just that the unexpected may happen at any time; it's how unexpected the unexpected is. At least now you've been warned that any time you put your socks on, you risk ending up in Accident and Emergency.

The reason the government collects these figures is so that they can spot increases in accidents related to different items, and run campaigns warning people of the dangers. Forewarned is forearmed, so they say.

There's a well-known story designed to forewarn people of danger. It's a story not so much of an accident in the home as an accident to the home. It goes like this:

Read or tell the story in **Matthew 7:24–27**. This is how Jesus ends his crucial teaching about everyday life that we call the Sermon on the Mount.

## Something to think about

An accident can change the course of your life. A disaster can end it. Jesus was saying, "If you want to avoid a certain kind of disaster in your life, listen to my teaching and put it into practice. Don't end up as one of life's casualties."

# 114 Are we blind?

## Theme
The dangers of taking something when we are not sure of what it is or what it might do to us.

## You will need
- a blindfold, a piece of fruit, a small packet of sweets.
- a plastic "doggy-doo" from a joke shop.

## Presentation
Ask for three volunteers to play a guessing game. Explain the rules: You are going to blindfold them one at a time, and ask them to hold out one hand, palm flat. An object will be placed on the outstretched palm. They must not close their fingers to feel it – appoint a referee to watch. They can ask you eight "yes or no" questions about the object (five if time is short). Each time the answer is "yes", they can have one guess as to what it is. Give a prize (or keep the object) for the correct answer.

The first two objects – fruit and sweets – are straightforward. The third is the "doggy-doo". This will occasion a lot of mirth in the audience – and revulsion when the contestant finds out what he is holding.

## Heroin re-branded
Thank the volunteers, and continue in this vein: Are we sometimes blind to what people are offering us?

For example, a study has shown that young people can be tricked into taking heroin, thinking it is a less harmful, "recreational" drug. Dealers can "re-brand" heroin and sell it in affordable, small bags. Sometimes they give it a different name.

The average age of users has dropped from 17–25 to 14–25. Children as young as ten to twelve years old have been found smoking and injecting the drug. Many are completely ignorant of the addictive powers of the Class A drug.

Talk about the dangers of taking "blind" anything that is offered to us. This could apply to tablets, or drink, or videos. Reinforce the message with the "doggy-doo" and the difficulties of cleaning ourselves up once we have been fouled.

# 115 Who's in control?

## Theme
A warning about those who try to control us, and a discussion of the virtue of self-control.

## You will need
• Watch some prime-time TV and take a note of the slogans or punch lines of a number of advertisements. Prepare a list of these with key words missing.

## Presentation
Either read out the ads and get everyone to call out the missing words, or make a bit more of it by recruiting two teams and running it as a quiz. (With a mixed-age group you will be chastened to note that children not long out of nappies will be able to do this.) Small prizes appropriate to one of the ads might be offered.

A successful advertising campaign is one that gets us to remember either a product name, or a slogan associated with a product. Of course, it costs a lot of money to run a major campaign. Car manufacturers, soft drinks companies, brewers, sportswear companies…these are some of the groups that spend millions of pounds trying to sell us an image that they want us to buy into.

Someone has written, "**The rich are always trying to control your lives.**" We can see the truth of that every day on our TV screens. Rich companies can afford the best ideas people, the best directors and actors to make their ads, the best prime-time TV slots.

## Influencing our thoughts
Their aim is to influence the way we think about ourselves and other people, and how we spend our money. In other words, they are trying to control our lives. We watch the ads, we buy the products – and the directors of the companies pay themselves huge salaries and retire with millions of pounds in the bank.

**"The rich are always trying to control your lives"** (James 2:6). That is bang up to date, but it was written nearly 2,000 years ago. It was James, probably the brother of Jesus, who wrote it in a letter to Christians all over the world.

It wasn't the only thing he had to say about the rich. He gave them a dire warning, too:

**You rich people, listen! Cry and be very sad because of the troubles that are coming to you. Your riches have rotted, and your clothes have been eaten by moths. Your gold and silver have rusted, and that rust will be a proof that you were wrong. It will eat your bodies like fire. You saved your treasure for the last days. Men worked in your fields but you did not pay them. They harvested your crops and are crying out against you. Now the Lord of heaven's armies has heard their cries.**

*James 5:1–4*

The pay-packets may be big, but if James is right, the future is not too bright for the rich who are trying to control our lives.

## Something to think about

Two of James' fellow leaders of the early church, Peter and Paul, urge us to be *self-controlled*. Self-control means stopping to think about what we do and why. It means deciding for ourselves how we spend our money, rather than letting rich companies do the thinking for us.

How often do we make fun of someone or call them names because they don't have the "right" trainers or the "right" brand of trousers or soft drinks or whatever? Whenever we do that we are playing right into the hands of the rich companies, strengthening the control they have over people's lives, doing their dirty work for them.

So how about starting a revolution? It's a revolution in which respect goes to the people who think for themselves. Respect for people who don't buy the big-name clothes because they don't want to make the fat cats fatter. Respect for people who can laugh at the ads but not get taken in by them.

It's a revolution that needs self-control. Get on board, because self-control equals self-respect. That's got to be better than allowing the rich to control our lives.

# 116 Sniff for success

## Theme
How to please God – and not create a stink.

## You will need
• a bottle of fragrance such as those widely available for aromatherapy or to put onto potpourri. Choose an unusual fragrance and spread enough around the room to make sure it is obvious to everyone as they enter.
• if possible, some incense and a censer, as used in some churches.

## Presentation
No, I've not had an accident with the after-shave or eau de toilette. This is essential oil of...[whatever – show bottle].

This is a serious tip for helping study for tests or exams or for learning that part in the Christmas play.

It has long been known that smells can call up memories of things that happened a long time in the past. (You could talk about something that brings back a memory for you.) Psychologists have shown that smells can also help you learn facts and remember them when you come to take a test.

You need something a little unusual. Perfume the room you are working in while you are revising or trying to learn something by heart. Then, on the day of the test or exam, have a drop on a handkerchief so that you can sniff it.

## Anxious about tests?
Research done by Dr Rachel Herz in Philadelphia[1] showed that volunteers using perfume like this were able to remember almost 20% more of the words they were given to learn for a test. It actually works better if you are the kind of person who normally gets rather anxious when it comes to tests.

In Old Testament times, when the Israelites brought some grain or cakes to offer as a sacrifice, part of it was mixed with oil and incense and burned on the altar. Incense is a mixture of gum and spices which gives off a sweet smell when burned.

Demonstrate, if you have incense.

---

1. Reported in *The Psychologist*, November 1997.

This part that was burned was known as the "memorial portion" (see Leviticus 2:1–10). The smell was said to be pleasing to God, and this was a way of asking God to "remember" the worshipper.

The idea of God being pleased by a smell might seem rather primitive to us, but it shows that even then, people were well aware of the link between smell and memory.

They also knew the importance of being right with God. That meant bringing something of value and offering it as a sacrifice to God, and doing it in the best way they knew how, including making it smell good.

Christians today believe that when Jesus died on the cross, he offered himself as a once-and-for-all sacrifice, and that now we can approach God through him.

So when we do something wrong – something that "stinks" – we can ask forgiveness. In this way, Christians rejoice that God only remembers the good in their lives, and not the stinks they have created.

## Something to do

How about trying this with a Bible verse or two in your church or group? Learn the passage one week and see how people do at recalling it – with fragrant assistance – a week later.

# 117 A winning combination

## Theme
A football illustration provides a talk based on Proverbs 20:29 – "The glory of young men is their strength; of old men, their experience."

## You will need
• up-to-date information about the current star players and managers.

## Presentation
A football enthusiast could be asked to prepare a report on a match, or you could begin with news of the latest sacking or appointing of a manager.

Our heroes are usually the young men – or women – on the pitch [such as…]. But equally important to the team's success is the manager. The manager has often been a successful player himself. He has had experience of the game, can analyze tactics, see players' strengths and weaknesses, and judge how to combine those strengths to build a team that is strong both in attack and defence.

He needs to be able to communicate effectively to the players so that they can understand the team strategy and tactics. He needs to be able to motivate them to give of their best (usually referred to in soccer as the mythical 110%).

Although they did not play soccer 3,000 years ago, King Solomon knew about successful team building. He wrote:

> **The glory of young men is their strength; of old men, their experience.**
> *Proverbs 20:29,* The Living Bible

A successful team combines the strengths of young people and the experience of older people.

Although most of us won't ever be professional sportsmen or women, we shall all be part of various "teams". Any group of people tackling a task together is a team. We shall be part of a team when we start work. If we join a club or voluntary organization we shall be part of a team.

## Good career move
As young people, what you have to offer the team is your "strength". That can be literally physical strength, or it can be skill, or knowledge, or enthusiasm. What you

287

will not have at first is experience. That can only come with years of doing a job. To be a successful part of the team, you need a good manager – someone who has the experience you lack and who can show you how to get the best out of your strengths.

Any young footballer would want to be part of a team with [current names] as the manager. He would know how much his career would benefit from being under such leadership.

So look for older men and women who are good "managers". When you find them, value their experience, listen to their advice, follow their example. See how much you can learn from them.

Solomon knew a trick or two. **"The glory of young men is their strength; of old men, their experience."** Put the two together and you get a winning combination.

## A prayer

**Lord God, I want to get the best out of the strengths you have given me. Send me some good managers as I go through life. Help me to recognize them, to listen to them, and to learn from their experience. Amen.**

# 118 Baby talk

## Theme
Good advice on how to avoid the mistakes our parents' generation made.

## You will need
- copies of the sketch (you can print them out from *www.77talks.co.uk*); two large faces painted onto card (this doesn't have to be great art); a large white towel as a nappy, and appropriate clothes for an outsize baby; the biggest teddy bear you can borrow; a pillow and a sheet or blanket.
- BABY DESMOND can say the words in the script, or they can be voiced over as his thoughts by someone with a microphone.

## Presentation
Ask the children what they are looking forward to about growing up… Who is fed up of being a child and would like to grow up quickly?… We are going to see someone who is very keen to grow up.

## Sketch
A table is covered with a sheet or blanket as a bed. MUM and AUNT BETTY are hidden behind the table with the two large faces and the teddy bear. BABY DESMOND, a leader or older child dressed as a baby, is revealed lying on the bed.

## BABY TALK

BABY    (*crying – pause – cries louder*)

MUM    (*first face appears and looks down at BABY*) What's a matter then, diddums? Who's making a lot of silly-willy noisey. Won't little Dessy-Wessy give his mummy a smile, then?

BABY    The name's Desmond, not Dessy-Wessy. You ought to know, you called me it. I can't stand all this stupid "Dessy-Wessy" business!

MUM    Oh dear, who's not a happy little chap today? Would he like his teddy? Nice cuddles with teddy. Mummy get teddy for Dessy-Wessy.

BABY    Oh no, not the teddy! Watch out, here it comes! Great hairy, ugly thing. It stinks something awful. I just can't wait to grow up. Get off, you great furry brute!

MUM Little Dessy-Wessy's got a temper on him today, hasn't he diddums? Has he got a pain in his little tummy, then?

BABY He's got something in his little tummy – and here it comes! *(loud rude noise)*

MUM Oh dear, he's filled his nappy. Who's a little pooey-pants, then? What a nasty smelly-welly! And just when Aunty Betty's coming to see him, as well.

BABY Oh no, not Aunty Betty. She'll have her big fat finger poking me all over. I wanna grow up!

BETTY *(second face appears)* Oooh! Just look at the little darling! Hasn't he grown! Oh, who's Aunty Betty's little sweetie-pie, then? Coochy-coochy-cooo!

BABY I'm not your little sweetie-pie, you old bat! You wait till I start walking. I'll crayon all over your walls! I'll stuff teddy down the toilet and flush it! Then we'll see who's a little sweetie-pie!

MUM Would he like his bottle, then? Some nice, warm milk to fill his little tummy. Mummy get Dessy-Wessy his bottle. *(MUM's face disappears)*

BABY Milk! Yuk! I want chocolate…and Coke…and greasy chips…and pizza. I wanna grow up. Help!

BETTY Who's got his daddy's eyes, then? And his daddy's hair?

BABY What do you mean, you daft old bat? Dad's hardly got any hair!

BETTY I think when he grows up he's going to look just like his daddy. And he's going to be a clever, clever, clever person like his mummy.

BABY You call that clever, the way she talks to me? And what do you mean, look like dad? I don't want to get wrinkly and bald and have hairs growing out of my nostrils. Wait a minute… You don't mean I'm going to grow up to be like you lot, do you? Oh no! I DON'T WANT TO GROW UP! I DON'T WANT TO GROW UP! *(starts screaming)*

\*   \*   \*

Sometimes, growing up looks very attractive, and we can't wait. But when you think what you might turn into, perhaps it's not such a good idea after all. Just think, you might end up like me!

And isn't it strange how grown-ups are always telling kids what to do, yet adults seem to make such a mess of things themselves. Just look at what grown-ups are doing to the world today.

How can we avoid making the same mistakes our parents' generation have made?

The wisest man who ever lived is supposed to have been King Solomon. Even he did some rather foolish things in his time, but on the whole he did a very good job of being king of Israel. Here is some advice he gave to young people.

Have a group of children read **Proverbs 3:1–8 (or –12)**. Split it into sections for different readers.

This was King Solomon's secret: **"Remember the Lord in everything you do. And he will give you success."**

How do we put his wise advice into practice? He said, **"...in everything you do."** So whatever it is we are doing, we can send up a quick prayer: "Please, Lord, show me...help me...forgive me...teach me..." or whatever it is we need at that moment. Then we pause and think before rushing into something.

As Solomon says just a bit further on,

> **Using his wisdom, the Lord made the earth.**     *Proverbs 3:19*

The God who has the wisdom and understanding to make the earth must be by far the best one to show us how to live on the earth and to care for it. If we can learn to remember him in everything we do, we are likely to grow up into people who make a much better job of things than our parents' generation has.

# 119 The collector card king

## Theme

A modern version of the parable of the three servants as told in Matthew 25:14–30. This is written for the World Cup, but it can be rewritten for other major competitions. Actions for the characters are obvious from the text. The fifth supporter is the one to do the swaps with. He/she needs extra items for swapping.

## You will need

- two narrators and five actors in football supporter gear.
- large medium and small cardboard boxes with pictures cut from magazines stuck on the outsides; card collections, scarves, etc. – whatever you can borrow.
- copies of the script. These can be printed out from *www.77talks.co.uk*.

## Sketch

NARRATOR 1   There was once a *Manchester United* fan who had the biggest collection of football gear in the country. He had mountains of collector cards, piles of programmes, books full of autographs, and wardrobes full of strips. He never missed an opportunity to add to his collection. His name was Dave, but everyone called him the Collector Card King.

NARRATOR 2   Of course, Dave wasn't going to miss out on the World Cup. It was the biggest collecting opportunity of his life. But he didn't want to miss out on things back home, either.

NARRATOR 1   Dave got three of his friends together: Stu, Debra, and Mick. He gave a great big boxful of gear to Stu. "Look after it carefully," he said. "And see what you can do while I'm away."

NARRATOR 2   He gave Debra a medium-size box with the same instructions…
And he gave Mick a boxful of World Cup cards…
Then he left in time for the opening match.

NARRATOR 1   Stu sorted his big box of gear and set about swapping, buying and selling. With a lot of hard work and clever deals he doubled what Dave had left him.

NARRATOR 2   Debra did the same with what she had. She also doubled her collection.

NARRATOR 1    But Mick was worried in case he lost some of Dave's prize cards. He put the box under his bed, safely buried among the smelly socks and old copies of *SHOOT* magazine.

NARRATOR 2    Weeks later, after the final, Dave came home. He called his three friends together and asked to see how they had done.

NARRATOR 1    Stu spoke first. "Look," he said. "You gave me a big box of gear and I've swapped and bought and sold – and doubled what you gave me."

NARRATOR 2    "That's awesome," said Dave. "You've shown that you've got a good head for business. I'm setting up a chain of football merchandising shops. I want you to be my managing director. We're going to be rich!"

NARRATOR 1    Next, it was Debra's turn. She showed him how much she had made.

NARRATOR 2    "That's great," said Dave. "Obviously, I can trust you, too. I want you to be my sales manager. Welcome to the company! We're all going to be rich!"

NARRATOR 1    Then Mick produced the box of cards. It smelled of dirty socks. "I know you're a really smart businessman," said Mick. "You expect people who work for you to get results. I was afraid if I lost any of your stuff you'd be really furious, so I hid it under the bed. Here it is."

NARRATOR 2    Dave went ballistic! "You're totally useless!" he shouted. "I gave you a chance and you blew it! People who use what they are given go up in the world. But people who don't use it lose everything. Get out! And don't come begging for a job in my shops – I wouldn't even let you sweep the floor!"

# After the sketch

You might ask the children to relate the main lines of the story, to ensure they have understood it. We have found a tendency for some children to be sympathetic to "Mick", so it may be helpful to point out that in real business situations, people are expected to turn in a profit – or find themselves out of a job.

In this story people are given an opportunity and expected to make something of it. Use it or lose it! This is like the skills of players in the World Cup. They have natural ability, but managers and coaches and supporters expect them to give maximum commitment, too.

You might be surprised to learn that this was a story Jesus told. We've just brought it up to date a bit. Jesus told stories like this to teach us something about life – and about God and ourselves. What was he trying to teach us in this story?... That this life is a shared responsibility: God gives us gifts, abilities, time, a planet rich in resources – our part is to make the best use of these.

For those who do make good use of them, there are rich rewards. Those who don't can't expect much sympathy.

# 120 The biggest explosion in history

## Theme
Trusting God in the most frightening circumstances.

## You will need
- a Bible: Psalm 46.
- possibly pictures of volcanoes erupting – see *www.77talks.co.uk*.

## Presentation
In 1628 BC there occurred the biggest explosion ever witnessed by human beings. The noise of that explosion was so loud that it echoed right round the world 16 times and made people deaf 500 kilometres (300 miles) away. It was a volcanic eruption. It was so fierce that it blew the greater part of a Mediterranean island away.

The island was Thera, north of Crete, south-east of Greece. Archaeologists today have discovered a mile-wide city on one of the parts of Thera that remains. By any standards, it was highly civilized – they even had showers and flush toilets. They were so advanced that some people think that there could have been TV by the time of Christ if their civilization had continued.

But in 1628 BC a volcano on the island started erupting. Clouds of dust and ash rained down on the town, totally burying it – but also protecting it for future generations to find. Then the mountain blew up. 80 cubic kilometres (50 cubic miles) of rock were blasted into the air. A tidal wave swept across the Mediterranean. In parts of the Nile delta, the wave was as high as a four storey building. But on one part of the Turkish coast, trapped between two arms of land like a funnel, the wave reached an incredible 250 metres (800 feet) high. It swept 50 kilometres (30 miles) inland, scouring the earth bare and leaving "scablands" that are still visible today.[1]

## Seven years without summer
Fine dust flung high into the atmosphere blocked out the sun and turned the following summer into winter. 5,000-year-old bristlecone pines in California bear the scars of the summer frosts on their growth rings for that year. Chinese records show that all the crops died and that the effects continued for seven years. Great numbers of people died of starvation in northern China, and that must have been true around the world.

---

1. Details about Thera from *Return to Sodom and Gomorrah*, Charles Pellegrino (TSP, 1994), chapter 9.

**Psalm 46** in the Bible may be a memory of that cataclysmic event.

Read the whole psalm, or selected verses from it.

## Something to think about

This ancient song shows the writer's confidence in God in the most frightening circumstances. Many people know the first sentence by heart: **"God is our refuge and strength, an ever-present help in trouble."** If someone could write that, after living through the biggest explosion in human history, then that is worth listening to. We shall all face disasters, either great or small. We shall all be in frightening situations. The sort of confidence that can trust God in the worst possible situations must be worth having. **"God is our refuge and strength, an ever-present help in trouble."**

# 121 Ways to praise

## Theme
There are many ways and reasons to praise God – and they are all good for you.

## You will need
- sports gear associated with a local or popular sports team, e.g. scarves, rattles.
- a book, a video, art reproduction etc., as below.

## Presentation
Talk about – or, better, get some fans to talk about – a favourite team and demonstrate how supporters react when the team wins.

That is one of the ways people behave when they think something or someone is really great.

Lots of us are fans of other things besides sports. How do we show we think something is great in these following cases?

- Music or theatre performance – we applaud.

- A book or a film or a song – we tell others how good it is and encourage them to read or see or buy it.

- A work of art – we gaze at it, take it in, see new things in it.

- A hero or an expert in a field we are interested in – we try to copy them, learn from them, be like them.

These are all different ways of praising people we appreciate. The bigger the group we are in, the noisier we tend to be in our appreciation and the more we can let our hair down. But no one way is really any better than another.

## Applaud a robin
If people are worth praising because of their skill or their creativity, how much more is God, the Creator of everything!… We don't normally scream and shout when we see a beautiful sunset, or applaud a robin singing, but we may pause to appreciate them.

The Bible is full of ways people have praised God, the book of Psalms especially.

- In **Psalm 150** people praise God with loud music and dancing, much like fans at a football match.

- In **Psalm 8** David praises God as he gazes at the stars and thinks about what it means to be a human being in the universe God has created.

- **Psalm 119** is full of praise for God's guidelines for living. The writer shows his appreciation by wanting to put them into practice and follow the guidelines.

- The writer of **Psalm 78** sees the great things God has done and wants to tell everyone about them.

So the way we praise depends on the kind of person we are, the sort of things we appreciate most, and whether we are alone or with a group of other people. But however we praise, it makes us feel good. And it makes us feel closer to the person we are praising; it creates a relationship between us. Praising God draws us closer to him and leaves us with a warm, peaceful feeling.

So if we want to make our day better – any day – let's try praising God. We can praise him for things we see in the natural world, people we appreciate, things he has done. We can praise silently or in words or song. We can praise by telling other people something or by putting into action something we have learned in the Bible. Try it. It does you good!

## Something to do

Put praise into practice with a noisy song or with quiet appreciation of a piece of music.

# 122 Here's mud in your eye!

## Theme
A mouth-watering introduction leads into the story of Jesus healing a blind man in John 9:1–11 and the conclusion that God treats us all as individuals.

## You will need
- possibly something good to eat; a 1.5 litre soft drink bottle.
- You could use the cartoon from the *www.77talks.co.uk* website.

## Presentation
Lovingly describe a meal that should appeal to your group, or eat something appetizing in front of them. Ask whose mouth is watering.

We make saliva – or spit – all the time, but especially when we start to think about food. Would anybody like to guess how much we produce in a day? A cupful?... Half a litre?... In fact, the average person produces 1.5 litres (2.5 pints) of saliva every day – enough to fill a large cola bottle. That is nothing compared to cows. [Show the cartoon if you have it.] A cow makes over 50 litres (85 pints) of spit a day!

Saliva is vital to turning the solid food we put into our mouths into a moist paste that we can swallow, but it also starts the digestive process. It has other uses as well. If you hurt your finger or get a splinter in it, what do you instinctively do?... Put it in your mouth and suck it. And if you fall over while you are out, you are likely to rub spit on the graze.

As so often, what we do instinctively is a good thing to do. Saliva is a natural antiseptic. Researchers at St Bartholomew's hospital in London got volunteers to lick their hands. They found that this produced a powerful microbe killer [nitric oxide]. We all carry around a useful emergency first-aid kit in our mouths!

It sounds strange, but Jesus once used spit when he healed a blind man. **Tell the story found in John 9:1–11.**

Another time, Jesus healed a blind man with just a word. Why did he use mud made with saliva this time? Was it because saliva is a good antiseptic, or was there another reason?

Nobody knows the answer to that. Perhaps this man needed something physical to happen to help him believe. When we look at the various stories of Jesus healing people, we find that they are all different. Sometimes he touched the person, sometimes he didn't. Sometimes he told them to do something, either before or after they were healed. What we can see is that he treated each one as an individual. He knew what would be helpful to each person.

## A prayer

Father God, we thank you for the first-aid antiseptic in our saliva that is always there, ready to use at a moment's notice. But we thank you more for the way you know each one of us personally and know just what we need. Help us to turn to you when we are in need and to trust you to heal our deepest hurts. Amen.

# Right for Me, Right for the World

Changing the world begins with changing our own hearts

# 123 Heart to change the world

## Theme
Cleaning up the mess inside us is just as important as cleaning up the world.

## You will need
- Make a giant heart as follows. Get a sheet of thick card, e.g. the side of a box. Fold a sheet of paper the same size in half; draw half a heart on it; cut out, open out, and trace onto the card. Cut out and paint red (auto spray paint is perfect for this). Glue a box, e.g. a cereal packet, to the back. On a discarded soft drink can write "GREEDY" with a marker pen. Similarly, write "CARELESS" on, for example, a yoghurt pot, and "SELFISH" on a piece of rag. Place this "rubbish" inside the box fixed to the back of the heart.

## Presentation
Do you have a heart to save the world? Every so often, politicians meet to try to agree on limiting emissions of greenhouse gasses. It is an uphill battle. There are too many people who don't want to change their lifestyle, too many who don't care what the world may be like in 50 or 100 years' time, because it doesn't affect them now.

Centuries ago, God gave the prophet Jeremiah a terrifying vision of a ruined world. This is what he saw:

> I looked at the earth. It was empty and had no shape! I looked at the sky. And its light was gone. I looked at the mountains, and they were shaking! All the hills were trembling. I looked, and there were no people! Every bird in the sky had flown away. I looked, and the good, rich land had become a desert! All its towns had been destroyed. The Lord and his great anger has caused this.
>
> *Jeremiah 4:23–26*

Although the situation was a different one then, the causes and results seem very similar. God said to the people, "**The way you have lived and acted has brought this trouble to you**" (Jeremiah 4:18). If global warming causes rising sea-levels and many other disasters, it will be because of the way we have lived and acted.

Do you have a heart to save the world? It's a big job; it needs a big heart.

[Produce your giant heart.]

Many children and young people obviously do have a heart to save the world. We can see that in things like recycling schemes. (Refer to anything you know the children are involved in.) But before we get too smug, we ought to look at our hearts very carefully.

[Ask for a volunteer to look inside the heart and pull out a piece of what he or she finds there.]

When we look at this heart, we find there's some rubbish inside. This cola can, what does it have written on it?… "GREEDY". Let's be honest – hands up – who is greedy sometimes?… All of us? Yes. Can any of us honestly say we weren't greedy in what we wanted for Christmas?

[A second volunteer takes out a piece of rubbish.]

What does this say?… "CARELESS". Hands up, who is careless sometimes?… Who throws a bit of litter down occasionally?… Who forgets to turn lights off, or leaves doors open in winter?… All of us.

[Third volunteer takes out the last piece of rubbish.]

What does this say?… "SELFISH". Who's selfish sometimes?… "Me first!" "It's all mine!" "I don't want to share!"…

## A clean heart

Greedy, careless, selfish – when we are honest we know that we've all got some of that kind of rubbish inside us. Just before that terrible vision of a ruined world, God said this through Jeremiah,

> **People of Jerusalem, clean the evil from your hearts and be saved.**     *Jeremiah 4:14*

The message is the same now as it was around 2,600 years ago. If you've got a heart to save the world, it has to be a clean heart. It's no good trying to clean up the problems out there if there is a mess inside. Sooner or later the rubbish inside starts to cause trouble, no matter how good our intentions are. To save the world will need some big changes in lifestyle for each one of us. Some of us may be surprised to find how greedy or selfish we really are when it comes to making those changes.

One of the lines in the Lord's Prayer is, "Forgive us our trespasses" or "Forgive us the wrongs we have done". That is really asking God to do a clean-up job on our hearts, to get rid of the rubbish there. So perhaps we might pray something like this:

## A prayer

> **Our Father in heaven, we have all put up our hands to confess that sometimes we are greedy, selfish and careless. Forgive us the wrong things we have done. Clean us up inside. And give us a big heart, a heart to save the world. Amen.**

# 124 Yoghurt race

## Theme
Wrong thinking leads to trouble.

## You will need
- runny (not "set") fruit yoghurts, preferably well coloured; two or three bowls and spoons; cloths to clean up with; carpet offcuts or cloth pads to go under people's heads; stable, flat-seated chairs.
- If the group is large, this needs to be done on a platform for visibility.

## Presentation

Ask for two or three tough volunteers for a yoghurt-eating race. Get each one to lie stomach-down across a chair with his head resting on the floor and his left hand behind his back (or right hand if left-handed). Place a bowl of yoghurt and spoon in front of each one's face. On the signal, they simply have to eat the yoghurt as fast as possible. First one to finish wins.

When finished, get them to stand up so the group can see their faces before they clean up. What a mess!

Maybe part of the reason the world is in a mess is because people try to do things while their *thinking* is all upside down.

Money is one example. There is nothing wrong with money, or earning it, or spending it. But when people put it *first*, it stops being a useful tool and leads them into all kinds of wrong. As Paul said in the Bible:

> **The love of money causes all kinds of evil. Some people have left the true faith because they want to get more and more money. But they have caused themselves a great deal of sorrow.**
> *1 Timothy 6:10*

Paul is talking there about the mess that can come from upside-down thinking about money.

Another example is freedom. As human beings, we are free to think, free to make choices, free to explore. It is one of the greatest privileges we have. But it is very easy to get our thinking about freedom upside-down and use it in the wrong way. That way lies disaster. Listen to Paul again:

**My brothers. God called you to be free. But do not use your freedom as an excuse to do the things that please your sinful self… If you go on hurting each other and tearing each other apart, be careful! You will completely destroy each other.**

*Galatians 5:13, 15*

A real-life example from your own experience of getting into a mess through misusing your freedom would be helpful here.

Hold up the towel that has been used to clean up someone's face. The great message of the Bible is that when we do get into a mess, God is always waiting to clean us up when we turn to him for help.

## A prayer

**Father God, please show us how to sort out our thinking before we get into a mess. But when we do do something stupid, help us to recognize our fault and say sorry. Remind us that you are always there, always ready with a towel to clean us up and turn our lives the right way up. Amen.**

# 125 The cost of water

## Theme
The importance of thinking about the real costs of what we do and say.

## You will need
- a bottle of mineral water and a jug of tap water.
- The Bible story is found in 1 Chronicles 11:15–19.

## Presentation
[Hold up the jug of water.] We each use nearly 4.5 litres of water a day for drinking and cooking. (Of course, we use much more for things like flushing the toilet and washing clothes.) Most of this water comes through pipes into our homes and all we have to do is turn on the tap and it flows out freely. But over the past few years, more and more people have started buying bottled water to drink. This is probably partly due to advertising and partly to people taking holidays in countries where it is more normal to drink bottled water, or necessary because of poor water quality.

If we are concerned about the environment, which one of these should we drink? Is it better to drink tap water or bottled water?… How did the bottled water get to the supermarket?… By lorry. It added to the congestion on the roads, used diesel, added to carbon dioxide emissions and pollution. Then there are the materials and energy used to make the bottle, and after use, the bottle is more waste to be disposed of or, perhaps, recycled. The cost of tap water to the environment is tiny by comparison.

## Water from Bethlehem
In the Old Testament there is a story about David – the one who killed Goliath – and a drink of water. After David became king of Israel, there was a war with the Philistines. The Philistines had taken Bethlehem – which was David's home town – and had a garrison of soldiers there.

David and his men were camped by a cave in the wilderness. It was a hot and dusty place. David had a real craving for some water from the well by the gate at Bethlehem, the well he had drunk from so often as a child. Some of his men overheard him, and three of them decided on a madcap mission. They broke through the enemy lines, drew some water from the well at Bethlehem and carried it back to David.

You might think that he would have been delighted. Not at all. He refused to drink it and poured it on the ground instead. Why? It seems very ungrateful! But David knew

307

what the real cost of that water was. His men might have been captured and killed. The lives of his friends were far more valuable to him than enjoying a drink of fresh water. He was not prepared for his men to risk their lives for his pleasure. The cost was far too great.

## Something to think about
The cost to the environment of a bottle of water is far greater than the cost of a jug of tap water. (It costs a lot more money, too!) Perhaps we should think about refusing to drink it, like David, because of the cost. It is only a small thing, but it is one of the many small things people need to think about in order to look after God's world properly.

# 126 Reactions and rewards

## Theme
One of the moral laws of the universe: we reap what we sow.

## You will need
- a ball to bounce.
- possibly a bicycle.

## Presentation
Come in bouncing a ball – save the reason for later. Ask for an athletic and fearless volunteer. The volunteer's mission – should they choose to accept it – is to put their head down and run as fast as they can into the side or back wall of the hall without stopping. Will they do it? Of course not! (But be prepared to stop the suicidal nutter who says yes!)

Why not? Because they know Newton's law of action and reaction. Don't they?... Well, perhaps not in words, but everyone knows it from experience. Sir Isaac Newton was one of the greatest scientists who ever lived. Newton's third law says that for every action, there is an equal and opposite reaction. In other words, if you hit the wall with your head, the wall hits you back equally hard. That's why it hurts. The good bit about this is that if you throw a ball on the floor, the floor obligingly hits it back to you. It's nice to have a floor that plays ball, isn't it? (Thank your hard-headed – or level-headed – volunteer and let him or her sit down.)

This law is one of the fundamental laws of the universe. Babies learn it the first time they bump their head against the table, but it takes a genius like Sir Isaac Newton to think it through and put it into words – or rather, into mathematics. Knowing the law stops us from riding our bicycles into the front of a bus.

## Road pushes cyclist
The law also enables the bike to work in the first place. You push on the pedal which moves the chain which turns the wheel which pushes against the road – and the road pushes back equally hard and sends you a few metres nearer the chip shop or the winning tape of the Tour de France.

Is there a similar law for the way people behave? If you punch someone in the playground will they punch you back equally hard? Not necessarily. They might punch you harder! Or they might not retaliate at all. Quite often, we do not seem to get any punishment for a bad action. We do something and "get away with it".

Equally, quite often we do not get any reward for a good action. Nobody notices the good thing we have done.

Or so it seems.

There is a famous thing that Jesus said about doing good. In this case, the good action he talked about was helping those in need. He said,

> **When you give to the poor, don't let anyone know what you are doing. Your giving should be done in secret. Your Father [God] can see what is done in secret and he will reward you.**
> *Matthew 6:3–4*

That reward isn't like Newton's "equal and opposite reaction". When you throw the ball on the floor, you don't have to wait ten minutes for the floor to decide to bounce it back to you. (Just think what a game of tennis would be like if you did!) God's rewards usually involve waiting. But what Jesus gives us here is a promise that the reward will come – in God's time. If we are quietly generous, God will be generous to us when the time is right.

## Planting selfishness

Does that also apply to bad or hurtful things we do? St Paul said it did, in one of his letters in the Bible. He uses a different picture, the picture of sowing seeds and waiting for the crop to grow. That gives a clearer idea of the time involved. He wrote,

> **Don't be misled: No one makes a fool of God. What a person plants, he will harvest. The person who plants selfishness, ignoring the needs of others – ignoring God! – harvests a crop of weeds. All he will have to show for his life is weeds!**
> *Galatians 6:7–8*, The Message

[Bounce the ball again.]

If you throw a ball against a wall, the wall bounces the ball back to you. If we do something hurtful or selfish, that will eventually bounce back on us as well – unless we say sorry and ask for forgiveness. But if we are generous and do good to others without making a fuss about it, God who sees everything will reward us for it. That's what Jesus promised.

## Something to think about

Paul went on to say:

> **The one who plants in response to God, letting God's Spirit do the growth work in him, harvests a crop of real life, eternal life.**

Let's have a few moments of quiet. We can ask God's Spirit to show us something generous, something kind, something helpful that we could do quietly today.

# 127 Animal welfare

## Theme
Our responsibility to take care of God's creation.

## You will need
- three children to read the Bible verses.
- recent examples of cruelty to animals – check the RSPCA website: *www.rspca.org.uk.*

## Presentation
Despite years of efforts by animal welfare campaigners, people go on being cruel to animals. (Give examples.)

The Bible teaches that this is not what God wants. He created the world, and we read in Genesis 1 that he was pleased with all he had made. Many other passages in the Bible teach us how God cares and provides for the living creatures he has made. Here are some extracts from **Psalm 104:**

READER A    "You make springs pour into the ravines; they flow between the mountains. They water all the wild animals; the wild donkeys come there to drink. Wild birds make nests by the water; they sing among the branches." (verses 10–12)

READER B    "You make the grass grow for cattle, and vegetables for the people. You make food grow from the earth." (verse 14)

READER C    "The lions roar for their prey and seek their food from God... These all look to you to give them their food at the proper time. When you give it to them, they gather it up; when you open your hand, they are satisfied with good things." (verses 21, 27–28)

That is God's part in creation, but looking after animals is *our* responsibility, too. Here are some guidelines which, although they were written two to three thousand years ago, are still helpful principles today:

READER A    "Good people take care of their animals." (Proverbs 12:10)

READER B    "If you happen to see your enemy's cow or donkey running loose, take it back to him. If his donkey has fallen under its load, help him get the donkey to its feet again; don't just walk off." (Exodus 23:4–5)

311

Some of the stories Jesus told, and the things he said, echo these important principles and reinforce the need for us to treat animals humanely. In fact, in John 10:14–15 Jesus says, **"I am the Good Shepherd who lays his life down for his sheep."** In this picture, Jesus says that because the shepherd cares so much for his sheep, he is even prepared to risk his life by defending them against wolves. As well as teaching us about God's love and protection for us, this gives us a perfect example of how Jesus wants us to care for those around us, animals as well as people.

The Bible makes it clear that God has trusted us to look after everything he has created. If we let him down, we are the ones who will have to answer to him. Relying on someone else to look after our world simply isn't good enough. If we sit back and watch while others destroy it, then we are as guilty as they are for spoiling it.

Whether we are talking about local traffic pollution, the treatment of animals in zoos, the felling of tropical rainforests, global warming, or Third World poverty, God has given us all a duty to stand up for what is right. Before it's too late.

# 128 Stop children

## Theme
God's big STOP signs – the Ten Commandments – are there for our protection.

## You will need
- to borrow a road-crossing "lollipop" and clothing from your local friendly school-crossing person.
- pictures of other road signs (e.g. printed out from a clip-art collection or at *www.77talks.co.uk*) and a copy of the Highway Code.

## Presentation
Show the "lollipop". It says, "STOP CHILDREN". Stop children what? Stop children using their mobile phones in class? Stop children watching too much TV? Stop children pestering adults? Or what?

Elicit from the children what the sign means: Stop...because there are children waiting to cross the road. Stop...to prevent an accident. Stop...to save someone from getting hurt.

In other words, it is not a sign to prevent us from doing something we like doing. It is a sign for our protection. How many children have been saved from being killed or seriously injured because of the lollipop woman or man on the way to school?

To develop this further, other road signs can be shown and the children asked what they mean. A sign like "Beware of the frogs" can cause a lot of amusement. There really is one! Give one child a copy of the *Highway Code* and see if he or she can find it. Emphasize that these signs are for our protection.

Get another child to come and hold up a Bible. God has a number of STOP signs, too. Things like: Stop telling lies about other people. Stop stealing. Stop using God's name as a swear word. Stop working seven days a week – take a day off to appreciate God's work in making this wonderful world.

There are ten big STOP signs like these in the Bible. Who knows what we call them?... Get the child with the Bible to find Exodus 20 and read the heading: The Ten Commandments. (Most Bibles have a heading like this. Check in advance.)

# Parents are old fuddy-duddies?

God's other big STOP signs are: Stop making anything other than me a "god" in your life. Stop worshipping anything that is merely made by human beings. Stop thinking that your parents are old fuddy-duddies who know nothing. Stop committing murder. Stop being unfaithful to the person you marry. Stop wanting what belongs to other people.

What are the STOP lollipop and the signs in the *Highway Code* for?… For our protection. To save lives. To stop children being injured. So what do you think God's big STOP signs are for?… Just the same. To protect us. To stop us getting hurt. Even to save our lives.

Some people don't think that road signs apply to them. They drive through red traffic lights. They ignore warning signs. They drive too fast.

Some people don't think the Ten Commandments apply to them. They ignore God's STOP signs and nothing seems to happen. But sooner or later, there's a crash. People get hurt. And it's often not just the one who ignored the signs who gets hurt. Others do, too.

So a big "Thank you" to the crossing lady who keeps us safe on the journey to school. And an even bigger "Thanks" to the one who made ten giant lollipop signs to keep us safe on our journey through life.

## Something to do

Make a series of lollipop STOP signs and write the Ten Commandments on them.

## NOTE

The authors wish to pay their respects to the woman in Barnsley who pointed out to a friend that the town council had provided a lollipop man on Sunday – when it was double-time, too. How kind of the council!

# 129 Tramp takes all

## Theme
God gave us seven days in a week and asked us to keep one specially for him.

## You will need
- to dress up as a tramp or a bag-lady. The more realistic you look the more effective the talk will be.

## Presentation
Be found curled up asleep when the meeting or service starts and don't be disturbed by people coming in. When the leader or minister (who is, of course, in the know) gets to the talk, you interrupt and say you will do the talking today. You make it quite clear that you are capable of doing a far better job than the one at the front!

(On one occasion during a church service, a woman went to fetch the police and had to be persuaded to desist by a well-known member of the congregation. Be prepared!)

Tell this story:

An old tramp visited a family, and the woman of the house took pity on him. She gave him something to eat, and then decided she would go further than that, and allowed him to have a bath. She agreed with him that he would throw away his old clothes – she found some of her husband's clothes, and fitted him up with a totally new outfit. He was very grateful. Then she decided that as he left, she would make him a flask of coffee and some sandwiches to help him on his way. He was even more grateful.

The tramp was so well mannered and so full of thanks that the woman was moved to do even more for him. "Now," she said, "I have a box here, and in it there are seven gold coins that my father gave to me. They have lain for many years doing nothing in this box. I am going to give you six of them, but I want to keep one of them for myself." The tramp was even more grateful and thanked her over and over again. Then he went on his way.

## All in a good cause
When her husband came home later, she told him that some of his clothes had been given to an old tramp, including his best gardening jacket, and a decent pair of boots. He frowned at first, but then said he supposed it was all in a good cause. They went to bed.

In the middle of the night, there was a noise and the woman said to her husband, "I think there's someone downstairs." He just grunted and turned over to go back to sleep, but then they both heard a bump. He got his cricket bat out of the wardrobe and crept downstairs. He peeked through the crack in the door.

Guess who it was?

[The children will all rush to tell you it was the tramp.] What do you think he was doing?… He was stealing that gold coin, the last one left in the box. What do you think of him and what he did?…

Of course, we would never do anything like that!… Would we?

God gave us seven days of the week and asked us to keep one specially for him. He said it was a day to rest from working, a holy day, a day to remember him and to give him honour. But people actually steal it and won't recognize the one who gave it. We are all so busy that we think we don't have time to take a day off from shopping, we don't have time to take a day off from getting jobs done, we don't have time to take a day to relax and come close to God.

Who is really the loser, God or us?

## A prayer

**Father God, you rested after you had made the world. You told us to rest on the seventh day, too. Help us to realize how foolish we are when we try to steal that day and use it to go on being busy. Help us to discover how much richer we are when we take time to come close to you. Amen.**

# Beyond Cyberspace

The ultimate in communication is as close as a whispered prayer or a summer daydream

'OK, vere is ze patient?'

# 130 Mobile phone 1

## Theme
We should keep on praying for justice, knowing that God will answer.

## You will need
- a mobile phone; a story that you can start reading or telling that gets interrupted.
- an assistant with a phone and your number, set for quick-dial. This assistant should be right at the back or in an adjoining room and have the phone hidden.

## Presentation
Start telling a story. When you have been going for half a minute or so, your assistant presses their quick-dial button to call you. You look round the group to see whose phone is ringing, realize it is yours, apologize, and answer it. You hold a quick conversation (imagining the other side so that your assistant does not have to speak and reveal himself), telling the other person where you are and that you can't help them just now.

Apologize again and continue with the story. The same thing happens a couple more times, and each time you get more forthright with the imaginary caller.

The final time it rings, you sigh in resignation and give the caller the information they want. (This could be an imaginary name, address and phone number or – for a laugh at your own expense – some information connected to what people know is an interest of yours.)

Now abandon your original story and tell a different one instead – the story of the persistent widow from **Luke 18:1–8**.

Underline the point that the judge in the story was a bad judge. If even a bad judge gave the woman justice because of her persistence, how much more will God answer prayers for justice! We may not see those answers immediately, but God's heart is for justice on earth, and we can be sure those prayers will receive an answer. Just keep dialling God's number!

## Prayers
A group of children could be asked in advance to prepare some prayers on a justice issue.

# 131 Mobile phone 2

## Theme
A practical and fun lesson in praying for people and blessing them.

## You will need
- a mobile phone.
- Do some detective work in advance and find a couple of relevant phone numbers in case the group can't come up with any themselves.

## Presentation
In a school assembly, for example, talk to the children and find out whose mum is at home and may be feeling a bit down or unwell. In a church situation, it is more likely to be a grandparent who is at home, perhaps alone.

Suggest that a phone call might cheer them up, and get out your mobile. Children will usually know their home number, so that is easy. In church, for a grandparent, often the parent is present and will know or have the number.

When you get through, chat to the person as though you know them. Then say that there are lots of people who want to say hello, and get all the children to shout, "Hello, Mrs Jones!" Then pass the phone to the child/grandchild for a quick word.

## A big amen
As this is church/worship, say you would like to pray for the person. Ask if you may (very few people refuse when one offers to pray for them), and if there is anything particular she would like prayer for. Then pray a simple prayer – with a big "Amen!" at the end from everyone with you.

This can be repeated two or three times. For subsequent calls, one of the children might offer to say the prayer.

Just doing this is such a strong and memorable lesson in itself that it doesn't really need anything added. If you wish, underline the point that praying is a natural thing that anyone can do anywhere and at any time. It always blesses people.

# NOTE

One of the authors used this in a different way and spoke to a father who was at home on a Sunday morning, doing odd jobs. Following a big "Hello" from the congregation and a word with the daughter, he asked him where he ought to be. "Well, at church, really." The father promised to come to church that evening, the author was invited to the home for tea, the man was converted – and is now a Methodist lay preacher!

# 132 Mobile phone 3

## Theme
People pray in different ways. The important thing is keeping in contact with God, not how you do it.

## You will need
• a mobile phone; a fixed-line phone (unplugged).

## Presentation
Ask some of the children what they like doing with friends. Playing will come out high on the list, but just chatting is usually close behind. Telling good news or sharing things that worry them are important things, too.

That's really what prayer is: talking to God, telling him about things that excite you, sharing worries and fears.

There are different ways of praying. For some people, the way they prefer is like this. [Produce the fixed-line phone.] This kind of phone stays in one place. If you want to talk to someone on it, you need to go to the phone. That means you can't use it when you are out and about. Some people pray mainly like this, at a particular time or in a particular place. It may be that they put aside some time to spend with God first thing in the morning or last thing at night. It may be that they find the best place to pray is in church or in a special quiet place at home. Perhaps they light a candle or use some prayers from a book.

## Always close
Others prefer to pray like this. [Produce the mobile phone.] They like to talk to God any time, any place. They may pray while they are on the move or doing other things. They find it very helpful to know that God is always around, always close, and that you can chat to him, just like a best friend.

One way of praying isn't better than another. It partly depends on the kind of person you are, and what you have learned from the example of other people or, if you go to church, the kind of church it is.

When Paul wrote to the church in Thessalonica, in Greece, he said:

> **Always be happy. Never stop praying. Give thanks whatever happens. This is what God wants for you in Christ Jesus.**
> *1 Thessalonians 5:16–18*

So put a smile on your face. Look around at all the things there are to be thankful for. And get on the phone to God!

# 133 The miracle well

## Theme
Answer to prayer can seem a long time coming, but when it does, God's generosity can surprise us.

## You will need
- A copy of the photo at *www.77talks.co.uk* printed onto an overhead transparency will help bring the story alive. It shows water gushing from the borehole.

## Presentation
In the south of France, in an old farmhouse perched on a mountain ridge, live an English couple, Tony and Georgina Clay, and their two children. Georgina is a district nurse who drives around the local villages caring for people in their homes. Tony looks after vines, renovates the house and writes songs – he used to have a band that toured schools in England.

Just north of their house is a mountainside that drops some 250 metres (800 feet) to the valley below. To the south, they look across valleys and ridges to the snow-capped peak of Mount Canigou in the Pyrenees. It is a beautiful spot to live in, but the nearest village is two kilometres away, the nearest shop is three kilometres down the mountainside, and they have no water or electricity!

When they bought the house in 1994 there was a small spring about 50 metres from the house for water, but it was only a trickle and it soon dried up. While Georgie collected drinking water on her rounds, from one of the village fountains, Tony fixed guttering and rigged up tanks and pipes and pumps to try to supply rainwater for washing and flushing the toilet. But there was never enough. To make matters worse, there has been less rainfall in recent years in the region, and even some whole villages are running out of water.

## Praying for a solution
Tony and Georgie loved the place and believed God wanted them there. There are very few Christians in the area and most people never give God a thought. As Georgie cared for the sick and elderly in the region, and as Tony demonstrated honesty and being a good neighbour, they were quietly showing God's love. They kept praying for a solution to the water problem, but it seemed to get worse, not better.

There is a bit in the book of Isaiah that talks about a person who does and says what is right. It goes on,

**...this is the man who will dwell on the heights, whose refuge will be the mountain fortress. His bread will be supplied, and water will not fail him.**

*Isaiah 33:16,* New International Version

That sounds like a good promise, but it gets hard to believe when you keep praying and nothing happens. At times things got really desperate, for example, when Tony fell off a horse and broke three ribs in his back. He was in severe pain for several months. It was winter and it was almost impossible for him to fetch water, start the electricity generator, or cut wood for the fire.

The only solution seemed to be to hire a company to drill a borehole. That is quite common in rural France, but it is very expensive. You have to pay for every metre that is drilled and there is no guarantee that you will hit water, especially living on a mountain ridge. And there is no technology that can tell you the right place to drill.

In 2000, with horses to water as well as their own needs, they decided to go for a borehole. They took the best advice they could get and started the drilling close to the house, only a few metres from the mountainside to the north. It was a Tuesday not long before Christmas. Tony asked the company to go down 35 metres (115 feet). By the end of the day, they had found just a trickle of water. What now? If they stopped they would waste the money they had spent so far. If they went on drilling, there was still no guarantee of finding water and they could waste even more money. What would you have done?

# Sleepless night

Tony and Georgie prayed, and got on the phone to ask friends to pray, too. Tony had a sleepless night. In the morning he had taken a decision. He told the drilling company to continue down to 45 metres (145 feet).

At 45 metres, nothing. But as the drill was in two-metre (six-foot) lengths, they went another metre for good measure – and the drill hit soft mud. A little bit deeper and water started rising up the borehole.

Was that an answer to prayer – or was it just coincidence?

That evening the engineers tested the flow of water. It was 6000 litres (1270 gallons) – six tonnes – of water per hour! The drilling company had never hit such a flow of water at such a height. They were 250 metres (800 feet) above the valley floor, but they seemed to have hit an underground river. The water must have been coming from many miles away. What a Christmas present!

Tony and Georgie now have enough water for themselves, the horses, a guest house when Tony has finished converting the barn – even a swimming pool. "**...This is the man who will dwell on the heights, whose refuge will be the mountain fortress. His bread will be supplied and water will not fail him.**"

## Something to think about

Jesus told stories to encourage people to go on praying even when it feels like God isn't listening. Tony and Georgie had six years of struggling and praying when it seemed like God wasn't listening. At times they were tempted to give up. If you feel like that sometimes, turn your tap on and remember the miracle well.

# 134 Arresting prayer

## Theme
Why isn't prayer always answered in the way we would like? A true story suggests one answer.

## You will need
• Nothing needed.

## Presentation
What happens if you pray and your prayer doesn't get answered? Do you think it's a waste of time and give up? Here is a true story about the head-teacher of a school and what happened when she prayed.

It was a fortnight into the summer holidays when Mrs Hammond[1] got a phone call from the school caretaker. Twenty-three windows at the back of the school had been broken. Mrs Hammond went to see and thought about how much it was going to cost to replace them.

She was also worried that whoever did it would come back and break into the school and do more damage inside.

Mrs Hammond has had lots of experience of God answering prayer, so she rang up two of her friends and asked them to come with her to the school the next evening and ask God to protect it. At the same time, Mrs Hammond took some letters to a house over the road. The letters asked people to keep an eye on the school and to phone for the police if they saw anyone inside the grounds. Some of the children were going to deliver the letters to all the houses near the school.

## Love your enemies
Then the three of them walked round the grass at the back and saw the place in the fence where people had probably climbed over. Mrs Hammond was fairly sure that it was some children who had broken the windows. They prayed, asking God to protect the school from more damage. They remembered that Jesus said that we should love our enemies and pray for those who hurt us (**Matthew 5:44**), so they asked God to bless the people who had broken the windows. They must be very unhappy people if the best they could think of to do in the summer holidays was to go round breaking school windows!

---

1. Name altered.

A week later, the phone rang again. Seventeen of the windows that had been mended had been broken again! Now Mrs Hammond was even more worried. The caretaker was on holiday and she was going on holiday herself the very next day. She had prayed for the school to be protected against more damage, and now there were 17 more windows to be paid for!

## A waste of time?

What would most of us have thought at that moment? Probably, that praying had been a waste of time. Maybe God isn't interested in school windows, or maybe he had more important things to do. But Mrs Hammond didn't think that like. She knew the bit in the Bible where Jesus says to go on praying and not stop. She went back to the school, and this time she took her husband with her.

They asked God to protect the school again, but Mr Hammond prayed a different prayer. He prayed that whoever was breaking the windows would be caught.

Then they went off, leaving the main gate unlocked because the gardeners were coming to work in the grounds that day. That meant they had to go back at the end of the afternoon to lock the gate again after the gardeners had finished. When they arrived, some of the children in the street asked if they could go round the back and see the broken windows. Mrs Hammond wasn't very keen, but these were children who were helping keep an eye on the school, so she said yes. They went round the back while Mr and Mrs Hammond went inside the school.

## We've caught them!

Suddenly, there was lots of shouting. "Mrs Hammond! Mrs Hammond! We've caught them! We've caught them!" Mr and Mrs Hammond ran round to the back of the school. Sure enough, the children had caught two boys. One of them had even got into the school through a broken window. They were two boys who had been at the school when they were younger. They confessed that it was them who had broken the windows. The police were called and came and took the boys away.

So what about the first prayer? Why wasn't that answered? Well, maybe it was. Maybe God knew that the best way to bless those boys was for them to get caught. Perhaps getting caught will stop them from doing something more serious later and getting into bigger trouble. Only God knows. That is one reason why, when we pray and don't seem to get an answer, we should not give up. God knows what is best. If we trust him and leave the way he answers prayer up to him, sooner or later we shall see some exciting answers.

# 135 Volcanoes and earthquakes

## Theme
Children rightly ask how a good God could allow volcanoes and earthquakes, with all the destruction and loss of life they cause. A part of the answer is that life on earth would be impossible without them.

## You will need
- pictures of volcanoes or destruction caused by earthquakes, from reference books or from links at *www.77talks.co.uk*.
- a piece of chalk.

## Presentation
Begin by referring to any recent news item, or discussing with children what they have seen on films or in books.

Many of us enjoy seeing the spectacular pictures of volcanoes, but when we hear about disasters in which towns get destroyed and people killed, we are bound to ask questions. "Why does God allow earthquakes?" "Why do people get killed when volcanoes erupt?"

Like all the questions about death and suffering, there are no simple answers. One of the things we do now know is that without earthquakes and volcanoes we would not even be alive to ask the questions. Here is why.

Who knows about greenhouse gases?... These are gases in the atmosphere that trap heat from the sun. At the present time, scientists are almost certain that the greenhouse effect is actually happening. A build-up of these gases in the atmosphere is leading to the earth warming up. Which is the gas which is the biggest cause of the problem? Breathe out!... Carbon dioxide, a gas we all pump into the atmosphere every time we breathe. Burning fossil fuels such as natural gas and petrol produces far more.

## The freezer effect
So we all know about the greenhouse effect and some of its possible dangers. But the effect also works in reverse. What would happen if the amount of carbon dioxide in the air decreased?... Yes, the earth would get colder. Some people call that "the freezer effect". Planet earth would become an ice-planet. No liquid seas, no rain...no life! No you and me!

Why should the amount of carbon dioxide in the atmosphere decrease? Well, it's happening all the time. Water in clouds, and carbon dioxide in the air, react together. They make a weak acid. When that acid falls as rain, it reacts with rock, and the carbon dioxide gets locked into solids known as carbonates. Here is an example. [Show a piece of chalk.] This is calcium carbonate. For example, the North and South Downs in the south of England are hills made of chalk. Where they meet the sea they are cut off, forming the famous white cliffs of Dover.

Millions of years of that happening and we would not even have been here to be worrying about the greenhouse effect! All the carbon dioxide would have been locked up in the earth's rocks. But something happens on earth that doesn't happen on a planet like Mars.

The earth's surface is made of vast plates that are slowly but surely moving, carrying the continents with them. When the edge of one plate rides up over another, mountains are formed. When one plate slides past another, it causes shocks – earthquakes. And when parts of plates carrying carbonates are pushed deep under the surface of the earth, they decompose, releasing carbon dioxide as gas once again.

And how does that carbon dioxide get back to the surface and into the atmosphere again? Anybody like to guess?... Through volcanoes! As they erupt, huge amounts of carbon dioxide are spewed back into the air.

The earth itself is a vast recycling machine. As carbon dioxide takes part in processes that are essential to life on earth, it gets locked away. But then the very structure of our planet recycles the carbon dioxide and releases it as gas again. Earthquakes happen because of that recycling, and volcanoes are an essential part of the process.

That process is one of the wonders of planet earth. It is one of the many reasons some scientists believe that there had to be a Creator God to design earth so precisely for life to be possible.

## A thought and a prayer

We still have big questions about the problem of death and suffering through natural disasters, but at least we now know that even earthquakes and volcanoes have their place. They are essential for our very existence here on earth. We might want to pray something like this:

> **Creator God, thank you for the ways science helps us to understand the world you made for us to live in. Please help scientists and governments to make the right discoveries and decisions so that less suffering is caused by natural disasters. Amen.**

For more on a similar theme, see "BUZZ OFF!" p. 117 and "Creepy-crawly or doctor's friend?" p. 129.

# 136 You've been framed!

## Theme
The need for forgiveness.

## You will need
- an old video cassette, a hammer and a waste bin.

## Presentation
Show the video cassette (or, if you have a camcorder, you could start by videoing the children).

Did you hear about the two burglars who videoed themselves committing crimes? They filmed each other breaking into houses, smashing up buildings and committing burglaries – more than 30 crimes in all. Then they carefully edited their tapes, adding subtitles and background music.

They reckoned without a visit from the police. Tamworth CID in Staffordshire were doing a routine search while investigating a completely unrelated matter. They noticed the videos, and their suspicions were aroused by the titles. When the men tried to keep them away from the police, it confirmed their suspicions.

So Tamworth police had a complete video record of a minor local crime wave. Guess who pleaded guilty when the case came to court!

Most sane people want to keep their wrongdoings well hidden, not make a film of them. Pause for a moment and think of some of the things each one of us would absolutely hate to have recorded on video for public show... Painful!

## God is not a policeman
In one of his letters in the New Testament, Paul wrote:

**Each of us will have to answer to God for what he has done.**     *Romans 14:12*

We don't have to be stupid enough to video our own foolishness – God is outside time and space and knows everything we have ever done. There is a record of our lives from start to finish. That is not because God is a big policeman in the sky, waiting to catch people. He simply knows everything.

Perhaps that's a good reason for taking seriously that bit in the Lord's Prayer that says, "Forgive us the wrongs we have done." Forgiveness means wiping the tape clean, erasing the record, making a new beginning.

[You could smash the video cassette at this point for dramatic effect, or simply throw it in a bin.]

But it is not a magic formula: we have to be genuinely sorry for what we have done and determined not to do it again. There's also that bit about forgiving other people for what they have done to us: we have to be prepared to let go of the "video" records we have in our heads of how other people have hurt us.

Do we want the record to stand? Or do we want it wiped away so we can make a fresh start? Those two criminals didn't have that choice. Jesus teaches us that we do.

## Something to do

Everyone, including leaders, could privately write on a piece of paper something they are sorry for, and then throw it in the bin.

# 137 A close shave

## Theme
A fun beginning leads to some serious reflection on what is involved when we pray, "Forgive us our sins."

## You will need
- a bowl of water, a towel, shaving foam, safety and cut-throat razors (borrow the latter from a barber if necessary).
- for a fun ending if you wish, two identical buckets and a packet of confetti. Empty the confetti into one of the buckets and hide this in advance behind the table you will use.

## Presentation
Announce that you have decided to take up a new trade and that you are sure the group is going to help you get started, by allowing you to practise on them. You are going to be a barber and you are going to start with the easy bit – shaving someone. If a parent doesn't volunteer, get the children to choose a "volunteer". (For a school assembly, prime a teacher.) Tell him to sit down; put the towel round his neck. Get the foam, and spray it liberally on him. Then show him the cut-throat razor, and do a bit of patter on how easy it looks, even though you have never tried using a cut-throat razor before. When sufficient effect has been created, the safety razor is produced (usually with its cover still on) so that you will lightly take off the foam and finish the "shave". Then pour the water into the empty bucket and put it down out of sight behind the table.

Tell the boys that when they grow up, shaving will be a daily routine (unless they grow a beard). And whether we need to shave or not, washing or showering is a daily must for everyone. (Boys may not agree with this!) We all have something else that needs dealing with on a daily basis. When Jesus' followers asked him to teach them how to pray, he gave them the model we call the Lord's Prayer. One of the things it includes is, "Forgive us our sins as we forgive those who sin against us."

## Blob of meanness
Like whiskers or dirt, sin builds up every day. A smear of selfishness here, a stain of untruth there, an ugly blob of meanness… How do we clean away this sort of dirt? It won't wash off with soap; you can't scrape it off with even the sharpest razor. It is ingrained into the very fibre of our being. Sin needs a more powerful cleanser – and there is only one place you can get it.

Several times in the Bible there is a word-picture of Jesus which includes something strange. For example, in the first chapter of the book of Revelation, verses 15 and 16 describe Jesus like this:

**His feet were like bronze that glows hot in a furnace. His voice was like the noise of flooding water. He held seven stars in his right hand. A sharp two-edged sword came out of his mouth. He looked like the sun shining at its brightest time.**

A sharp two-edged sword coming out of his mouth? It sounds odd, but remember this is a word-picture. This is a symbol, a way of saying that the words that come out of Jesus' mouth are powerful. With a word he created the universe. With a word he can strike down a whole nation.

One time, some friends brought a paralyzed man to Jesus. Jesus healed him, but first he said,

**Son, your sins are forgiven.**   *Mark 2:5*

The religious leaders were furious. They knew that only God has the power to forgive sins. But Jesus was God. The words of his mouth had the power to clean that man inside-out.

So when we pray, "Forgive us our sins", we are asking for something much more powerful, much sharper than this cut-throat razor, to clean us up. We are asking God to say the words to us, **"Your sins are forgiven."**

When I showed *John* [your volunteer] this razor, he was scared. And he was right to be scared! It's dangerous. And we are right to fear the sharp two-edged sword that comes out of the mouth of Jesus – the words that have power to create or to destroy. The wonder of it is, no matter what we may have done, when we come to Jesus genuinely wanting to be right with him, he uses that sharp sword so gently that he removes all the wrong from us and leaves us clean and whole and unharmed.

# Prayer
A time of quiet would be appropriate here for people to bring anything to Jesus they want to say sorry for and, perhaps, to imagine him as in the word-picture from Revelation.

# Fun ending
Pick up the bucket containing the confetti. Hold it up so that people can see – they will think it is the bucket with the water in it. Swish it round, wander down the middle of your audience, trip and throw the bucket full of confetti into the gathering. They will part like the Red Sea!

# 138 Daydreaming

## Theme
Research shows that daydreaming may not be such a bad thing after all. The reaction of Nathanael when Jesus said he had seen him under the fig-tree (John 1:47–49) suggests that the young man may have been doing a spot of divinely-inspired daydreaming.

## You will need
• to read the story in John 1:43–51.

## Presentation
Hands up – who has ever got into trouble for daydreaming in class?...

Is it just some people who daydream, while others get on with the job in hand undistracted? Is daydreaming a bad thing, a waste of time? (You might describe one of your own favourite daydreams.)

It would probably surprise most of us to know that the average person spends more than one third of their waking hours daydreaming. We actually spend more of our waking hours daydreaming than we spend of our time asleep in night-dreaming. Our daydreams can be anything from a passing thought to a full-blown reverie that lasts a few minutes. It is the last that gets us into trouble when we are supposed to be concentrating on our maths!

It has been shown that daydreaming has some quite beneficial effects. It helps us to relax, and sometimes it even lowers our blood pressure. It can be quite helpful if you have a problem to solve, and it can also be creative, so daydreaming in class might not always be a waste of time, after all.

## A bit of a hero
There was a young man in the Bible who was doing a spot of daydreaming one time. His name was Nathanael, and he had found a nice spot to daydream on a hot Mediterranean spring day – underneath a shady fig-tree. His daydream was like many of ours: imagining ourselves a bit of a hero, being centre stage in some important event. It looks as though he was daydreaming about being a real top-of-the-class Israelite and being a bit like Israel himself, the man from whom the nation took its name. Israel himself had a dream in which he saw heaven open and God's messengers – angels – going up and down between earth and heaven. (Genesis 28:10–15. This was before his name was changed from Jacob to Israel – see Genesis 32:28.)

While Nathanael was in the middle of this daydream, one of his friends turned up, Philip. Philip insisted on taking him to see someone he had just met, Jesus of Nazareth. Nathanael was a bit cross at being disturbed – daydreamers will know how he felt! But when he met Jesus he was in for a big shock. Jesus told him exactly what he had been daydreaming about under the fig-tree. Not only that, but Jesus said his daydream was going to come true! He would see angels. "I tell you the truth," said Jesus to his new friends. "You will all see heaven open. You will see 'angels of God going up and coming down' on the Son of Man." (By "Son of Man" Jesus meant himself.)

And Nathanael did see remarkable things. At the end of John's story of Jesus, we learn that Nathanael was with some of the other disciples when Jesus appeared on the beach at the Sea of Galilee after his resurrection. (See John 21:2.) Imagine being one of the people who saw Jesus after he came back from the dead!

So try a spot of daydreaming. Unplug the telly, switch off the mobile, stretch out somewhere comfortable and enjoy the pictures inside your head. Remember Nathanael. You never know what it might lead to!

## Something to do
If the children are in the mood, you could finish with some quiet music and a couple of minutes' quiet "daydreaming time".

# 139 Blind man sees

## Theme

Asking God to guide our dreams. This could follow on from "Daydreaming".

## You will need

- a stick, a piece of cloth for a cloak, a bowl, some coins.
- to prepare the story of Bartimaeus in Luke 18:35–43. (Luke does not tell us his name, but Mark does. It means Son of Timaeus.)

## Presentation

Tell the story as an impromptu drama, recruiting volunteers to play different parts as you go along.

[Set the scene.] Jericho is a town just north of the Dead Sea. It is extremely hot there most of the year, but springs provide water, and tall palm trees carry great bunches of bright red and yellow dates. In Jesus' time, the main trade route from Arabia to Damascus passed through the town. Caravans of laden camels arrived regularly. There was a tax-collection booth and a large Roman garrison.

Ask for a volunteer to be Bartimaeus. Describe him sitting on his cloak in the shade of a palm tree, with his begging bowl in front of him. Get a couple of children to drop coins in his bowl.

Bartimaeus had plenty of time for daydreaming. Ask for suggestions as to the kind of daydreams he might have had (e.g. good food…a rich merchant giving him a big gift…getting his sight back).

Jesus was on his way to Jerusalem. He had walked down the road beside the river Jordan from Galilee. From Jericho he would begin the long, hot climb uphill to the capital. Have more volunteers play the parts of Jesus, his disciples, and the people in the crowd, as you tell the rest of the story.

Getting his sight restored meant big changes for Bartimaeus. He would have to stop begging and start working. What kind of work would he do? There would be all kinds of things other people had done for him or helped him with, that now he would have to do for himself. He was praising God, but his new life would not be easy.

## Something to think about

We need to think carefully about our daydreams and what it would mean if they came true. Jesus asked Bartimaeus what he wanted and then gave him what he asked for. Perhaps the best thing we can do is to ask God to guide our daydreams, so that what we dream about is what he knows is best for us.

# Expert Futurologists

The future is bright – if we know how to prepare for it

# 140 Like him

## Theme

A glimpse into that amazing future when we shall see Jesus – and find that we are like him.

## You will need

- There is an easy option and a time-consuming option. See below for the former. For the latter, it is probably best to get a computer-literate young person to do it for you! You need some familiar faces – either from scanned photos of people in your group or of people known to them, or from, for example, a TV magazine. These should have effects applied to them in a photo programme to make them hard to recognize, for example, artistic effects. Finally, they need to be printed on transparencies or prepared to show on a computer screen.
- Easy option. Print out some historical characters from *www.77talks.co.uk*.

## Presentation

Get volunteers or the whole group to guess who the people are in the doctored photos. Or divide the group into teams and let them do it competitively.

Comment on how easy – or how hard – it has been to recognize the faces in the photos. If we know a face well, we can often recognize it in even a badly distorted picture.

One face people have wanted to see down the centuries is the face of Jesus. Many artists have painted him, but nobody actually knows what he looked like. There is no description of his human appearance in the Bible.

It seems from reading the Bible that what Jesus looked like when he was here on earth doesn't really matter. What does matter is what he is like as a person. And we can know that. We can know that by reading about him in the gospel stories, by talking to him in prayer, by being his follower, his disciple, his apprentice. There is no doubt then that we shall know him when we see him.

But one of the people who did know what he looked like, John, one of his first disciples, says something strange about that moment when we see him as he really is. He says we shall be like him! Listen to this:

Have a child read **1 John 3:1–3**.

## Something to think about

John says that we have not yet been shown what we will be like in the future. That is still a mystery. But we are going to be like Jesus! When we think about Jesus, we think about his amazing love, his infinite wisdom, his unbelievable power that created the universe. He is perfect, pure, glorious – and yet he is the closest and best friend anyone ever had. And we are going to be like him. Just how, we don't know yet. It's like the biggest Christmas present you ever dreamed of, waiting to be unwrapped. It is a mystery – but what an exciting mystery! No wonder John exclaims, **"The Father has loved us so much! He loved us so much that we are called children of God."**

So treasure this thought in your heart: "One day I am going to see my Lord, the King of kings, the Son of God. I am going to see Jesus as he really is. And when I see him, I am going to be like him. Wow!"

# Purpose in all that we do

## Theme

When we see a purpose in all we do, every part of our lives becomes valuable.

## You will need

- some pieces of paper with numbers written on them as shown here.
- an OHP, an acetate with the sum below, a pen, and a prize of some kind.

## Presentation

You need to do the first part of this talk one week – it only takes a couple of minutes – and the main part the following week.

### Week 1

(This can be at the end of another talk.) Announce that you have something valuable to give away. In fact, you have ten (or more) of them to give away freely to people who want them.

Give out the pieces of paper with these five numbers on. When children ask why they are valuable, simply say that hopefully they will find out sometime. Tell them to do what you usually do with something valuable: keep it safe. Refuse to say any more.

```
2
8
5
3
9
```

### Week 2

Announce that you have a prize which – hopefully – is going to be won by someone in the room. Show the prize. Display an acetate showing a sum with missing numbers on the OHP, as shown below. Explain that it is a simple addition sum, but some of the numbers are missing. There are several possible combinations of numbers that would fit, but you are looking for one particular set of numbers. Provide a pen. The first person who can come and write in the missing numbers will win the prize.

```
  7 3 _ 5 9
  4 0 _ 4 6
  3 6 _ 0 4
+ 9 5   7 2
2 4 5 _ 8 1
```

What happens at this moment is unpredictable. Perhaps someone will realize quickly that the missing numbers are on the pieces of paper that you gave out last week. Or it may need a little prompting. If nobody has the numbers with them, the prize will have to wait until someone brings it.

Hold up a copy of the original piece of paper. It doesn't look much. It has no value on its own and is totally uninteresting. We had to wait a week to find out what its value was. There are lots of things in life which are like that. There are lessons at school which do not interest us much and do not seem to have much purpose. There are things our parents ask us to do which we find boring. We may have to wait a long time before we find out their real value.

There is a secret, known to some Christians, that can turn any lesson, any job, into something valuable. A poet who was born more than 400 years ago knew the secret and wrote it in a poem that is also a prayer. His name was George Herbert.

> **Teach me, my God and King,**
> **In all things Thee to see,**
> **And what I do in any thing**
> **To do it as for Thee.**

In this poem George Herbert is praying to see God in everything. Because he knows God created the world and everything in it with a purpose, he knows that nothing is without value or without meaning. If we do everything as though it was God himself teaching us or telling us what to do, then every single part of our lives becomes valuable. Everything becomes like this piece of paper – a thing of value to be stored up until its worth becomes clear.

## A prayer

Read the words of the poem again as a prayer that the children can join in with, if they want to make it their own.

# 142 Growing into responsibility

## Theme
Taking on larger responsibilities is an essential part of growing up. It's God's plan, too.

## You will need
- two prepared OHP transparencies; coloured pens. Draw a table as in the model (see p. 228) or print it from the *www.77talks.co.uk* website. In the left-hand column, list responsibilities appropriate to the age of the group. For under-11s, for example, *Chores at home, Keep bedroom tidy, Run errands, Look after pets, Thank you letters, Register or dinner monitor*, etc. For over-11s, some of the above plus: *Babysitting, Clothing allowance, Caring for ill parent, Part-time job, Music practice, Team captain*, etc. Prepare a second table with responsibilities suitable for the next phase of life, i.e. for under-11s make an over-11s table; for over-11s make a young adult table. Leave some rows blank.
- Prepare to tell the parable of the three servants, **Matthew 25:14–30**. The *Good News Bible* is a helpful basic translation, but both *The Living Bible* and *The Message* have some great lines. Avoid the misleading word "talents".

## Presentation
Display the chart appropriate to the age-group and ask for a volunteer. Work down the left-hand column, looking at the different responsibilities, and asking the volunteer to say whether he or she has no responsibility in that area, or some, or a lot, or too much. Colour in the chart accordingly. If there are blank rows, children might suggest other ways in which some of them carry responsibility. Ask how they feel about these responsibilities. Good? Proud? Too much bother?...

| Responsibility | None | Some | A lot | Too much |
|---|---|---|---|---|
| Jobs in school | | | | |
| Keep room tidy | | | | |
| Run errands | | | | |
| Look after pet(s) | | | | |

Ask for some suggestions as to what extra or increased responsibilities they expect to take on in the next few years. After a few suggestions, show your second table. Point out the ideas you had, and add any others they indicated. Are they looking forward to some of these new responsibilities? Or scared about some of them?...

A major part of growing up is taking on more responsibility. It began when we first took responsibility for putting the food in our own mouths instead of Mum feeding us, and it has been increasing in large and small steps ever since. Big ones in the future include things like driving a car, living on your own, getting married, starting a family. As a general rule, increased responsibility at work means a bigger pay-packet. New responsibilities can be exciting, but they can also be scary and time-consuming. Ducking them is like saying you don't want to grow up.

Jesus told a famous story about some people rising to the challenge of new responsibilities – and one who didn't.

Retell the parable of the three servants from **Matthew 25:14–30**.

Draw out the contrast. For the first servant, one translation reads:

> **His master praised him for good work. "You have been faithful in handling this small amount," he told him, "so now I will give you many more responsibilities. Begin the joyous tasks I have assigned to you."** *verse 21,* The Living Bible

But as for the third:

> **"That's a terrible way to live! It's criminal to live cautiously like that!"** *verse 26,* The Message

It seems that growing into more and more responsibility is part of God's plan for human beings. And for those ready to take on responsibilities willingly, he has planned big-time rewards. Who knows, you might even end up being responsible for a whole galaxy!

# 143 How will you manage your £1m?

## Theme

A surprising message on being streetwise from perhaps Jesus' most "difficult" parable: the story of the crooked manager. The figures are obviously approximate, but broadly realistic.[1]

## You will need

- a board or OHP and pens.
- Luke 16:1–9 in *The Message* (Peterson's version provides an illuminating commentary on this passage).

Presentation

Ask the children how much they think they will earn during their lifetime… On average earnings at today's rate it will be something like £1 million. With inflation this means that everyone will earn well over that – and some people very much more.

How much will you spend, and on what?… (Write figures on OHP.) About a quarter will go on taxes of various kinds – say £250,000.

Housing: at least £200,000.

Living: (food, transport, entertainment, clothes, etc.) – £320,000.

Pension: (everyone will have to buy their own) – £130,000.

What does this add up to? £900,000.

| £1 million | |
|---|---|
| Tax | £250,000 |
| Housing | £200,000 |
| Living | £320,000 |
| Pension | £130,000 |
| Sub-total | £900,000 |
| ? ? ? | £100,000 |

That leaves £100,000. This could go on a bigger house, better holidays – or something else you choose. We'll leave that to think about later.

## Good managers

If you went for a job that involved handling £1m you would certainly be expected to be a good manager. As each of us is really going to handle at least that much in our

---

1. Originally, every third year, the tithe of the harvest was kept in storehouses for distribution to the poor and needy (see Deuteronomy 14:22–29). Taxation could be seen as partially accomplishing this end today. On this basis you might want to adjust the figures to leave £75,000 rather than £100,000.

lives, we all need to be good managers. Jesus told a story that had some surprising advice on how to handle our money.

Read **Luke 16:1–9** in *The Message*, then reinforce the main lines of the story to make sure the children understand.

Jesus wasn't suggesting that we should be crooks. He was advising us to use what we have wisely, in order to plan for our future. Wise people know they have to put some money aside for a pension – even though it's a lifetime away for people of your age.

## Long-term future

People who are even wiser know that they should be planning for life beyond this life. If life on earth is just episode 1 of something much greater, then the future beyond the future needs some thought, too. One thing many Christians do is to take 10% of their earnings [point to the £100,000 on the OHP] and give it away. They look for opportunities to use that money in ways that will really help other people in need. Jesus talked about this as "storing up treasure in heaven". As he says here (in a different translation): **"Make friends for yourselves with worldly wealth, so that when it gives out, you will be welcomed in the eternal home."**

Most of the people we help with our money will probably never know us personally, but God knows. The money we give away is banked for us – in heaven.

So enjoy your £1 million. But be a bit streetwise with it. Invest some in your long-term future – the future beyond the future.

# 144 Bumps on the head

## Theme
One discredited "science" opens the door for a little undermining of the modern equivalents of explaining human behaviour and telling the future – astrology and palmistry.

## You will need
• You could use the phrenology picture from the *www.77talks.co.uk* website.

## Presentation
Ask the children to feel their heads and note where there are bumps on their skulls. If the group won't get out of hand, they could feel their neighbour's head and do a comparison.

Do bumps in different places tell you something about your abilities or your character? People in the 19th century thought they did.

It was an Austrian doctor, Franz Gall, who first proposed the idea. He believed that if you were good at music, for example, the music-centre in your brain would be larger than normal and cause a bump at a particular place on your skull. Being good at maths would cause a bump somewhere else.

It wasn't just skills that the bumps were supposed to show. Gall thought they could provide a guide to the kind of person you were. A bump in one place might show, for example, that you would love your children. A bump somewhere else might show that you were likely to be a thief.

The name given to this study of personality through bumps on the head was *phrenology*.

Phrenology became hugely popular in Europe and America. Queen Victoria of England was one of the people to believe in it. Books and leaflets were published. Models and pictures of the head were produced, showing the areas linked to different abilities. Some people made lots of money out of it.

One of the reasons it was so popular was that it seemed to give a scientific explanation for the way people behaved. People who were losing interest in the church liked that. Instead of saying, "I've done something wrong. I'm sorry", you could say, "It's not my fault. It's just the way I'm made. The bumps on my head show that."

# History of ignorance

These days we know that Franz Gall was completely wrong. Brain-scanning machines show that the brain is an amazingly complex web of connections. There is no simple pattern of different parts controlling different activities. And there is absolutely no link whatsoever between the bumps on your head and the kind of person you are.

Very few people believe in phrenology today. It is just part of the history of ignorance. We wouldn't be so silly as to be taken in by anything like that today. Or would we?

What about astrology – "Your future in the stars" – or palmistry, or other kinds of fortune-telling? Aren't they very similar? They claim to be able to tell your character by the time and place you were born or by the lines on your hand. And there is lots of money to be made by selling books and writing newspaper columns on "your stars".

There seems to be an awful lot of people around who don't want to take responsibility for their own choices or actions. They would much rather believe that things can be explained by their stars, or their tarot card readings, or something similar.

Centuries and centuries ago people knew that astrology was a waste of time. Isaiah, one of the prophets whose words we have in the Bible, said:

> **You have advisors by the ton – your astrologers and stargazers, who try to tell you what the future holds. But they are as useless as dried grass burning in the fire.**
> *Isaiah 47:13–14,* The Living Bible

So why do people go on believing in them? Well, here's one theory. Maybe they had a bump on the head when they were children!

# APPENDIX 1
# Communication Guidelines

# GUIDELINE 1:
# Start by holding hands

Much of the great teaching of Jesus springs from the moment. It starts from where people are at. Jesus takes people by the hand in their actual — but restricted — perspective and leads them a few steps to where a breathtaking vista opens up before their eyes.

The day after the feeding of the five thousand, for instance, the crowd catches up with Jesus on the far side of the Sea of Galilee. Clearly hoping for a repeat of the free picnic, they ask him what miraculous sign he will perform. "Our forefathers ate the manna in the desert," they say, "as it is written: 'He gave them bread from heaven to eat.'"

"**I am the bread of life,**" replies Jesus, revealing to them the eternal in the immediate. "**He who comes to me will never go hungry.**"

We must fall far short of Jesus in his gift, but we can ensure that we start from where the children are at. We can come alongside them in their interests and concerns and lead them by the hand into a wider perspective.

Here are some examples from this book:

- children love humour: HOLY JOKER and KANGAROOS AND MANNA both start with different kinds of jokes.

- daily concerns like bullying provide starting points for ESCAPE.

- children are curious and love puzzles: WITH OUR OWN EYES and A TALE OF TWO FISH begin with intriguing puzzles.

- many of them find the natural world fascinating: THUNDER FROM HEAVEN and BEAUTY AND THE BEAST draw on this interest.

- everybody enjoys stories of human behavior outside the norm: COURAGE TO GO BLIND and UNDER THE KNIFE are two such.

# GUIDELINE 2:
# The illustration is the message

"The Lord is my shepherd," said David unforgettably. He did not start with a five-point abstract treatise on the nature of God and then throw in an illustration to help the slower-of-mind get the point. The illustration was the message.

The death of Jesus is the pivot of Christianity. Yet Jesus gave hardly any teaching about the meaning of his death. He simply took a piece of Passover bread and said, "This is my body." Then he took a cup of wine and said, "This is my blood."

*When you get the picture, you've got the message.*

It is not easy for Western-educated minds to put their faith in the power of the picture (which is strange considering we have been brought up with the matchless examples given above). And yet we are told that society is moving strongly in the direction of the image being more important than the word. This is the world our children live in. We had better learn how to use the image before we get left behind.

At the very least we can endeavour not to underestimate the place of illustrations in the talks we give to children. Take two examples from this book, A LOVEABLE TEDDY and ARE YOU DISPOSABLE? In each case there is a strong image. It is that image which is likely to remain in the minds of the children even if our explanations make little impact.

Seek out strong illustrations like these. After all, it is the biblical way.

# GUIDELINE 3:
# Get them involved

When we have a talk to prepare, let's ask ourselves, "Am I treating the children as just an audience — literally 'hearers' only — or am I inviting them to be active participants?" The latter leads to far more effective communication.

One way of making them active participants is to actually involve one or two, as in MOTHER'S DAY PET or GIVING AND RECEIVING. This effects the whole group, not just the chosen volunteers. The other children identify with their friends out in the front and think how they would react if it was them.

If you want to know how to milk this effect for all its worth, watch a few TV game or quiz shows and pick up some tips. A good game show host gets terrific involvement from the audience. Of course, the one thing we should never do with a child volunteer is to make him or her a victim of ridicule.

Another way of getting active involvement is to raise a question in the minds of the children. SWIMMING AGAINST THE CURRENT does this: everyone wants to know what the dead fish is there for. Similarly in MOTHER'S DAY PET, the desire to know what this strange creature is in the box keeps everyone on the edge of their seats. It is the kind of technique the prophet Ezekiel used to great effect (see Ezekiel 4 and 5 for some dramatic examples).

Involving children in these ways (and in others in this volume) opens mental doors and increases receptivity to the messages we want to convey.

# GUIDELINE 4:
# Visualize it!

Look at UP IN SMOKE on page 89. The basis of this talk is a few figures found in one news item and a quote from another. Given as a straight talk it would be fairly dull. The trick with this sort of material is to ask, "How can I translate some of the elements visually?"

The key element here is: 5.7 billion tons of carbon going up in smoke each year. Where do we find carbon in a form that children will be familiar with? A little thought turns up the answer: in barbecue charcoal. If there isn't a bag in the garage already, one can soon be picked up. Some elementary maths translates tons into bags, but it is such a large number as to be almost meaningless. Writing it onto a roll of paper and slowly unrolling it for dramatic effect creates the necessary impact.

Copying the quote, "They didn't pay God's creation enough respect," on to OHP acetate adds a further visual element and helps reinforce the key teaching.

Another example is in 1 IN 14,000,000 in the DON'T GET CAUGHT section. Visualizing the chance of winning the lottery as the same as finding one dime in a pile 26 km (16 miles) high is staggering. I had to repeatedly run the figures through a calculator and ask a mathematician to check them before I could convince myself it was true!

The principle is simple and well known, but too often forgotten. Yet the time spent in thought and preparation is repaid many times over by the impact made. Visualize it!

# GUIDELINE 5:
# Enjoy yourself!

The blindfold fishing game in HOOKED! is great fun. In a different way, so is the story of Hungry Hagar in BEASTLY BULLFROG. Both create ripples of laughter.

Laughter is a great way of coming alongside children. It establishes common ground, is a beginning of friendship, and breaks down possible barriers.

When we enjoy presenting a talk to children, that in itself communicates a very positive message about the ideas and lifestyle we are advocating. After all, joy is a keynote of the kingdom of God.

And there is no contradiction in having fun and presenting a serious message at the same time. Indeed, it models a very healthy and balanced approach to life. This is especially important when we are tackling issues of potentially harmful vices such as those in this section. Coming across as too serious – being seen as a killjoy – can actually provoke in children the opposite reaction to that intended.

So relax and have fun. Enjoy yourself!

# GUIDELINE 6:
# Surprise them

I love the reaction you get in a group of children when you pray, "Thank you, God, for pain!"

*Is this guy just mildly nutty or final proof of the failure of Care in the Community?*

Surprise is a great way of getting genuine attention. It can range from the shock tactic of a loud noise or shout, to the gentler effect of producing a strange object, or to unexpected actions or words as above. It often provokes laughter.

Surprise can raise a question in the minds of children so that they keep listening until they get an answer. It can persuade them to see things from a fresh viewpoint. It helps make a message memorable.

Jesus used shock and surprise in his teaching. Telling people to behave like a hated Samaritan is one example; an employer paying his workers as much for one hour as for a whole day is another.

The day Jesus arrived in Jericho on his final journey to Jerusalem was a day of surprises. Here was a man being talked about as the promised Messiah choosing to stay with that despised collaborator with Romans, Zacchaeus! The message Jesus gave through that choice was very much the same as the surprising conclusion of BUZZ OFF!

# GUIDELINE 7:
# The "YUK!" factor

You don't need to be unusually squeamish to get a shiver from the thought of the eccentric food additives in LIZARD MUESLI or the benign attentions of the maggots in CREEPY-CRAWLY.

The "Yuk!" factor in a talk plays much the same part as laughter or surprise. It gains attention, creates questions, and ensures memorability. You can be sure that horse-dung pizza and flesh-munching maggots are going to get talked about in the playground and over the take-out.

As recorded in John 6, Jesus so offended people with his words about eating his flesh and drinking his blood that it drove many of them away. Yet there can be no doubt that this teaching lodged in their minds.

The "Yuk!" factor is one to be used sparingly, but is a helpful addition to any communicator's toolbag.

# GUIDELINE 8:
# Avoid the hard sell

How many of us have the courage to simply tell a story or give an illustration and then walk away, leaving our hearers to work it out for themselves? Yet Jesus did it all the time. According to his historians, he never spoke to the crowds without using parables. His puzzled inner circle of followers sometimes had to badger him afterwards for explanations.

Jesus clearly wanted people to think things through, come to their own conclusions, and respond at their own pace. He knew that a free response is of infinitely greater value than a coerced response. I find that a hard act to follow!

At the very least, we can resist the temptation to deliver the "moral" with hammer blows. Try finishing with a question rather than a statement; or by saying, "That's my opinion. What do you think?"

Allow stories like HEALED OF DYSLEXIA to speak for themselves. We can severely weaken the impact of a story by spinning lots of words or trying to reinforce the message. It requires trust. But that is the way the Master did it.

# GUIDELINE 9:
# Carrying conviction

"The best lack all conviction," wrote Yeats, "while the worse are full of passionate intensity."

How do we convey conviction without putting our hearers off with the hard sell? How do we persuade a post-modern generation that what we believe is vitally relevant to them, too, and not just a personal choice of our own creation?

Perhaps the answer lies in having an attitude modelled on that of Jesus as he talked to two of his followers on the road to Emmaus. This is the story featured in HARD TO RECOGNIZE.

Jesus used their knowledge of the Hebrew scriptures (he started from where they were at) to lead them into understanding and to impart a burning conviction of truth to them. Then when they reached the village, "Jesus acted as if he were going further." It was their free choice to invite him to stay, and only after they had made that choice did he reveal his identity to them.

Each child we speak to has a God-given freedom to weigh what we say and to respond in their own time and their own way. (The parable of the sower has shown us in advance the broad outline of those responses.) We have to respect that freedom absolutely, just as Jesus did — even on the day of his resurrection.

So we use persuasion, not manipulation; truth, not enticement; the appeal of love, not the coercion of superiority. Then we pray that, like young Andrew Pickering in ANDREW'S LAST WORDS, the time will come for each one's eyes to be opened and that each will recognize Jesus as the risen Lord and Savior.

# GUIDELINE 10:
# Don't patronize

It is better not to talk to children at all than to talk down to them.

Christmas is one of those times when it is easy to slip into "This is for the children" mode. In fact there are very few messages for children in the Bible. There is only truth for all people. And all people have to come as children before our Father in heaven.

Children ask big questions and are capable of wrestling with difficult ideas. Our task is to find the language and the pictures which will help them in their thinking.

CHRISTMAS FAITH 4 introduces the concept of the incarnation. The incarnation is all about God coming alongside us in the form of Jesus and finding the words and pictures to communicate to us. As I read the Gospels and see Jesus doing this I feel uplifted, never patronized.

Here are two ways of avoiding being patronizing. One is an attitude, the other a technique.

The right attitude when talking to children is knowing that to do so is an awesome privilege. Each one of them is a precious and unique creation who will one day, God willing, be a being in a world outside space and time and beyond our present comprehension. To be responsible for helping them take a step on that journey — or for hindering them by our own pride or folly — is a humbling responsibility.

The technique is one to be used when talking to a wide age-range of children: aim for the oldest. Providing the talk is entertaining or has good visual elements, it will hold the younger one's attention. If they don't understand everything but are left with a sense that there are good things for them to grow into, that's fine. It is much better than the older ones feeling that this is all beneath them and that they have already grown out of Christianity.

# Biblical index

## OLD TESTAMENT

## NEW TESTAMENT